NEW YORK REVIEW BOOKS
CLASSICS

GROWING UP ABSURD

PAUL GOODMAN (1911–1972) was an American social critic, psychologist, poet, novelist, and anarchist. His writings appeared in *Politics*, *Partisan Review*, *The New Republic*, *Commentary*, *The New Leader*, *Dissent*, and *The New York Review of Books*. He published several well-regarded books in a variety of fields—including city planning, Gestalt therapy, literary criticism, and politics—before *Growing Up Absurd*, cancelled by its original publisher and turned down by a number of other presses, was brought out by Random House in 1960.

CASEY NELSON BLAKE is Professor of History and American Studies at Columbia University and the author of several studies in American intellectual and cultural history. He writes regularly for *Commonweal*, *Dissent*, *Raritan*, and other publications.

SUSAN SONTAG (1933–2004) was a novelist, playwright, filmmaker, and one of the most influential critics of her generation. Her books include *Against Interpretation*, *On Photography*, *Illness as Metaphor*, and *The Volcano Lover*.

GROWING UP ABSURD

Problems of Youth in the Organized Society

PAUL GOODMAN

Foreword by
CASEY NELSON BLAKE

With an essay by
SUSAN SONTAG

NEW YORK REVIEW BOOKS

New York

THIS IS A NEW YORK REVIEW BOOK
PUBLISHED BY THE NEW YORK REVIEW OF BOOKS
435 Hudson Street, New York, NY 10014
www.nyrb.com

Portions of this volume appeared under the following titles: "Youth in the
Organized Society" (February, 1960), "The Calling of American Youth"
(March, 1960), and "In Search of Community" (April, 1960) in *Commentary*;
"Growing Up Absurd" (1960) in *Dissent*; "The Freedom to Be Academic" in
i.e., The Cambridge Review; "Freedom to Go" in *Liberation*; "Patriotism" (July,
1960) in *Mademoiselle* ; "Wingless Wandervogel" and "The Crime of Our
Century" in *Midstream*.

Goodman, Paul, 1911–1972.
 Growing up absurd / by Paul Goodman ; introduction by Casey Nelson Blake ;
with an essay by Susan Sontag.
    p. cm. — (New York Review Books classics)
 Originally published: New York : Random House, [1960]
 ISBN 978-1-59017-581-1 (alk. paper)
 1. Youth—United States. I. Title.
 HQ796.G645 2012
 305.2350973—dc23

                         2012012241

ISBN 978-1-59017-581-1

Printed in the United States of America on acid-free paper.
1 0 9 8 7 6 5 4 3

CONTENTS

Foreword by Casey Nelson Blake · vii

Preface · 5

Introduction · 13

I. JOBS · 25

II. BEING TAKEN SERIOUSLY · 41

III. CLASS STRUCTURE · 54

IV. APTITUDE · 70

V. PATRIOTISM · 91

VI. SOCIAL ANIMAL · 111

VII. FAITH · 123

VIII. AN APPARENTLY CLOSED ROOM · 145

IX. THE EARLY RESIGNED · 155

X. THE EARLY FATALISTIC · 173

XI. THE MISSING COMMUNITY · 194

Conclusion · 213

Appendices · 217

"On Paul Goodman" by Susan Sontag · 273

FOREWORD

Paul Goodman, Anarchist and Patriot*

TO THE MEMORY OF CHRIS LANIER

I.

"THE WORST feature of our present organized system of doing things," Paul Goodman wrote in *Growing Up Absurd*, is "its blurring of the object." Authorities were evasive about "crying objective public needs" such as education, meaningful work, and spaces for democratic self-government. "Everybody talks nice," but public discussion refused to acknowledge what everyone knew. As a result, the young grew up in "a society in which one's important problems are treated as nonexistent." They were "early resigned" and stayed that way.

Honesty, even to the point of cruelty, was Goodman's way to cut through the fog of official speech. Goodman wrote *Growing Up Absurd* in a colloquial style he had perfected in fifteen years of prolific work as a polemicist and critic. His 1960 book was his bid to join the great Anglo-American tradition of plain speech and pamphleteering. The timing couldn't have been better. It appeared just as the baby boom generation was entering colleges and universities and became an overnight success among young people chafing at the constraints of Cold War culture. Denouncing a culture unworthy of Americans' allegiance, Goodman had a blunt eloquence that recalls William Cobbett, Thomas Paine, the Populists, and William James.

---

*A version of this essay appeared in the Summer 2012 issue of *Raritan*. I am grateful to Taylor Stoehr, Sarah Leonard, and Tim Barker for helping me on my way.

The book is "homespun of oatmeal gray," as he titled one of his last collections of poetry. He could write too fast, sometimes churning out clotted prose that provoked ridicule. But at its best, his language conveyed simple truths that his readers dared not utter lest they look unsophisticated—or because they could not admit how the organized system had broken their hearts. Goodman didn't care if he seemed naïve or sentimental. Who else among the New York intelligentsia upheld earnestness as a virtue? He believed that people required fulfilling work, sociability, love of place, and faith that the world was responsive to their strivings. It took courage to be utopian, to call for a society "where people are not afraid to make friends." It took even greater courage to offer "dumb-bunny" solutions to the problems of everyday life. Proposals poured out in book after book: seersuckers for nurses who wasted hours ironing starchy white uniforms; a ban on cars in Manhattan; tiny neighborhood schools run at a fraction of public school budgets; and more. To Goodman, these were commonsense projects a free people could agree on and pursue that very day. Gaining confidence in their own competence, citizens could then take on the democratization of the workplace and nuclear disarmament. Irving Howe observed in *Partisan Review* in 1962 that "Goodman continues to write as if it were still possible to move people: perhaps not sufficiently or in sufficient numbers, yet with some sense that speech remains a power."

What makes *Growing Up Absurd* especially original all these years later is its unique synthesis of anarchist utopianism with unabashed cultural conservatism. That combination bewildered many reviewers but no doubt appealed to the generation that founded both the Young Americans for Freedom and Students for a Democratic Society soon after its publication. Half a million copies of the book sold by the time Goodman died of a heart attack in 1972 at age sixty. Goodman had made a serious study of the Founders in the late 1950s, and the Jeffersonian vision of a republic of small producers figured prominently in all the social criticism he wrote from that point forward. "I rely heavily on the following method of argument," he noted in his journal as he worked on *Growing Up Absurd*:

"I make a list of unaccomplished or lost causes and accumulate them as a program for action.... the Missing Community of social stability is found by summing up the modern revolutionary aims that were in their time compromised and unfulfilled." "Socially and psychologically," this strategy "has the effect of making my radical rejection of the *status quo* seem spectacularly conservative. (In fact, I am conservative.)" Indeed he was. Reading George Washington's Circular Letter gave him the courage to write the book. He whistled "The Star-Spangled Banner" as he delivered the last chapter to his publisher.

To call Goodman one of the great cultural conservatives of the twentieth century will strike many as preposterous. After all, Goodman co-authored the founding document of gestalt therapy and championed Wilhelm Reich against the neo-Freudians; had two common-law marriages and raised children while cruising New York's waterfront and hitting on virtually every young man he encountered; and lost one teaching job after another over his open bisexuality. Even Black Mountain College, of all places, sent him packing. Then there was the party in the 1950s at the apartment of a prominent psychiatrist when he started French-kissing a dog, in a grotesque attempt to shock guests into recognition of their animal nature. (Goodman protested when his host pulled the dog away and locked him in the bedroom. "It's *my* dog, Paul," he had to be told.) Jonathan Lee's 2011 documentary, *Paul Goodman Changed My Life*, makes clear how much this self-proclaimed "queer" mattered to gay men in the pre-Stonewall era. And of course he was an anarchist from the day he first read Peter Kropotkin in the 1930s. Not a Marxist, not a sober social democrat, not a liberal "realist"—an anarchist. He opposed World War II, the Cold War, all wars. With Randolph Bourne he believed "war is the health of the state." The 1945 *May Pamphlet* he wrote for his fellow war resisters offered a succinct statement of anarchist change: "A free society cannot be the substitution of a 'new order' for the old order; it is the extension of spheres of free action until they make up most of the social life."

This is hardly the life one associates with a conservative critic of modernity. Yet the chapters on jobs, patriotism, and faith that form the moral center of *Growing Up Absurd* are a traditionalist's lament of loss and waste that T. S. Eliot and even the Southern Agrarians might have endorsed. Americans floundered without "manly" work, a love of country and place, and the grateful acceptance of a creaturely existence that alone made possible a creative life. The corruption of patriotism by state power especially disabled the young as they launched themselves into adulthood. In a patriotic culture children learned stories of civic heroism that gave them confidence in their country's possibilities, and their own. Without that "patriotic opportunity," the young came with "a fatal emptiness to the humane culture of science, art, humanity and God." "I am an anarchist and a patriot," he wrote in his journal in 1958—"a curious kind of thing."

Goodman's fierce indictment of "our abundant society" in the introduction went to the heart of the matter:

> It is lacking in enough man's work. It is lacking in honest public speech, and people are not taken seriously. It is lacking in the opportunity to be useful. It thwarts aptitude and creates stupidity. It corrupts ingenuous patriotism. It corrupts the fine arts. It shackles science. It dampens animal ardor. It discourages the religious convictions of Justification and Vocation and it dims the sense that there is a Creation. It has no Honor. It has no Community.

Goodman was obtuse in thinking the maladies he diagnosed in his book were irrelevant to the experiences of girls and women. That was another side of his conservatism. But he was not obtuse in insisting that all those capitalized words mattered, and that their waning was a source of profound sadness for many Americans. "Tradition has been broken, yet there is no new standard to affirm. Culture becomes eclectic, sensational, or phony."

II.

Though now nearly forgotten, *Growing Up Absurd* was an enormous success in its day and for years to come. Well into the 1970s, the book was a fixture in the libraries of aspiring intellectuals and young professionals living in college towns and still-affordable urban neighborhoods. It stood on shelves alongside other books the postwar "paperback revolution" made available to readers seeking to understand the roots of modern domination and the resources available to resist it. There, stacked on plywood planks laid down on cinder blocks, were Hannah Arendt's *Eichmann in Jerusalem* and *On Revolution*, Norman O. Brown's *Life Against Death*, Albert Camus's *The Myth of Sisyphus* and *The Rebel*, Walter Kaufmann's existentialism anthology, Erich Fromm's *Escape from Freedom*, and an edition of the young Marx. Those with theological leanings found room for Niebuhr, Tillich, and Buber. Marcuse, Mills, and Chomsky soon claimed a place on the shelves of leftists seeking a more incisive critique of advanced capitalism, alongside James Baldwin's *The Fire Next Time*, Betty Friedan's *The Feminine Mystique*, and *The Autobiography of Malcolm X*. Then, starting in the 1980s, those paperbacks would be swept away—replaced by translations of the French structuralists, then the Western Marxists, then Foucault and Derrida, and Judith Butler. The books Goodman and his contemporaries wrote are literally devouring themselves half a century later, as acid turns their pages into dust.

The success of Goodman's book reflected the ascendancy after World War II of a humanistic intellectual left that broke sharply with the economic ideology of the old 1930s left. As Daniel Bell observed in *The End of Ideology*, many postwar socialists concluded that "dehumanization" had superseded exploitation as the greatest threat to ordinary citizens, rendering older political categories obsolete. The task for radicals was to find some core of human nature unscarred by a murderous century as the foundation for a new politics. Dwight Macdonald anticipated much of what was to come in his 1946 essay, "The Root Is Man." "We feel," he wrote, "that the firmest ground from which to struggle for that human liberation which was the goal of the old Left is the ground not of History but of those non-historical values (truth, justice, love, etc.) which Marx has made unfashionable among socialists." The search for a meaningful way of life was as important as an economic program, maybe more so. "We must emphasize the emotions, the imagination, the moral feelings, the primacy of the individual human being, must restore the balance that has been broken by the hypertrophy of science in the last two centuries." Camus argued in an essay of the same year, "Neither Victims nor Executioners," that the cultivation of human decency was both the condition and goal of political action. The challenge was "to fight within History to preserve from History that part of man which is not its proper province."

Such defenses of the human resounded in the manifestoes of the early New Left. *Liberation*'s "Tract for the Times" and the SDS's "Port Huron Statement" joined the revival of direct democracy to a search for "a meaning in life that is personally authentic," as Tom Hayden and friends put it. Mario Savio, the Berkeley Free Speech Movement leader, gave voice to that radical humanism in his famous speech calling on students to throw their bodies on the gears of the Machine. We are not the "raw materials" of the knowledge industry, he shouted to the protesters outside Sproul Hall in 1964. "We're human beings!"

Savio surely knew *Growing Up Absurd*, as did all budding radicals of the day, and he spoke the same humanistic language as its author. Goodman launched his inquiry into the "Youth Problems in the Organized System" with a polemic against social scientists who discarded the idea of human nature in the name of culture, delivering adolescents to a regime of "socialization" that wasted their talents and stunted genuine growth. "Socialization to what?" Goodman demanded. To the cynicism and indifference that pervaded schools, corporations, and state bureaucracies? The self-image of American society was of an "apparently closed room" with a "rat race" at its center. All the talk of finding productive channels for youthful discontent carried the same underlying message: there are no alternatives. It was time to ask if "the harmonious organization to which the young are inadequately socialized" was "against human nature, or not worthy of human nature."

III.

After a decade spent writing books no one read, Goodman received an advance from a small publisher for a book about juvenile delinquency. The $500 check from Criterion Books was no small sum for a man who had lived for years in near-poverty, and the subject was a natural. Goodman had gotten to know many street kids and gang members in games on New York's handball courts. A social category invented after World War II by psychiatrists and police, juvenile delinquents sparked hysteria (the Kefauver hearings on comic books) and obsession (*Rebel Without a Cause*, *West Side Story*)—or both (*The Wild One*). The manuscript Goodman produced by the end of October was rejected by Criterion, only to be snatched up by the Random House editor Jason Epstein on the recommendation of his friend Norman Podhoretz, who at age thirty had just taken over the editorship of *Commentary*. Podhoretz serialized three chapters in advance of the book's publication, signaling the magazine's revival as a forum for social criticism. *Growing Up Absurd* was "everything I wanted for the new *Commentary*, and more," he later recalled: "it was the very incarnation of the new spirit I had been hoping would be at work in the world, as it had been in me."

Goodman wrote about "J.D.'s" with great attentiveness and compassion, but *Growing Up Absurd* took on much more than juvenile delinquency. Readers expecting a sociology of troubled youth found instead an excoriating account of America's spiritual desolation. Goodman's powerful insight was that Organization Men, delinquents, and bohemian adventurers "on the road" suffered together in an organized society that stifled their capacities as human beings. The elevation of consumption over satisfying work had fostered a base cynicism among Americans of all backgrounds. Seemingly at odds, the junior executive, the gang member, and the Beat were united in thinking that role-playing composed the sum total of human relations. An "organized system of reputations" had displaced older standards of excellence that challenged adolescents to master and surpass what they had inherited from previous generations. The young had lost the very idea of an "objective changeable world," the "conviction that there is a Creation of the Six Days, a real world rather than a system of social rules that indeed are often arbitrary."

The aspects of *Growing Up Absurd* that feel most dated today are those it shared with other social criticism of the period. David Riesman's *The Lonely Crowd*, William H. Whyte's *The Organization Man*, John Kenneth Galbraith's *The Affluent Society*, and Vance Packard's *The Hidden Persuaders* had popularized critiques of consumerism and white-collar conformism among the very people who had most benefited from the postwar boom. Like those books, *Growing Up Absurd* overestimated the extent of postwar prosperity and assumed a Fordist, mass-production economy was the logical endpoint of capitalist development. The problem with the organized system was that it functioned too well, in Goodman's account, not that it left millions in desperate straits. Goodman was too quick to dismiss labor unions as co-opted, too slow to see the gathering force of the resurgent, pseudo-populist right that had begun a decade earlier with Nixon and McCarthy. He was a religious seeker who returned again and again to Buber and Laotzu but took no notice of the Christian revival around him in so many forms, from Billy Graham's evangelicalism to the growing Catholic left.

In other words, his was a book of its moment, above all in its assumption that the human nature in need of defending was male. A girl did not grow up absurd because she had a meaningful vocation ahead of her, Goodman asserted in the book's introduction. "She will have children, which is absolutely self-justifying, like any other natural or creative act." The problems of male youth were nonetheless "intensely interesting to women, for if the boys do not grow up to be men, where shall the women find men?" One of the most visible bisexuals in American history traded on the panic over "feminized" white-collar men that rattled Cold War culture. "If the husband is running the rat race of the organized system," Goodman warned, "there is not much father for the children." Then he let the matter drop. It tells us a great deal about the times that Goodman shoehorned his rationale for omitting girls and women into the final edits of the manuscript, and even more that many of his male *and* female admirers from the 1960s now shake their heads in astonishment that this exclusion passed by them unnoticed.

What sets Goodman's book apart from other social criticism of the day is the account of "missed and compromised revolutions" that gave his work its historical ballast. The concluding chapter ran through a list of lost causes since the dawn of the modern age—from the Protestant ideal of vocation, republican self-government, and agrarianism to urban functionalism, workers' control of production, and progressive education. The corruption of progressive pedagogy especially appalled him; it figured in all his social criticism as a microcosm of an Enlightenment perverted into its opposite. Goodman read John Dewey as a radical betrayed by managerial liberals, his democratic theory recast as a strategy for "adjusting" youth to existing social roles. Such people had likewise transformed William James's instrumentalism into an ideology of technocratic control. Goodman admitted the radical programs he admired were inconsistent, often at odds with one another, and each in its own way flawed. But the time had come to "achieve them all." "We have no recourse to going back, there is nothing to go back to."

This was the paradox and challenge Goodman faced. There was no going back, and yet Goodman the conservative wanted to go back. The realization of the "modern spirit"—of the entire radical agenda at once—was the way to recover the traditional community ravaged by the organized system. His heroes Kropotkin and William Morris had seen a radical decentralism as a means to recover a culture of mutuality, craft skills, and local autonomy they associated with medieval towns. Their recuperation of a precapitalist past anticipated the efforts by Dewey, Bourne, Thorstein Veblen, and Lewis

Mumford to translate the republican ethic of craftsmanship into a modern idiom. Such ideas continued to shape the work of contemporaries Goodman may well have found uncongenial—Edmund Wilson, Dorothy Day, and Jane Jacobs—as well as his anarchist comrades Macdonald and Ivan Illich. Several of those thinkers pushed back harder against the secular and cosmopolitan culture of modern America than Goodman did. Some beat a path to religious orthodoxy or rejected the progressive faith in planning and expertise with a fury that far exceeded his misgivings about the course Western societies had taken since the eighteenth century. Goodman was a modernist and a conservative, just as he was an anarchist and a patriot. The problem was how to chart a way forward, achieving all the lost modern revolutions at once, that was also a way back to the past.

IV.

The long arc of Goodman's career reveals successive efforts to resolve that problem, as he joined the Jeffersonian and anarchist traditions to psychotherapy, urban planning, educational reform, and professional ethics. As early as the 1945 *May Pamphlet*, he was including "group psychotherapy" in his "revolutionary program." Two years later he and his architect brother, Percival, published *Communitas*, a manifesto for a utopian urbanism that regarded "community life as a continuous group-psychotherapy in our sick society, in which just the anxieties and tensions of living together become the positive occasions to change people and release new energy altogether." Harold Rosenberg, one of Goodman's few advocates among the New York intellectuals, understood his friend was both pedagogue and therapist. In fact, Goodman's proposal for a new university curriculum in *The Community of Scholars* culminated "in a course of group therapy for the senior year"—a successor of sorts to the required course in moral philosophy taught by college presidents in the early nineteenth century. "I envisage groups of less than ten for a two-hour weekly session," Goodman told readers. "Of course such a course must not be called 'psychology' but preferably be put in the Humanities, where indeed it belongs."

Although Goodman's commitment to "group sesh" is less visible in *Growing Up Absurd*, the book still draws deeply on his theoretical and practical involvement with psychotherapy in its assault on socialization. Taylor Stoehr's *Here Now Next*—still the best study of Goodman—demonstrates the centrality of the 1951 book on gestalt theory Goodman co-authored with Fritz Perls and Ralph Hefferline for everything that followed. Goodman was chiefly responsible for the theoretical apparatus of *Gestalt Therapy*, in which he detailed an interactive model of the self reminiscent of James's psychology. Human experience was at its best an ongoing, dynamic process in which the individual probed and expanded the boundary separating the self and environment. Therapy itself was an exercise in testing boundaries, as therapist and patient cultivated awareness of the possibilities of the present situation and collaborated on practical measures to further individual autonomy. "The aware self does not have fixed boundaries," he explained.

When Goodman lashed out at manipulative strategies for "adjusting" children to existing social roles or bemoaned a culture of role-playing, he was writing as "socio-therapist of the body politic," in Stoehr's words. The great tragedy of mid-century America was how few of its citizens imagined that "the society I live in is my own," the title Goodman used for a collection of open letters to public officials. Elders owed adolescents the chance to take on a concrete task and mold their world more to their liking. That's how they learned there was in fact an "objective changeable world" out there, as opposed to role-playing. He elaborated on this theme in *The Community of Scholars*: "there is no other way for them to grow up to be free citizens, to commence, except by discovering, in an earnest moment, that some portion of the objective culture is after all natively their own; it is usable by *them*."

Goodman was not alone, of course, in plumbing the psychic sources of domination in advanced industrial societies: Norman O.

Brown and Herbert Marcuse offered competing accounts by weaving together Marxism and psychoanalysis. The New Left, counterculture, and feminist movements all insisted on the simultaneous transformation of private and public life. Goodman departed from these explorations in his assumption that group therapy was the natural complement to his communitarian anarchism. Group therapy loomed large in his criticism as the modern equivalent of the Athenian agora, medieval university, and New England town meeting, its practitioners equipped with insights into humans' emotional and libidinal needs that those earlier face-to-face communities ignored. It was the site where Buber's unmediated "I-Thou" relationship flourished, a psycho-spiritual analogue to anarchism in its commitment to experimental self-fashioning and effective action.

Yet there was greater tension than Goodman acknowledged between the robust civic life he sought and a therapeutic process that ultimately had individuals' psychological needs as its goal. If the premodern institutions Goodman admired worked—with all their exclusions—they did so precisely because they insisted participants set aside their interior, emotional lives as they entered into public deliberation. They were not patients in the civic arena, or therapists for that matter, but citizens, scholars, and neighbors. Goodman might well have argued that psychotherapy equipped people for self-government, but the public life often demands that "I" defer to "Thou" for the sake of the commonweal. Therapy may not always teach that discipline. Sadly, Goodman's own life provides a cautionary lesson on this score. The edited volume of his journals from the late 1950s, *Five Years*, documents the insatiable neediness that drove many friends away. The journals, Rosenberg wrote in an introduction, were "a chronicle of hunger" for sex, recognition, community, and transcendence. He regretted that Goodman reordered his notes for publication under thematic headings, asking "how many of the notes belong under any but 'Myself.'"

Whatever its psychological benefits, group therapy could not bear the weight of Goodman's political expectations. The agora and town hall were explicitly political institutions in a way therapy groups are not. They were sites for factional contestation as well as deliberation, and operated in a larger landscape of social conflict and competition (with the army and the church, kings and merchants, slaves and serfs). Group therapy fell short as an anarchist program for extending "spheres of free action until they make up most of the social life" in the face of entrenched opposition.

The same might be said of Goodman's courageous defense of professional ethics in his last work of social criticism, published in 1970. Written after the democratic promise of the early New Left curdled into a crude rhetoric of "revolution" and "armed resistance," *The New Reformation* revealed a man weary of the young people he'd formerly embraced as his "crazy young allies," tired of the endless round of protests and speeches, and simply burned out from the public life he'd lived since *Growing Up Absurd*. The contempt late-1960s students displayed for liberal learning, so different from the spirit of the early teach-ins and Free Speech Movement, left him sick at heart. "There was no knowledge" for such students, he concluded, "only the sociology of knowledge."

Knowing the odds were against him, Goodman made one last attempt to reclaim the modern project as a way of reviving older communal values. His goal was not revolutionary overthrow of the existing order but a "Reformation" of modernity comparable to Luther's assault on Rome in the name of Christian principles. Goodman had long shared Veblen's belief that honest professionalism provided a bulwark against the consumerist impulses of the leisure class. Now he called on professionals to save secular, scientific culture from itself. To be faithful to their vocation and useful to their communities, professionals had to resist the subordination of their work to corporate and military agendas—and at the same time ignore demands they put down their books and join the Revolution. Professionals had come to assume for Goodman the role craftsmen and peasants played in earlier anarchist movements and that small farmers did for the Populists. Their organizations might yet serve as the craft guilds and granges of the twentieth century, modeling high standards and mutual aid for a society enthralled by power.

Much of what Goodman wanted from professionals was in fact the ethic of an older middle class, which he extolled elsewhere for its "independence, initiative, scrupulous honesty, earnestness, utility, respect for thorough scholarship." The new class of salaried professionals was a different animal altogether, the product of a society that subordinated such virtues to the demands of centralized organization. Most professional organizations demanded a monopoly on specialized knowledge indistinguishable from the technocratic claims Goodman denounced in business and government. Reformation of the professions required a more searching investigation of the intertwining of corporate power, expertise, and education.

Goodman's appeal to professional integrity was a noble conclusion to his own career as a public intellectual. He wanted teachers to educate "for keeps," scientists to pursue disinterested inquiry, and architects to interrogate the ethical assumptions in their functionalist designs. He had tried to speak plainly and honorably as an old-fashioned man of letters, and he expected professionals to do the same. Yet one closes *The New Reformation* with the sense that Goodman himself knew it was not enough. The author of *Growing Up Absurd* described himself as an "Angry Middle-Aged Man, disappointed but not resigned." A decade later that disappointment had deepened.

Goodman's last years were a time of despair. The death of his son from a hiking accident devastated him. Radical students ignored him in the rush to revolution. The hurricane of the 1960s had blown away much of his career as a literary artist. He wrote his best poetry at the end, but essentially gave up on fiction. His health declined, and then his heart gave way. A posthumously published essay summed up Goodman's "crazy hope" for a world made "tolerable" for human life. "Politically I want only that the children have bright eyes, the river be clean, food and sex be available, and nobody be pushed around."

V.

Goodman's story illuminates several of the most important episodes of mid-century American intellectual culture—the deployment of humanism in the service of a radical program; the felt connections between culture, personal life, and political change that gave so many movements of the period their unusual moral and emotional charge; and the leading role that intellectuals of the era played as voices of civic conscience. Goodman brought to that moment a belief in the necessary connection between self-reconstruction and social reconstruction that had been the common faith of Dewey, Bourne, and Mumford. Those thinkers differed on many issues, but if they shared one core idea it was what Robert Westbrook has called "democratic self-realization." Real personal growth meant entering into a dialogue with other citizens, expressing oneself in public debate and art, and in the end making both private and public life more human—more *personal*—through the creation of a shared civic culture. "I believe in a rounded, symmetrical development of both the human personality and the community itself," Mumford wrote in 1930, in a statement that sums up nicely the orientation of this generation.

Goodman believed that as well, but it was no easy thing to reinvent the wheel that Dewey and his contemporaries had designed only a few decades earlier. The collapse of the left, the Second World War, McCarthyism, the consolidation of a consumer culture: together these constituted a break in historical memory that made the earlier language of a Dewey or Mumford unrecognizable by mid-century. "The young are honorable and see the problems," Goodman wrote in 1968, "but they don't know anything because we have not taught them anything." Goodman tried to teach his young readers the progressive language of self-reconstruction and social reconstruction but did so with arguments his predecessors would have found puzzling or unpalatable—an appeal to timeless human needs (as opposed to their historicism) and a gestalt psychology that made for an uneasy fit with a larger political or social program. Mumford's credo assumed a more unified self, and a more holistic culture, than postwar conditions allowed. And although Goodman sought to keep faith with that credo, his own work registered the psychic turbulence of a culture that witnessed the vogue of psychoanalysis, restlessness with fixed gender roles, and a search for "authentic" ways of being. By the time Deweyan pragmatism returned to prominence in American intellectual life in the 1980s, the idea of democratic self-realization had largely dropped by the wayside. Richard Rorty's *Contingency, Irony, and Solidarity* insisted on a stark division of the public good and private needs that Dewey himself would never have countenanced. Rorty's politics were in any event closer to New Deal liberalism than the Populist and communitarian commitments that had motivated Dewey's generation, and which Goodman fought for in the postwar period. In retrospect, Goodman's boundary-testing self appears to stand midway between the holism of Dewey, Bourne, and Mumford and the fractured, contingent self of Rorty's liberal-ironist utopia.

Goodman's clear and persistent voice allowed him to keep his audience for much of the 1960s, as the intellectual ground was shifting beneath his feet. The appeal to "the human" so many postwar radicals had articulated was losing its hold even at the height of Goodman's popularity. Pop and minimalist art prefigured the antihumanism that quickly burned through the culture of the left, as radicals embraced structuralist and Marxist theory and academics began to assimilate Foucault's early work. By the turn of the decade, first radical feminism and then other social movements interrogated humanism for its alleged marginalization of difference. Even before his death in 1972, Goodman's unique synthesis of modernism and conservatism was unraveling. Many who once thrilled to his plain-spoken moralism stopped listening.

There are signs that Goodman may find a new audience half a century after his emergence as a public intellectual. Occupy Wall Street activists practice a "horizontal" politics identical to Goodman's anarchist communitarianism. They are not alone. Other social movements emerging in the last decade demonstrate moral and civic commitments Goodman would no doubt have wanted to explore with care. The enthusiasm of young people for organic farming, efforts to carve out smaller sustainable communities from the ruins of deindustrialized heartland cities, experiments in cohousing, parents' home-schooling of children, civic engagement curricula in higher education, even the tentative embrace of environmentalism by evangelicals all scramble the usual left-right categories and assume that people can take hold of an "objective changeable world" for their own purposes. Recent intellectual currents likewise have a Goodmanian flavor. Graduate students and Ph.D.s in the humanities and social sciences are organizing schools such as Brooklyn Brainery and other free-standing "communities of scholars" instead of waiting for tenure-track jobs that will never come. And as the initial euphoria over Barack Obama's election in 2008 collapsed into the old braindead politics, young writers for blogs such as *The New Inquiry* or *Front Porch Republic* turned for inspiration to thinkers indifferent to political conventions. Much of their work beats a path back to the sturdy tradition of American social and cultural criticism that nearly disappeared from the university in the decades after Goodman's death. In reclaiming that tradition, they set aside irony for the earnestness he treasured (a risky move for the young and ambitious). To their credit, few of those involved share Goodman's faith in therapy as the key to active citizenship. *Growing Up Absurd* is more likely to capture their imagination as a work of social criticism free of right-left pieties, not as a gestalt manifesto. Meanwhile, Goodman's rhetorical style—his deployment of "high" intellectual culture in public argument, his combination of do-it-yourself remedies and searching radical criticism—fits the public culture that is emerging out of the wreckage of the academy and traditional journalism. Its practitioners aspire to write in the vernacular; and there is a passion and urgency in their words that recalls Goodman at his best. Maybe his "crazy young allies" have arrived a generation later than he imagined.

VI.

"Everybody talks nice," Goodman complained in *Growing Up Absurd*. "At most there is some unruliness and dumb protest, and some withdrawal." There was a lot more unruliness after 1960, and as the movement exploded Goodman found himself in demand everywhere. Very important people wanted him to speak at very important forums on the Problems of Youth, popular magazines and newspapers solicited articles, he appeared on television, lectured at campuses, testified before school boards, joined one demonstration after another. Celebrity brought with it strange invitations, including one from the National Security Industrial Association—a consortium of arms manufacturers that asked him to speak at its October 1967 symposium in Washington on "Research and Development in the 1970s." In a comic collision of events, the meeting took place just as antiwar protesters gathered in the capital. While his friends picketed outside locked doors, Goodman tore into his hosts as enemies of American democracy. "You are the military industrial of the United States, the most dangerous body of men at present in the world, for you not only implement our disastrous policies but are an overwhelming lobby for them, and you expand and rigidify the wrong use of brains, resources, and labor so that change becomes difficult." He continued as the audience sat in stunned silence: "the best service you people could perform is rather rapidly to phase yourselves out, passing on your relevant knowledge to people better qualified, or reorganizing yourselves with entirely different sponsors and commitments, so that you learn to think and feel in a different way. Since you are most of the R&D that there is, we cannot do without you as people, but we cannot do with you as you are." Then the laughter and booing began, along with scattered applause, but Goodman would not be stopped. The assembled napalm and bomb makers claimed they defended the American way of life, "but we believe, however, that that way of life is unnecessary, ugly, and un-American." Shouts from the audience: "Who are 'we'?"

Goodman pressed on: "we are I and those people outside—we cannot condone your present operations; they should be wiped off the slate."

Anarchist, patriot, conservative moralist, and champion of the modern, Paul Goodman was not one for talking nice.

—CASEY NELSON BLAKE

GROWING UP ABSURD

For
Lore Perls

PREFACE

I.

IN EVERY day's newspaper there are stories about the two subjects that I have brought together in this book, the disgrace of the Organized System of semimonopolies, government, advertisers, etc., and the disaffection of the growing generation. Both are newsworthily scandalous, and for several years now both kinds of stories have come thicker and faster. It is strange that the obvious connections between them are not played up in the newspapers; nor, in the rush of books on the follies, venality, and stifling conformity of the Organization, has there been a book on Youth Problems in the Organized System.

Those of the disaffected youth who are articulate, however—for instance, the Beat or Angry young men—are quite clear about the connection: their main topic is the "system" with which they refuse to co-operate. They will explain that the "good" jobs are frauds and sells, that it is intolerable to have one's style of life dictated by Personnel, that a man is a fool to work to pay installments on a useless refrigerator for his wife, that the movies, TV, and Book-of-the-Month Club are beneath contempt, but the Luce publications make you sick to the stomach; and they will describe with accuracy the cynicism and one-upping of the "typical" junior executive. They consider it the part of reason and honor to wash their hands of all of it.

Naturally, grown-up citizens are concerned about the beatniks and delinquents. The school system has been subjected to criticism. And there is a lot of official talk about the need to conserve our

5

human resources lest Russia get ahead of us. The question is why the grownups do not, more soberly, draw the same connections as the youth. Or, since no doubt many people *are* quite clear about the connection that the structure of society that has become increasingly dominant in our country is disastrous to the growth of excellence and manliness, why don't more people speak up and say so, and initiate a change? The question is an important one and the answer is, I think, a terrible one: that people are so bemused by the way business and politics are carried on at present, with all their intricate relationships, that they have ceased to be able to imagine alternatives. We seem to have lost our genius for inventing changes to satisfy crying needs.

But this stupor is inevitably the baleful influence of the very kind of organizational network that we have: the system pre-empts the available means and capital; it buys up as much of the intelligence as it can and muffles the voices of dissent; and then it irrefutably proclaims that itself is the only possibility of society, for nothing else is thinkable. Let me give a couple of examples of how this works. Suppose (as is the case) that a group of radio and TV broadcasters, competing in the Pickwickian fashion of semimonopolies, control all the stations and channels in an area, amassing the capital and variously bribing Communications Commissioners in order to get them; and the broadcasters tailor their programs to meet the requirements of their advertisers, of the censorship, of their own slick and clique tastes, and of a broad common denominator of the audience, none of whom may be offended: they will then claim not only that the public wants the drivel that they give them, but indeed that nothing else is being created. Of course it is not! not for *these* media; why should a serious artist bother? Or suppose again (as is not quite the case) that in a group of universities only faculties are chosen that are "safe" to the businessmen trustees or the politically appointed regents, and these faculties give out all the degrees and licenses and union cards to the new generation of students, and only such universities can get Foundation or government money for research, and research is incestuously staffed by the same sponsors and according to the same policy, and they allow no one but those they choose, to have access to either the classroom or expensive apparatus: it will then be claimed that there is no other learning or professional competence; that an inspired teacher is not "solid"; that the official projects are the direction of science; that progressive education is a failure; and finally, indeed—as in Dr. James Conant's report on the high schools—that only 15 per cent of the youth are "academically talented" enough to be taught hard subjects. This pre-empting of the means and the brains by the organization, and the shutting out of those who do not conform, can go so far as to cause delusions, as when recently the president of Merck and Company had the effrontery to warn the Congress that its investigation of profiteering in drugs might hinder the quest of scientific knowledge! as if the spirit of Vesalius and Pasteur depended on the financial arrangements of Merck and Company.

But it is in these circumstances that people put up with a system because "there are no alternatives." And when one cannot think of anything to do, soon one ceases to think at all.

To my mind the worst feature of our present organized system of doing things is its indirectness, its blurring of the object. The idea of directly addressing crying objective public needs, like shelter or education, and using our immense and indeed *surplus* resources to satisfy them, is anathema. For in the great interlocking system of corporations people live not by attending to the job, but by status, role playing, and tenure, and they work to maximize profits, prestige, or votes regardless of utility or even public disutility—e.g., the plethora of cars has now become a public disutility, but automobile companies continue to manufacture them and persuade people to buy them. The indispensable premise of city planning, according to a vice president of Webb and Knapp, is to make a "modest long-term profit on the promoter's investment." (His exact sentence, to a meeting of young planners, was, "What we're going to have built will be built only if some developer is going to make a profit from it.") Obviously he is not directly interested in housing people or in city convenience and beauty; he is directly interested in being a good vice president of Webb and Knapp. That is his privilege, but it is not a useful goal, and an idealistic young fellow would not want to be such a man. Another example: Some earnest liberal Congressmen are baffled "how to give Federal aid to education and not interfere in the curriculum and teaching." But when the teaching *function* is respected and assayed by the teacher's peers-in-skill, no one *can* interfere, no one would dare (just as Harvard tossed out McCarthy). The sole function of administration is to smooth the way, but in this country we have the topsy-turvy situation that a teacher must devote himself to satisfying the administrator and financier rather than to doing his job, and a universally admired teacher is fired for disobeying an administrative order that would hinder teaching. (See Appendix A.) Let me give another example, because I want to make this point very clear: These same Congressmen are concerned "how to discourage low-level programming in private TV stations without censorship." Their question presupposes that in communication the prior thing is the existence of networks and channels, rather than something to communicate that needs diffusing. But the prior thing *is* the program, and the only grounds for the license to the station is its ability to transmit it. Nothing could be more stupid than for the communications commission to give to people who handle the means of broadcasting the inventing of what to broadcast, and then, disturbed at the poor quality, to worry about censorship.

We live increasingly, then, in a system in which little direct attention is paid to the object, the function, the program, the task, the need; but immense attention to the role, procedure, prestige, and profit. We don't get the shelter and education because not enough mind is paid to *those* things. Naturally the system is inefficient; the overhead is high; the task is rarely done with love, style, and excitement, for such beauties emerge only from absorption in real objects; sometimes the task is not done at all; and those who could do it best become either cynical or resigned.

2.

In the light of this criticism, the recent scandalous exposures of the advertisers, the government, and the corporations are heartening rather than dismaying. (I am writing in the winter of 1959–60 and we have been hearing about TV, the FCC, Title I, and the Drug Industry; by the time this is published there will be a new series.) The conditions exposed are not new, but now the public skepticism and disgust are mounting; to my ear there is even a new ring; and the investigations are being pushed further, even further than intended by the investigators. The effect of this must be to destroy for many people the image of inviolability and indispensability of the kind of system I have been discussing, to show its phony workings and inevitable dangers. It is the collapse of "public relations."

When the existing state of things is suddenly measured by people against far higher standards than they have been used to, it is no longer the case that there are no alternatives. People are forced by their better judgment to ask very basic questions: Is it possible, *how* is it possible, to have more meaning and honor in work? to put wealth to some real use? to have a high standard of living of whose quality we are not ashamed? to get social justice for those who have been shamefully left out? to have a use of leisure that is not a dismaying waste of a hundred million adults? The large group of independent people who have been out of the swim, with their old-fashioned virtues, suddenly have something admirable about them; one is surprised that they still exist, and their existence is relevant. And from the members of the Organized System itself come acute books criticizing the shortcomings of the Organized System.

It is my belief that we are going to have a change. And once the Americans can recover from their mesmerized condition and its astounding political apathy, our country will be in a most fortunate situation. For the kinds of radical changes we need are those that are appropriate to a fairly general prosperity. They are practicable. They can be summed up as simply restoring, in J. K. Galbraith's phrase,

the "social balance" that we have allowed to become lopsided and
runaway in the present abuse of the country's wealth. For instance,
since we have a vast surplus productivity, we can turn to finding jobs
that will bring out a youth's capacity, and so really conserve human
resources. We can find ways to restore to the worker a say in his production, and so really do something for manly independence. Since
we have a problem of what to do with leisure, we can begin to think
of necessary community enterprises that want doing, and that people can enthusiastically and spontaneously throw themselves into,
and be proud of the results (e.g., beautifying our hideous small
towns). And perhaps thereby create us a culture again. Since we have
the technology, the capital, and the labor, why should we not have
livable cities? Should it be hard to bring back into society the 30 per
cent who are *still* ill fed and ill housed, and more outcast than ever?
What is necessary is directly addressing definite objective needs and
using available resources to satisfy them; doing things that are worth
while just because they are worth while, since we can. Politically,
what we need is government in which a man offers himself as a candidate because he has a new program that he wants to effectuate,
and we choose him because we want that good, and judge that he is
the best man to effectuate it. Is that outlandish?

3.

The present widespread concern about education is only superficially a part of the Cold War, the need to match the Russian scientists. For in the discussions, pretty soon it becomes clear that people
are uneasy about, ashamed of, the world that they have given the
children to grow up in. That world is not manly enough, it is not
earnest enough; a grownup may be cynical (or resigned) about his
own convenient adjustments, but he is by no means willing to see his
children robbed of a worth-while society. With regard to the next
generation, everybody always has a higher standard than the one he
is used to. The standard is ceasing to be one of money and status and

is becoming a standard of the worth of life. But worth, like happiness, comes from bona-fide activity and achievement.

My stratagem in this book is a simple one. I assume that the young *really* need a more worth-while world in order to grow up at all, and I confront this real need with the world that they have been getting. This is the source of their problems. *Our* problem is to remedy the disproportion. We can. Our inheritance, our immense productivity, has been pre-empted and parceled out in a kind of domainal system; but this grandiose and seemingly impregnable feudalism is vulnerable to an earnest attack. One has the persistent thought that if ten thousand people in all walks of life will stand up on their two feet and talk out and insist, we shall get back our country.

INTRODUCTION

"Human Nature" and the Organized System

I.

GROWING up as a human being, a "human nature" assimilates a culture, just as other animals grow up in strength and habits in the environments that are for them, and that complete their natures. Present-day sociologists and anthropologists don't talk much about this process, and not in this way. Among the most competent writers, there is not much mention of "human nature." Their diffidence makes scientific sense, for everything we observe, and even more important, our way of observing it, is already culture and a pattern of culture. What is the sense of mentioning "human nature" if we can never observe it? The old-fashioned naïve thought, that primitive races or children are more natural, is discounted. And the classical anthropological question, What is Man?—"how like an angel, this quintessence of dust!"—is not now asked by anthropologists. Instead, they commence with a chapter on Physical Anthropology and then forget the whole topic and go on to Culture.

On this view, growing up is sometimes treated as if it were acculturation, the process of giving up one culture for another, the way a tribe of Indians takes on the culture of the whites: so the wild Babies give up their "individualistic" mores and ideology, e.g., selfishness or magic thinking or omnipotence, and join the tribe of Society; they are "socialized." More frequently, however, the matter is left vague: we start with a *tabula rasa* and end up with "socialized" and cultured. ("Becoming cultured" and "being adjusted to the social group" are taken almost as synonymous.) Either way, it follows that

13

you can teach people anything; you can adapt them to anything if you use the right techniques of "socializing" or "communicating." The essence of "human nature" is to be pretty indefinitely malleable. "Man," as C. Wright Mills suggests, is what suits a particular type of society in a particular historical stage.

This fateful idea, invented from time to time by philosophers, seems finally to be empirically evident in the most recent decades. For instance, in our highly organized system of machine production and its corresponding social relations, the practice is, by "vocational guidance," to fit people wherever they are needed in the productive system; and whenever the products of the system need to be used up, the practice is, by advertising, to get people to consume them. This works. There is a man for every job and not many are left over, and the shelves are almost always cleared. Again, in the highly organized political industrial systems of Germany, Russia, and now China, it has been possible in a short time to condition great masses to perform as desired. Social scientists observe that these are the facts, and they also devise theories and techniques to produce more facts like them, for the social scientists too are part of the highly organized systems.

2.

Astonishingly different, however, is the opinion of experts who deal with human facts in a more raw, less highly processed, state. Those who have to cope with people in small groups rather than statistically, attending to *them* rather than to some systematic goal—parents and teachers, physicians and psychotherapists, policemen and wardens of jails, shop foremen and grievance committees—these experts are likely to hold stubbornly that there is a "human nature." You can't teach people some things or change them in some ways, and if you persist, you're in for trouble. Contrariwise, if you *don't* provide them with certain things, they'll fill the gaps with eccentric substitutes.

This is immediately evident when something goes wrong; for instance, when a child can't learn to read because he has not yet developed the muscular accommodation of his eyes; if you persist, he withdraws or becomes tricky. Such a case is clear-cut (it is "physical"). But the more important cases have the following form: the child *does* take on the cultural habit, e.g., early toilet training, and indeed the whole corresponding pattern of culture, but there is a diminishing of force, grace, discrimination, intellect, feeling, in specific behaviors or even in his total behavior. He may become too obedient and lacking in initiative, or impractically careful and squeamish; he may develop "psychosomatic" ailments like constipation. Let me give an instance even earlier in life: an infant nurtured in an institution without a particular nurse attending him during the first six months, does not seem to develop abnormally; but if during the end of the first year and for some time thereafter he is not given personal care, he will later be in some ways emotionally cold and unreachable—either some function has failed to develop, or he has already blocked it out as too frustrated and painful. In such examples, the loss of force, grace, and feeling seems to be evidence that somehow the acquired cultural habits do not draw on unimpeded outgoing energy, they are against the grain, they do not fit the child's needs or appetites; *therefore* they have been ill adapted and not assimilated.

That is, on this view we do not need to be able to say what "human nature" *is* in order to be able to say that some training is "against human nature" and you persist in it at peril. Teachers and psychologists who deal practically with growing up and the blocks to growing up may never mention the word "human nature" (indeed, they are better off without too many a priori ideas), but they cling stubbornly to the presumption that at every stage there is a developing potentiality *not* yet cultured, and yet not blank, and that makes possible the taking on of culture. We must draw "it" out, offer "it" opportunities, not violate "it" except for unavoidable reasons. What "it" is, is not definite. It is what, when appealed to in the right circumstances, gives behavior that has force, grace, discrimination, intellect, feeling. This vagueness is of course quite sufficient for education, for education is an art. A good teacher feels his way, looking for response.

3.

The concept of "human nature" has had a varied political history in modern times. If we trace it, we can see the present disagreement developing.

In the eighteenth century, the Age of Reason and the early Romantic Movement, the emphasis was on "*human* nature," referring to man's naturally sympathetic sentiments, his communicative faculties, and unalienable dignity. (Immanuel Kant immortally thought up a philosophy to make these cohere.) Now this human nature was powerfully enlisted in revolutionary struggles against courts and classes, poverty and humiliation, and it began to invent progressive education. Human nature unmistakably demanded liberty, equality, and fraternity—and every man a philosopher and poet.

As an heir of the French Revolution, Karl Marx kept much of this concept. Sympathy recurred as solidarity. Dignity and intellect were perhaps still in the future. But he found an important new essential: man is a maker, he must use his productive nature or be miserable. This too involved a revolutionary program, to give back to man his tools.

During the course of the nineteenth century, however, "human nature" came to be associated with conservative and even reactionary politics. The later Romantics were historical minded and found man naturally traditional and not to be uprooted. A few decades later, narrow interpretations of Darwin were being used to support capitalist enterprise; and racial and somatic theories were used to advance imperial and elite interests. (The emphasis was now on "*nature*"; the humanity became dubious.) It was during this later period that the social scientists began to be diffident about "human nature"; for, politically, they wanted fundamental social changes, different from those indicated by the "natural" theory of the survival of the fittest; and, scientifically, it was evident that many anthropological facts were being called natural which were overwhelmingly cultural. Most of the social scientists began to lay all their stress on political organization, to bring about reform. Nevertheless, scientifically trained anarchists like Kropotkin insisted that "human nature"—which had now become mutual-aiding, knightly, and craftsman-like—was still on the side of revolution.

In our own century, especially since the Twenties and Thirties, the social scientists have found another reason for diffidence: it seems to them that "human nature" implies "not social" and refers to something prior to society, belonging to an isolated individual. They have felt that too much importance has been assigned to Individual Psychology (they were reacting to Freud) and this has stood in the way of organizing people for political reform. It is on this view, finally, that growing up is now interpreted as a process of socializing some rather indefinite kind of animal, and "socializing" is used as a synonym for teaching him the culture.

4.

Let us now proceed more carefully, for we are approaching our present plight. *Is* "being socialized," no matter what the society, the same as growing up and assimilating human culture? The society to which one is socialized would have to be a remarkably finished product.

There are here three distinct concepts, which sometimes seem the same but sometimes very different: (1) society as the relations of human social animals, (2) the human culture carried by society, and (3) a particular society, like ours, formed by its pattern of culture and institutions, and to which its members are socialized or adjusted.

In ordinary, static circumstances, and especially when a dominant system in a society is riding high (as the organized system is with us), socializing to that society seems to provide all valuable culture. But *as soon as we think of a fundamental social change*, we begin to say that people are being adjusted, "socialized," to a very limited kind of human society; and our notion of "human culture" at once broadens out to include ancient, exotic, and even primitive models as superior to the conventional standards (as, e.g., our disaffected groups lay store by the Japanese or the Samoans and Trobriand Islanders). Then at once "human nature" is again invoked to prove the necessity of change, for "human nature" has been thwarted or insulted by the dominant system. "Man" can no *longer* be defined as what suits the dominant system, when the dominant system apparently does not suit men.

I think many social scientists have been making an error in logic. Certainly only society is the carrier of culture (it is not inborn). But it does not follow that socialized and cultured are synonymous. What follows, rather, is that, since culture is so overwhelmingly evident in observing mankind, social properties must be of the essence of original "human nature," and indeed that the "isolated individual" is a product of culture.

This, of course, was just the line that Freud really took. Far from having an Individual Psychology, he tended to exaggerate the social nature of the baby by reading into it preformed traits of his own society. From the earliest infancy, imitation and emulation, love, striving to communicate, rivalry, exclusiveness and jealousy, punishment, introjected authority, identification, growing up on a model, finding safety in conforming—these were among the conflicting elementary functions of the "human nature" that must grow into culture. And Freud, with magnificent originality, tried to show that by their very conflict they made it possible to assimilate culture; only such a social animal could become cultured. Every step of education was the resolution of a difficult social conflict. As might have been expected, from this hectic theory of human nature were drawn the most various political implications. Some, in the interests of community and sex reform, have wanted fundamental social changes, like Ferenczi and Reich. Others, to save religion, have been ul-

tratraditionalist, like Jung or Laforgue. The run of orthodox psychoanalytic practice has been quietist, as the social scientists claimed. But the most surprising implication has been drawn by the social scientists themselves, when they finally got around to making use of modern psychology: they have found in it techniques for harmoniously belonging to the organized system of society!

A curious thing has occurred. Unlike the majority of their predecessors for a century and a half, most of our contemporary social scientists are not interested in fundamental social change. To them, we have apparently reached the summit of institutional progress, and it only remains for the sociologists and applied-anthropologists to mop up the corners and iron out the kinks. Social scientists are not attracted to the conflictful core of Freud's theory of human nature; a more optimistic theory, like Reich's, is paid no attention at all. But they have hit on the theory I mentioned at the beginning: that you can adapt people to anything, if you use the right techniques. Our social scientists have become so accustomed to the highly organized and by-and-large smoothly running society that they have begun to think that "social animal" means "harmoniously belonging." They do not like to think that fighting and dissenting are proper social functions, nor that rebelling or initiating fundamental change is a social function. Rather, if something does not run smoothly, they say it has been improperly socialized; there has been a failure in communication. The animal part is rarely mentioned at all; if it proves annoying, it too has been inadequately socialized.

5.

Nevertheless, we see groups of boys and young men disaffected from the dominant society. The young men are Angry and Beat. The boys are Juvenile Delinquents. These groups are not small, and they will grow larger. Certainly they are suffering. Demonstrably they are not getting enough out of our wealth and civilization. They are not growing up to full capacity. They are failing to assimilate much of the culture. As was predictable, most of the authorities and all of the public spokesmen explain it by saying there has been a failure of socialization. They say that background conditions have interrupted socialization and must be improved. And, not enough effort has been made to guarantee belonging, there must be better bait or punishment.

But perhaps there has *not* been a failure of communication. Perhaps the social message has been communicated clearly to the young men and is unacceptable.

In this book I shall therefore take the opposite tack and ask, "Socialization to what? to what dominant society and available culture?" And if this question is asked, we must at once ask the other question, "Is the harmonious organization to which the young are inadequately socialized, perhaps against human nature, or not worthy of human nature, and *therefore* there is difficulty in growing up?" If this is so, the disaffection of the young is profound and it will not be finally remediable by better techniques of socializing. Instead, there will have to be changes in our society and its culture, so as to meet the appetites and capacities of human nature, in order to grow up.

This brings me to another proposition about growing up, and perhaps the main theme of this book. *Growth, like any ongoing function, requires adequate objects in the environment* to meet the needs and capacities of the growing child, boy, youth, and young man, until he can better choose and make his own environment. It is not a "psychological" question of poor influences and bad attitudes, but an objective question of real opportunities for worthwhile experience. It makes no difference whether the growth is normal or distorted, only real objects will finish the experience. (Even in the psychotherapy of adults one finds that many a stubborn symptom vanishes if there is a real change in the vocational and sexual opportunities, so that the symptom is no longer needed.) It is here that the theory of belonging and socializing breaks down miserably. For it can be shown—I intend to show—that with all the harmonious belonging and all the tidying up of background conditions that you please, our abundant society is at present simply deficient in many of the most elementary objective opportunities and worth-while goals that could make growing up possible. It is lacking in enough man's work. It is lacking in honest public speech, and people are not taken seriously. It is lacking in the opportunity to be useful. It thwarts aptitude and creates stupidity. It corrupts ingenuous patriotism. It corrupts the fine arts. It shackles science. It dampens animal ardor. It discourages the religious convictions of Justification and Vocation and it dims the sense that there is a Creation. It has no Honor. It has no Community.

Just look at that list. There is nothing in it that is surprising, in either the small letters or the capitals. I have nothing subtle or novel to say in this book; these are the things that *everybody* knows. And nevertheless the Governor of New York says, "We must give these young men a sense of belonging."

Thwarted, or starved, in the important objects proper to young capacities, the boys and young men naturally find or invent deviant objects for themselves; this is the beautiful shaping power of our human nature. Their choices and inventions are rarely charming, usually stupid, and often disastrous; we cannot expect average kids to deviate with genius. But on the other hand, the young men who conform to the dominant society become for the most part apathetic, disappointed, cynical, and wasted.

(I say the "young men and boys" rather than the "young people" because the problems I want to discuss in this book belong primarily, in our society, to the boys: how to be useful and make something of oneself. A girl does not *have* to, she is not expected to, "make something" of herself. Her career does not have to be self-justifying, for she will have children, which is absolutely self-justifying, like any other natural or creative act. With this background, it is less important, for instance, what job an average young woman works at till she is married. The quest for the glamour job is given at least a little substance by its relation to a "better" marriage. Correspondingly, our "youth troubles" are boys' troubles—female delinquency is sexual: "incorrigibility" and unmarried pregnancy. Yet as every woman knows, these problems are intensely interesting to women, for if the boys do not grow to be men, where shall the women find men? If the husband is running the rat race of the organized system, there is not much father for the children.)

6.

This essay is on "Youth Problems." But the reader will find, perhaps to his surprise, that I shall make little distinction in value between talking about middle-class youths being groomed for ten-thousand-dollar "slots" in business and Madison Avenue, or underprivileged hoodlums fatalistically hurrying to a reformatory; or between hard-working young fathers and idle Beats with beards. For the salient thing is the sameness among them, the waste of humanity. In our society, bright lively children, with the potentiality for knowledge, noble ideals, honest effort, and some kind of worth-while achievement, are transformed into useless and cynical bipeds, or decent young men trapped or early resigned, whether in or out of the organized system. My purpose is a simple one: to show how it is desperately hard these days for an average child to grow up to be a man, for our present organized system of society does not want men. They are not safe. They do not suit.

Our public officials are now much concerned about the "waste of human resources." Dr. Conant, the former president of Harvard, has surveyed the high schools. But our officials are not serious, and Dr. Conant's report is superficial. For the big causes of stupidity, of lack of initiative and lack of honorable incentive, are glaring; yet they do not intend to notice or remedy these big causes. (This very avoidance of the real issues on the part of our public officials is, indeed, one of the big causes.) Our society cannot have it both ways: to maintain a conformist and ignoble system *and* to have skillful and spirited men to man that system with.

7.

It is not my purpose in this essay to outline a better world. But I think it requires no deep wisdom or astonishing imagination to know what we need, and in a later chapter of this book I shall even list some points of a rough program. The prevalent sentiment that it is infinitely impractical to follow the suggestions of common reason, is not sound. If it is impractical, it is because some people don't want to, and the rest of us don't want to enough.

For instance, there is a persistent presumption among our liberal statesmen that the old radical-liberal program has been importantly achieved, and that therefore there is no familiar major proposal practical to remedy admittedly crying ills. This is a false presumption. Throughout the nineteenth and twentieth centuries, the radical-liberal program was continually compromised, curtailed, sometimes realized in form without content, sometimes swept under the rug and heard of no more. I shall later list more than twenty fundamental liberal demands that have gone unfulfilled which would still be live and salutary issues today if anybody wanted to push them. This has occurred, and keeps occurring, by the mutual accommodation of both "liberals" and "conservatives" in the interests of creating our present coalition of semimonopolies, trade unions, government, Madison Avenue, etc. (including a large bloc of outlaw gangsters); thriving on maximum profits and full employment; but without regard for utility, quality, rational productivity, personal freedom, independent enterprise, human scale, manly vocation, or genuine culture. It is in this accommodation that our politicians survive, but it does not make for statesmanship. Even so mild a critic as Henry Steele Commager, in the *New York Times*, judges that we have had only three reputable statesmen in fifty years, the last of whom died fifteen years ago. While one may not agree with his number and examples, there is no doubt that we have been living in a political limbo.

Naturally this unnatural system has generated its own troubles, whether we think of the unlivable communities, the collapse of public ethics, or the problems of youth. I shall try to show in this essay that these ills are by no means inherent in modern technological or ecological conditions, nor in the American Constitution as such. But they have followed precisely from the betrayal and neglect of the old radical-liberal program and other changes proposed to keep up with the advancing technology, the growth of population, and the revolution in morals. Important reforms did not occur when they were ripe, and we have inherited the consequences: a wilderness of unfinished situations, unequal developments and inconsistent standards, as well as new business. And now, sometimes the remedy must be stoically to go back and carry *through* the old programs (as we are having to do with racial integration), e.g., finally to insist on stringent master-planning of cities and conserving of resources, or on really limiting monopolies. Sometimes we must make changes to catch up—e.g., to make the laws more consistent with the sexual revolution, or to make the expenditure on public goods more commensurate with the geometrically increasing complications of a more crowded population. And sometimes, finally, we have to invent really new devices—e.g., how to make the industrial technology humanly important for its workmen, how to use leisure nobly, or even how, in a rich society, to be decently poor if one so chooses.

This book is not about these great subjects. But they hover in the background of the great subject that it is about. For it is impossible for the average boy to grow up and use the remarkable capacities that are in every boy, unless the world is for him and makes sense. And a society makes sense when it understands that its chief wealth *is* these capacities.

I. JOBS

IT'S HARD to grow up when there isn't enough man's work. There is "nearly full employment" (with highly significant exceptions), but there get to be fewer jobs that are necessary or unquestionably useful; that require energy and draw on some of one's best capacities; and that can be done keeping one's honor and dignity. In explaining the widespread troubles of adolescents and young men, this simple objective factor is not much mentioned. Let us here insist on it.

By "man's work" I mean a very simple idea, so simple that it is clearer to ingenuous boys than to most adults. To produce necessary food and shelter is man's work. During most of economic history most men have done this drudging work, secure that it was justified and worthy of a man to do it, though often feeling that the social conditions under which they did it were *not* worthy of a man, thinking, "It's better to die than to live so hard"—but they worked on. When the environment is forbidding, as in the Swiss Alps or the Aran Islands, we regard such work with poetic awe. In emergencies it is heroic, as when the bakers of Paris maintained the supply of bread during the French Revolution, or the milkman did not miss a day's delivery when the bombs recently tore up London.

At present there is little such subsistence work. In *Communitas* my brother and I guess that one-tenth of our economy is devoted to it; it is more likely one-twentieth. Production of food is actively discouraged. Farmers are not wanted and the young men go elsewhere. (The farm population is now less than 15 per cent of the total population.)

Building, on the contrary, is immensely needed. New York City needs 65,000 new units a year, and is getting, net, 16,000. One would think that ambitious boys would flock to this work. But here we find that building, too, is discouraged. In a great city, for the last twenty years hundreds of thousands have been ill housed, yet we do not see science, industry, and labor enthusiastically enlisted in finding the quick solution to a definite problem. The promoters are interested in long-term investments, the real estate men in speculation, the city planners in votes and graft. The building craftsmen cannily see to it that their own numbers remain few, their methods antiquated, and their rewards high. None of these people is much interested in providing shelter, and nobody is at all interested in providing new manly jobs.

Once we turn away from the absolutely necessary subsistence jobs, however, we find that an enormous proportion of our production is not even unquestionably useful. Everybody knows and also feels this, and there has recently been a flood of books about our surfeit of honey, our insolent chariots, the follies of exurban ranch houses, our hucksters and our synthetic demand. Many acute things are said about this useless production and advertising, but not much about the workmen producing it and their frame of mind; and nothing at all, so far as I have noticed, about the plight of a young fellow looking for a manly occupation. The eloquent critics of the American way of life have themselves been so seduced by it that they think only in terms of selling commodities and point out that the goods are valueless; but they fail to see that people are being wasted and their skills insulted. (To give an analogy, in the many gleeful onslaughts on the Popular Culture that have appeared in recent years, there has been little thought of the plight of the honest artist cut off from his audience and sometimes, in public arts such as theater and architecture, from his medium.)

What is strange about it? American society has tried so hard and so ably to defend the practice and theory of production for profit and not primarily for use that now it has succeeded in making its jobs and products profitable and useless.

2.

Consider a likely useful job. A youth who is alert and willing but not "verbally intelligent"—perhaps he has quit high school at the eleventh grade (the median), as soon as he legally could—chooses for auto mechanic. That's a good job, familiar to him, he often watched them as a kid. It's careful and dirty at the same time. In a small garage it's sociable; one can talk to the customers (girls). You please people in trouble by fixing their cars, and a man is proud to see rolling out on its own the car that limped in behind the tow truck. The pay is as good as the next fellow's, who is respected.

So our young man takes this first-rate job. But what when he then learns that the cars have a built-in obsolescence, that the manufacturers do not want them to be repaired or repairable? They have lobbied a law that requires them to provide spare parts for only five years (it used to be ten). Repairing the new cars is often a matter of cosmetics, not mechanics; and the repairs are pointlessly expensive—a tail fin might cost $150. The insurance rates therefore double and treble on old and new cars both. Gone are the days of keeping the jalopies in good shape, the artist-work of a proud mechanic. But everybody is paying for foolishness, for in fact the new models are only trivially superior; the whole thing is a sell.

It is hard for the young man now to maintain his feelings of justification, sociability, serviceability. It is not surprising if he quickly becomes cynical and time-serving, interested in a fast buck. And so, on the notorious *Reader's Digest* test, the investigators (coming in with a disconnected coil wire) found that 63 per cent of mechanics charged for repairs they didn't make, and lucky if they didn't also take out the new fuel pump and replace it with a used one (65 per cent of radio repair shops, but *only* 49 per cent of watch repairmen "lied, overcharged, or gave false diagnoses").

There is an hypothesis that an important predisposition to juvenile delinquency is the combination of low verbal intelligence with high manual intelligence, delinquency giving a way of self-expression where other avenues are blocked by lack of schooling. A lad so endowed might well apply himself to the useful trade of mechanic.

3.

Most manual jobs do not lend themselves so readily to knowing the facts and fraudulently taking advantage oneself. In factory jobs the workman is likely to be ignorant of what goes on, since he performs a small operation on a big machine that he does not understand. Even so, there is evidence that he has the same disbelief in the enterprise as a whole, with a resulting attitude of profound indifference.

Semiskilled factory operatives are the largest category of workmen. (I am leafing through the U.S. Department of Labor's *Occupational Outlook Handbook*, 1957.) Big companies have tried the devices of applied anthropology to enhance the loyalty of these men to the firm, but apparently the effort is hopeless, for it is found that a thumping majority of the men don't care about the job or the firm; they couldn't care less and you can't make them care more. But this is *not* because of wages, hours, or working conditions, or management. On the contrary, tests that show the men's indifference to the company show also their (unaware) admiration for the way the company has designed and manages the plant; it is their very model of style, efficiency, and correct behavior. (Robert Dubin, for the U.S. Public Health Service.) Maybe if the men understood more, they would admire less. The union and the grievance committee take care of wages, hours, and conditions; these are the things the workmen themselves fought for and won. (Something was missing in that victory, and we have inherited the failure as well as the success.) The conclusion must be that workmen are indifferent to the job because of its intrinsic nature: it does not enlist worth-while capacities, it is not "interesting"; it is not his, he is not "in" on it; the product is not really useful. And indeed, research directly on the subject, by Frederick Herzberg on Motivation to Work, shows that it is defects in the intrinsic aspects of the job that make workmen "unhappy." A survey of the literature (in Herzberg's *Job Attitudes*) shows that Interest is second in importance only to Security, whereas Wages, Conditions, Socializing, Hours, Ease, and Benefits are far less important. But foremen, significantly enough, think that the most important thing to the workman is his wages. (The investigators do not seem to inquire about the usefulness of the job—as if a primary purpose of *working* at a job were not that it is good *for* something! My guess is that a large factor in "Security" is the resigned reaction to not being able to take into account whether the work of one's hands is useful for anything; for in a normal life situation, if what we do is useful, we feel secure about being needed. The other largest factor in "Security" is, I think, the sense of being needed for one's unique contribution, and this is measured in these tests by the primary importance the workers assign to being "in" on things and to "work done being appreciated." (Table prepared by Labor Relations Institute of New York.)

Limited as they are, what a remarkable insight such studies give us, that men want to do valuable work and work that is somehow theirs! But they are thwarted.

Is not this the "waste of our human resources"?

The case is that by the "sole-prerogative" clause in union contracts the employer has the sole right to determine what is to be produced, how it is to be produced, what plants are to be built and where, what kinds of machinery are to be installed, when workers are to be hired and laid off, and how production operations are to be rationalized. (Frank Marquart.) There is *none* of this that is inevitable in running a machine economy; but *if* these are the circumstances, it is not surprising that the factory operatives' actual code has absolutely nothing to do with useful service or increasing production, but is notoriously devoted to "interpersonal relations"; (1) don't turn out too much work; (2) don't turn out too little work; (3) don't squeal on a fellow worker; (4) don't act like a big-shot. This is how to belong.

4.

Let us go on to the Occupational Outlook of those who are verbally bright. Among this group, simply because they cannot help asking more general questions—e.g., about utility—the problem of finding man's work is harder, and their disillusion is more poignant.

> He explained to her why it was hard to find a satisfactory job of work to do. He had liked working with the power drill, testing the rocky envelope of the shore, but then the employers asked him to take a great oath of loyalty.
>
> "What!" cried Rosalind. "Do you have scruples about telling a convenient fib?"
>
> "No, I don't. But I felt uneasy about the sanity of the director asking me to swear to opinions on such complicated questions when my job was digging with a power drill. I can't work with a man who might suddenly have a wild fit."
>
> … "Why don't you get a job driving one of the big trucks along here?"
>
> "I don't like what's in the boxes," said Horatio sadly. "It could just as well drop in the river—and I'd make mistakes and drop it there."
>
> "Is it bad stuff?"
>
> "No, just useless. It takes the heart out of me to work at something useless and I begin to make mistakes. I don't mind putting profits in somebody's pocket—but the job also has to be useful for something."
>
> … "Why don't you go to the woods and be a lumberjack?"
>
> "No! they chop down the trees just to print off the New York Times!"
>
> (*The Empire City*, III, i, 3.)

The more intelligent worker's "indifference" is likely to appear more nakedly as profound resignation, and his cynicism may sharpen to outright racketeering.

"Teaching," says the *Handbook*, "is the largest of the professions." So suppose our now verbally bright young man chooses for teacher, in the high school system or, by exception, in the elementary schools if he understands that the elementary grades are the vitally important ones and require the most ability to teach well (and of course they have less prestige). Teaching is necessary and useful work; it is real and creative, for it directly confronts an important subject matter, the children themselves; it is obviously self-justifying; and it is ennobled by the arts and sciences. Those who practice teaching do not for the most part succumb to cynicism or indifference—the children are too immediate and real for the teachers to become callous—but, most of the school systems being what they are, can teachers fail to come to suffer first despair and then deep resignation? Resignation occurs psychologically as follows: frustrated in essential action, they nevertheless cannot quit in anger, because the task is necessary; so the anger turns inward and is felt as resignation. (Naturally, the resigned teacher may then put on a happy face and keep very busy.)

For the job is carried on under impossible conditions of overcrowding and saving public money. *Not* that there is not enough social wealth, but first things are not put first. Also, the school system has spurious aims. It soon becomes clear that the underlying aims are to relieve the home and keep the kids quiet; or, suddenly, the aim is to produce physicists. Timid supervisors, bigoted clerics, and ignorant school boards forbid real teaching. The emotional release and sexual expression of the children are taboo. A commercially debauched popular culture makes learning disesteemed. The academic curriculum is mangled by the demands of reactionaries, liberals, and demented warriors. Progressive methods are emasculated. Attention to each case is out of the question, and all the children—the bright, the average, and the dull—are systematically retarded one way or another, while the teacher's hands are tied. Naturally the pay is low—for the work is hard, useful, and of public concern, all three of which qualities tend to bring lower pay. It is alleged that the low pay is why there is a shortage of teachers and why the best do not choose the profession. My guess is that the best avoid it because of the certainty of miseducating. Nor are the best *wanted* by the system, for they are not safe. Bertrand Russell was rejected by New York's City College and would not have been accepted in a New York grade school.

5.

Next, what happens to the verbally bright who have no zeal for a serviceable profession and who have no particular scientific or artistic bent? For the most part they make up the tribes of salesmanship, entertainment, business management, promotion, and advertising. Here of course there is no question of utility or honor to begin with, so an ingenuous boy will not look here for a manly career. Nevertheless, though we can pass by the sufferings of these well-paid callings, much publicized by their own writers, they are important to our theme because of the model they present to the growing boy.

Consider the men and women in TV advertisements, demonstrating the product and singing the jingle. They are clowns and mannequins, in grimace, speech, and action. And again, what I want to call attention to in this advertising is not the economic problem of synthetic demand, and not the cultural problem of Popular Culture, but the human problem that these are human beings working as clowns; that the writers and designers of it are human beings thinking like idiots; and the broadcasters and underwriters know and abet what goes on—

Juicily glubbily
Blubber *is dubbily*
delicious and nutritious
—eat it, Kitty, it's good.

Alternately, they are liars, confidence men, smooth talkers, obsequious, insolent, etc., etc.

The popular-cultural content of the advertisements is somewhat neutralized by *Mad* magazine, the bible of the twelve-year-olds who can read. But far more influential and hard to counteract is the *fact* that the workmen and the patrons of this enterprise are human beings. (Highly approved, too.) They are not good models for a boy looking for a manly job that is useful and necessary, requiring human energy and capacity, and that can be done with honor and dignity. They are a good sign that not many such jobs will be available.

The popular estimation is rather different. Consider the following: "As one possible aid, I suggested to the Senate subcommittee that they alert celebrities and leaders in the fields of sports, movies, theater and television to the help they can offer by getting close to these [delinquent] kids. By giving them positive 'heroes' they know and can talk to, instead of the misguided image of trouble-making buddies, they could aid greatly in guiding these normal aspirations for fame and status into wholesome progressive channels." (Jackie Robinson, who was formerly on the Connecticut Parole Board.) Or again: when a mass cross-section of Oklahoma high school juniors and seniors was asked which living person they would like to be, the boys named Pat Boone, Ricky Nelson, and President Eisenhower; the girls chose Debbie Reynolds, Elizabeth Taylor, and Natalie Wood.

The rigged Quiz shows, which created a scandal in 1959, were a remarkably pure distillate of our American cookery. We start with the brute facts that (a) in our abundant expanding economy it is necessary to give money away to increase spending, production, and profits; and (b) that this money must not be used for useful public goods in taxes, but must be plowed back as "business expenses," even though there is a shameful shortage of schools, housing, etc. Yet when the TV people at first tried simply to give the money away for nothing (for having heard of George Washington), there was a great Calvinistic outcry that this was demoralizing (we may gamble on the horses only to improve the breed). So they hit on the notion of a real contest with prizes. But then, of course, they could not resist making the show itself profitable, and competitive in the (also rigged) ratings with other shows, so the experts in the entertainment-commodity manufactured phony contests. And to cap the climax of fraudulence, the hero of the phony contests proceeded to persuade himself, so he says, that his behavior was educational!

The behavior of the networks was correspondingly typical. These business organizations claim the loyalty of their employees, but at the first breath of trouble they were ruthless and disloyal to their employees. (Even McCarthy was loyal to his gang.) They want to maximize profits and yet be absolutely safe from any risk. Consider their claim that they knew nothing about the fraud. But if they watched the shows that they were broadcasting, they could not *possibly*, as professionals, not have known the facts, for there were obvious type-casting, acting, plot, etc. If they are not professionals, they are incompetent. But if they don't watch what they broadcast, then they are utterly irresponsible and on what grounds do they have the franchises to the channels? We may offer them the choice: that they are liars or incompetent or irresponsible.

The later direction of the investigation seems to me more important, the inquiry into the bribed disk-jockeying; for this deals directly with our crucial economic problem of synthesized demand, made taste, debauching the public and preventing the emergence and formation of natural taste. In such circumstances there cannot possibly be an American culture; we are doomed to nausea and barbarism. And *then* these baboons have the effrontery to declare that they give the people what the people demand and that they are not responsible for the level of the movies, the music, the plays, the books!

Finally, in leafing through the *Occupational Outlook Handbook*, we notice that the armed forces employ a large number. Here our young man can become involved in a world-wide demented enterprise, with personnel and activities corresponding.

6.

Thus, on the simple criteria of unquestioned utility, employing human capacities, and honor, there are not enough worthy jobs in our economy for average boys and adolescents to grow up toward. There are of course thousands of jobs that are worthy and self-justifying, and thousands that can be made so by stubborn integrity, especially if one can work as an independent. Extraordinary intelligence or special talent, also, can often carve out a place for itself—conversely, their usual corruption and waste are all the more sickening. But by and large our economic society is *not* geared for the cultivation of its young or the attainment of important goals that they can work toward.

This is evident from the usual kind of vocational guidance, which consists of measuring the boy and finding some place in the economy where he can be fitted; chopping him down to make him fit; or neglecting him if they can't find his slot. Personnel directors do not much try to scrutinize the economy in order to find some activity that is a real opportunity for the boy, and then to create an opportunity if they can't find one. To do this would be an horrendous task; I am not sure it could be done if we wanted to do it. But the question is whether anything less makes sense if we mean to speak seriously about the troubles of the young men.

Surely by now, however, many readers are objecting that this entire argument is pointless because people in *fact* don't think of their jobs in this way at all. *Nobody* asks if a job is useful or honorable (within the limits of business ethics). A man gets a job that pays well, or well enough, that has prestige, and good conditions, or at least tolerable conditions. I agree with these objections as to the fact. (I hope we are wrong.) But *the question is what it means to grow up into such a fact as: "During my productive years I will spend eight hours a day doing what is no good."*

7.

Yet, economically and vocationally, a very large population of the young people are in a plight more drastic than anything so far mentioned. In our society as it is, there are not enough worthy jobs. But if our society, being as it is, were run more efficiently and soberly, for a majority there would soon not be any jobs at all. There is at present nearly full employment and there may be for some years, yet a vast number of young people are rationally unemployable, useless. This paradox is essential to explain their present temper.

Our society, which is not geared to the cultivation of its young, *is* geared to a profitable expanding production, a so-called high standard of living of mediocre value, and the maintenance of nearly full employment. Politically, the chief of these is full employment. In a crisis, when profitable production is temporarily curtailed, government spending increases and jobs are manufactured. In "normalcy"—a condition of slow boom—the easy credit, installment buying, and artificially induced demand for useless goods create jobs for all and good profits for some.

Now, back in the Thirties, when the New Deal attempted by hook or crook to put people back to work and give them money to revive the shattered economy, there was an outcry of moral indignation from the conservatives that many of the jobs were "boondoggling," useless made-work. It was insisted, and rightly, that such work was demoralizing to the workers themselves. It is a question of a word, but a candid critic might certainly say that many of the jobs in our present "normal" production are useless made-work. The tail fins and built-in obsolescence might be called boondoggling. The $64,000 Question and the busy hum of Madison Avenue might certainly be called boondoggling. Certain tax-dodge Foundations are boondoggling. What of business lunches and expense accounts? fringe benefits? the comic categories of occupation in the building trades? the extra stagehands and musicians of the theater crafts? These jolly devices to put money back to work no doubt have a demoralizing effect on somebody or other (certainly on me, they make me green with envy), but where is the moral indignation from Top Management?

Suppose we would cut out the boondoggling and gear our society to a more sensible abundance, with efficient production of quality goods, distribution in a natural market, counterinflation and sober credit. At once the work week would be cut to, say, twenty hours instead of forty. (Important People have already mentioned the figure thirty.) Or alternately, half the labor force would be unemployed. Suppose too—and how can we not suppose it?—that the automatic machines are used generally, rather than just to get rid of badly organized unskilled labor. The unemployment will be still more drastic.

(To give the most striking example: in steel, the annual increase in productivity is 4 per cent, the plants work at 50 per cent of capacity, and the companies can break even and stop producing at *less than 30 per cent* of capacity. These are the conditions that forced the steel strike, as desperate self-protection. (Estes Kefauver, quoting Gardiner Means and Fred Gardner.)

Everybody knows this, nobody wants to talk about it much, for we don't know how to cope with it. The effect is that we are living a kind of lie. Long ago, labor leaders used to fight for the shorter work week, but now they don't, because they're pretty sure they don't want it. Indeed, when hours are reduced, the tendency is to get a second, part-time, job and raise the standard of living, *because* the job is meaningless and one must have something; but the standard of living is pretty meaningless, too. Nor is this strange atmosphere a new thing. For at least a generation the maximum sensible use of our productivity could have thrown a vast population out of work, or relieved everybody of a lot of useless work, depending on how you take it. (Consider with how little cutback of useful civilian production the economy produced the war goods and maintained an Army, economically unemployed.) The plain truth is that at present very many of us are useless, not needed, rationally unemployable. It is in this paradoxical atmosphere that young persons grow up. It looks busy and expansive, but it is rationally at a stalemate.

8.

These considerations apply to all ages and classes; but it is of course among poor youth (and the aged) that they show up first and worst.

They are the most unemployable. For a long time our society has not been geared to the cultivation of the young. In our country 42 per cent have graduated from high school (predicted census, 1960); less than 8 per cent have graduated from college. The high school trend for at least the near future is not much different: there will be a high proportion of drop-outs before the twelfth grade; but *markedly more* of the rest will go on to college; that is, the stratification will harden. Now the schooling in neither the high schools nor the colleges is much good—if it were better more kids would stick to it; yet at present, if we made a list we should find that a large proportion of the dwindling number of unquestionably useful or self-justifying jobs, in the humane professions and the arts and sciences, require education; and in the future, there is no doubt that the more educated will have the jobs, in running an efficient, highly technical economy and an administrative society placing a premium on verbal skills.

(Between 1947 and 1957, professional and technical workers increased 61 per cent, clerical workers 23 per cent, but factory operatives only 4½ per cent and laborers 4 per cent.—Census.)

For the uneducated there will be no jobs at all. This is humanly most unfortunate, for presumably those who have learned something in schools, and have the knack of surviving the boredom of those schools, could also make something of idleness; whereas the uneducated are useless at leisure too. It takes application, a fine sense of value, and a powerful community-spirit for a people to have serious leisure, and this has not been the genius of the Americans.

From this point of view we can sympathetically understand the pathos of our American school policy, which otherwise seems so inexplicable; at great expense compelling kids to go to school who do not want to and who will not profit by it. There are of course unpedagogic motives, like relieving the home, controlling delinquency, and keeping kids from competing for jobs. But there is also this desperately earnest pedagogic motive, of preparing the kids to take *some* part in a democratic society that does not need them. Otherwise, what will become of them, if they don't know anything?

Compulsory public education spread universally during the nineteenth century to provide the reading, writing, and arithmetic necessary to build a modern industrial economy. With the overmaturity of the economy, the teachers are struggling to preserve the elementary system when the economy no longer requires it and is stingy about paying for it. The demand is for scientists and technicians, the 15 per cent of the "academically talented." "For a vast majority [in the high schools]," says Dr. Conant in *The Child, the Parent, and the State*, "the vocational courses are the vital core of the program. They represent something related directly to the ambitions of the boys and girls." But somehow, far more than half of these quit. How is that?

9.

Let us sum up again. The majority of young people are faced with the following alternative: Either society is a benevolently frivolous racket in which they'll manage to boondoggle, though less profitably than the more privileged; or society is serious (and they hope still benevolent enough to support them), but they are useless and hopelessly out. Such thoughts do not encourage productive life. Naturally young people are more sanguine and look for man's work, but few find it. Some settle for a "good job"; most settle for a lousy job; a few, but an increasing number, don't settle.

I often ask, "What do you want to work at? If you have the chance. When you get out of school, college, the service, etc."

Some answer right off and tell their definite plans and projects, highly approved by Papa. I'm pleased for them, but it's a bit boring, because they are such squares.

Quite a few will, with prompting, come out with astounding stereotyped, conceited fantasies, such as becoming a movie actor when they are "discovered"—"like Marlon Brando, but in my own way."

Very rarely somebody will, maybe defiantly and defensively, maybe diffidently but proudly, make you know that he knows very well what he is going to do; it is something great; and he is indeed already doing it, which is the real test.

The usual answer, perhaps the normal answer, is "I don't know," meaning, "I'm looking; I haven't found the right thing; it's discouraging but not hopeless."

But the terrible answer is, "Nothing." The young man doesn't want to do anything.

—I remember talking to half a dozen young fellows at Van Wagner's Beach outside of Hamilton, Ontario; and all of them had this one thing to say: "Nothing." They didn't believe that what to work at was the kind of thing one *wanted*. They rather expected that two or three of them would work for the electric company in town, but they couldn't care less. I turned away from the conversation abruptly because of the uncontrollable burning tears in my eyes and constriction in my chest. Not feeling sorry for them, but tears of frank dismay for the waste of our humanity (they were nice kids). And it is out of that incident that many years later I am writing this book.

II. BEING TAKEN SERIOUSLY

I.

THE SIMPLE job plight of these adolescents could not be remedied without a social revolution. Therefore it is not astonishing if the most well-intentioned public spokesmen do not mention it at all. In this book we shall come on other objective factors that are not mentioned. But it is hard to grow up in a society in which one's important problems are treated as nonexistent. It is impossible to belong to it, it is hard to fight to change it. The effect must be rather to feel disaffected, and all the more restive if one is smothered by well-meaning social workers and PAL's who don't seem to understand the real irk. The boys cannot articulate the real irk themselves.

For instance, what public spokesman could discuss the jobs? The ideal of having a real job that you risk your soul in and make good or be damned, belongs to the heroic age of capitalist enterprise, imbued with self-righteous beliefs about hard work, thrift, and public morals. Such an ideal might still have been mentioned in public fifty years ago; in our era of risk-insured semimonopolies and advertised vices it would be met with a ghastly stillness. Or alternately, to want a job that exercises a man's capacities in an enterprise useful to society, is utopian anarcho-syndicalism; it is labor invading the domain of management. No labor leader has entertained such a thought in our generation. Management has the "sole prerogative" to determine the products and the machines. Again, to speak of the likelihood or the desirability of unemployment, like Norbert Wiener or J. K. Galbraith, is to be politically nonprofessional. Yet every kid somehow knows that if he quits school he won't get ahead—and the majority quit.

During, let us say, 1890–1936, on Marxist grounds, the fight for working conditions, for security, wages, hours, the union, the dignity of labor, *was* mentioned, and it gave the worker or the youth something worth while. But because of their historical theory of the "alienation of labor" (that the worker *must* become less and less in control of the work of his hands) the Marxist parties never fought for the man-worthy job itself. It is not surprising now if workmen accept their alienation, and are indifferent also to Marxist politics.

2.

When the objective factors cannot be mentioned, however, other rhetoric is used instead, and in this chapter let us examine its style, as applied, for instance, to juvenile delinquency, on which there is a good deal of oratory.

In our times the usual principle of such speech is that the others, the delinquent boys, are not taken seriously as existing, as having, like oneself, real aims in a real world. They are not condemned, they are not accepted. Instead they are a "youth problem" and the emphasis is on their "background conditions," which one can manipulate; they are said to be subject to "tensions" that one can alleviate. The aim is not to give human beings real goals that warrant belief, and tasks to share in, but to re-establish "belonging," although this kind of speech and thought is precisely calculated to avoid contact and so makes belonging impossible. When such efforts don't work, one finally takes some of the boys seriously as existing and uses force to make them not exist.

Let me give a childish but important illustration of how this works out. A boy of ten or eleven has a few great sexual adventures— *he* thinks they're great—but then he has the bad luck to get caught and get in trouble. They try to persuade him by punishment and other explanations that some different behavior is much better, but he knows by the evidence of his senses that nothing could be better. If he gives in, he lives on in a profound disbelief, a disbelief in their candor and a disbelief even of his own body feelings. But if he persists and proves incorrigible, then the evidence of his senses is attached to what is socially punished, explained away; he may even be put away. The basic trouble here is that they do not really believe he has had the sexual experience. That objective factor is inconvenient for them; therefore it cannot exist. Instead, this is *merely* a case of insecure affection at home, slum housing, comic books, and naughty companions: tensions and conditions. My hunch, as I shall discuss later, is that this kind of early sexual adventure and misadventure is fairly common in delinquency. It is called precocious, abnormal, artificially stimulated, and so forth—an index of future delinquency. In my opinion that's rubbish, but be that as it may; what is important in a particular case is that there is a stubborn new fact. Attempting to nullify it makes further growth impossible (and *creates* the future delinquency). The sensible course would be to accept it as a valuable part of further growth. But if this were done, they fear that the approved little hero would be a rotten apple to his peers, who now would suddenly *all* become precocious, abnormal, artificially stimulated, and prone to delinquency.

The sexual plight of these children is officially not mentioned. The revolutionary attack on hypocrisy by Ibsen, Freud, Ellis, Dreiser, did not succeed this far. Is it an eccentric opinion that an important part of the kids' restiveness in school from the onset of puberty has to do with puberty? The teachers talk about it among themselves, all right. (In his school, Bertrand Russell thought it was better if they had the sex, so they could give their undivided attention to mathematics, which was the main thing.) But since this objective factor does not *exist* in our schools, the school itself begins to be irrelevant. The question here is not whether the sexuality should be discouraged or encouraged. That is an important issue, but far more important is that it is hard to grow up when existing facts are treated as though they do not exist. For then there is no dialogue, it is impossible to be taken seriously, to be understood, to make a bridge between oneself and society.

In American society we have perfected a remarkable form of censorship: to allow every one his political right to say what he believes, but to swamp his little boat with literally thousands of millions of newspapers, mass-circulation magazines, best-selling books, broadcasts, and public pronouncements that disregard what he says and give the official way of looking at things. Usually there is no conspiracy to do this; it is simply that what he says is not what people are talking about, it is not newsworthy.

(There is no conspiracy, but it is *not* undeliberate. "If you mean to tell me," said an editor to me, "that *Esquire* tries to have articles on important issues and treats them in such a way that nothing can come of it—who can deny it?" Try, also, to get a letter printed in the *New York Times* if your view on the issue calls attention to an essential factor that is not being generally mentioned.)

Naturally, the more simply true a statement is in any issue about which everybody is quite confused, the less newsworthy it will be, the less it will be what everybody is talking about. When the child in the story said, "But the Emperor has no clothes!" the newspapers and broadcasts surely devoted many columns to describing the beautiful new clothes and also mentioned the interesting psychological incident of the child. Instead of being proud of him, his parents were ashamed; but on the other hand they received $10,000 in sympathetic contributions toward his rehabilitation, for he was a newsworthy case. But he had a block in reading.

Where there is official censorship it is a sign that speech is serious. Where there is none, it is pretty certain that the official spokesmen have all the loud-speakers.

3.

But let us return to our theme of vocation and develop it a step further. Perhaps the young fellows *really* want to do something, that is, something worthwhile, for only a worth-while achievement finishes a doing. A person rests when he has finished a real job. (The striking illustration of this is that, statistically, the best mental health used to be found among locomotive engineers, and is now found among airline pilots! The task is useful, exacting, it sets in motion a big machine, and when it is over, it is done with.) If the object is important, it gives structure to many a day's action and dreaming—one might even continue in school. Unfortunately our great society balks us, for it simply does not take seriously the fact, or the possibility, that people want this; nor the philosophic truth that except in worthwhile activity there is no way to be happy. For instance, in a standard questionnaire for delinquents, by Milton Barron, in a hundred headings there do not appear the questions, "What do you want to be? What do you want to work at? What do you want to achieve?" (But Donald Taft's *Criminology*, which Barron is adapting, has the sentence: "Absence of vocational interest at the age when it is normal . . . is tell-tale of a starved life.")

In despair, the fifteen-year-olds hang around and do nothing at all, neither work nor play. Without a worth-while prospect, without a sense of justification, the made-play of the Police Athletic League is not interesting, it is not their own. They do not do their school work, for they are waiting to quit; and it is hard, as we shall see, for them to get part-time jobs. Indeed, the young fellows (not only delinquents) spend a vast amount of time doing nothing. They hang around together, but don't talk about anything, nor even—if you watch their faces—do they passively take in the scene. Conversely, at the movies, where the real scene is by-passed, they watch with absorbed fantasy, and afterward sometimes mimic what they saw.

If there is nothing worth while, it is hard to do anything at all. When one does nothing, one is threatened by the question, *is* one nothing? To this insulting doubt, however, there is a lively response: a system of values centering around threatened grownupness and defensive conceit. This is the so-called "threatened masculinity," not in the sense of being called a girl, but of being called, precisely, "boy," the Negro term of insult. With this, there is an endless compulsion to prove potency and demand esteem. The boys don't talk about much of interest, but there is a vast amount of hot rhetoric to assert that oneself is "as good as anybody else," no more useless, stupid, or cowardly. For instance, if they play a game, the interest in the game is weak: they are looking elsewhere when the ball is served, there are lapses in attention, they smoke cigarettes even while playing handball. The interest in victory is surprisingly weak: there is not much glow of self-esteem. But the need for proof is overwhelming: "I won you, didn' I? I won you last week too, didn' I?"

During childhood, they played games with fierce intensity, giving themselves as a sacrifice to the game, for play was the chief business of growth, finding and making themselves in the world. Now when they are too old merely to play, to what shall they give themselves with fierce intensity? They cannot play for recreation, since they have not been used up.

The proving behavior is endless. Since each activity is not interesting to begin with, its value does not deepen and it does not bear much repetition. Its value as proof quickly diminishes. In these circumstances, the inevitable tendency is to raise the ante of the compulsive useless activity that proves one is potent and not useless. (This analysis applies equally to these juveniles and to status-seeking junior executives in business firms and on Madison Avenue.)

It is not surprising then, that, as Frederic Thrasher says in *The Gang*, "Other things being equal, the imaginative boy has an excellent chance to become the leader of the gang. He has the power to make things interesting for them. He 'thinks up things for us to do.'"

At this point let us intervene and see what the Official Spokesmen say.

4.

Last summer, after a disastrous week when there were several juvenile murders, the Governor of New York made the following statement (*New York Times*, September 2, 1959):

We have to constantly devise new ways to bring about a challenge to these young folks and to provide an outlet for their energies and give them a sense of belonging.

The statement is on the highest level of current statesmanship—that is why I have chosen it. It has been coached by sociologists and psychologists. It has the proper therapeutic and not moralistic attitude, and it does not mention the cops. (The direct appeal to force came a couple of weeks later, when there were other incidents.)

The gist of it is that the Governor of New York is to play the role that Thrasher assigns to the teen-age gang leader. He is to think up new "challenges." (The word could not have been more unfortunate.) But it is the word "constantly" that is the clue. A challenge can hardly be worth while, meaningful, or therapeutic if another must constantly and obsessively be devised to siphon off a new threat of "energy." Is not this raising the ante? Solidly meeting a real need does not have this character.

("The leader," says Thrasher, "sometimes controls the gang by means of summation, i.e., by progressively urging the members from one deed to another, until finally an extreme of some sort is reached.")

My guess is that in playing games the Governor will not have so lively an imagination as the lad he wants to displace as leader; unlike the grownups, the gang will never select him. One of the objective factors that make it hard to grow up is that Governors are likely to be men of mediocre humane gifts.

The psychology of the Governor's statement is puzzling. There are no such undifferentiated energies as he speaks of. There are energies of specific functions with specific real objects. In the case here they might be partly as follows: In adolescents a strong energy would be sexual reaching. For these boys, as for other adolescents, it is thwarted or imperfectly gratified, but these have probably not learned so well as others to cushion the suffering and be patient; so that another strong energy of the delinquents would be diffuse rage of frustration, perhaps directed at a scapegoat. If they have been kept from constructive activity making them feel worth while, a part of their energy might be envious and malicious destructiveness of property. As they are powerless, it is spite; and as they are humiliated, it is vengeance. As they feel rejected and misunderstood, as by governors, their energy is woe; but they react to this with cold pride, and all the more fierce gang-loyalty to their peers. For which of these specific energies does the Governor of New York seriously plan to devise an outlet? Their own imaginative gang leader presumably does devise challenges that let off steam for a few hours.

What is the sociology of "belonging" here? In the great society they are certainly uprooted. But in the gang their conformity is sickeningly absolute; they have uniform jackets and uniform morals. They speak a jargon and no one has a different idea that might brand him as queer. Since they have shared forbidden behavior, they are all in the same mutually blackmailing plight and correspondingly guilty and suspicious toward the outsider. It is a poor kind of community they have; friendship, affection, personal helpfulness are remarkably lacking in it; they are "cool," afraid to display feeling; yet does the Governor seriously think that he can offer a good community that warrants equal loyalty?

5.

More aware of what challenging means, the New York Youth Board has had a policy more calculated to succeed. Its principle is provisionally to accept as *given* the code of the gang and the kids' potency-proving values and prejudices; and then, as an immediate aim, to try to distract their overt behavior into less annoying and dangerous channels. This immediate aim is already valuable, for it diminishes suffering. For instance, there is less suffering if a youth's addiction is changed from heroin to alcohol, so long as heroin is illegal and alcohol is legal; the youth is less in danger and the store that he would rob to pay for the criminally overpriced narcotic is out of danger.

Then there is the further hope that, accepted by the wise and permissive adult, the adolescents will gradually come to accept themselves and the spiral of proving will be arrested. Further, that the friendship of the trusted adult will evoke a love (transference) that can then be turned elsewhere. I take it that this is the Youth Worker philosophy. In many cases it should succeed.

I am skeptical that it can widely succeed. For here again the young people are not taken seriously as existing, as having real aims in the same world as oneself. To the Youth Board, in their own real world (such as it is), the code is *not* acceptable, and the teen-age vaunts and prejudices cannot lead to growth in any world. To pretend otherwise is playing games and continuing to exclude them from one's own meant world. How then can the boys be trusting and feel they are understood? Not being morons, they know they *cannot* be understood in their own terms, which are empty to themselves. They know there is another world beyond, as square and sheepish as they might please to rationalize it, but which is formidable and enviable. (Actually, apart from the code itself and the sphere of their delinquencies, the kids are models of conventionality in their tastes, opinions, and ignorance.) And though they have a childish need for sympathetic attention and are proud of having compelled it—"We're so bad they give us a youth worker"—they are too old not to demand being taken seriously.

There is a valuable nondirective approach which makes no judgments or interpretations and gives no advice, but which simply draws the patient out and holds up a mirror; and this is no doubt also part of the philosophy of the Youth Board. But then, it must be a therapy, it must hold up the mirror and risk the explosion of shame and grief, or the impulsive defenses against them, violent retaliation or flight. In youth work this is very impractical. It is a different thing to go *along* with the patient, or worse to seem to go along with him, and provide only the reassurance of attention.

The philosophy of the Youth Board can succeed only if the worker can hold out some real objective opportunity, something more than "interpersonal relations," and make the boy finally see it. (E.g., at P.S. 43 in New York there has been an experiment of simply urging the kids to go to college—a far-off goal—showing that it is economically possible for them, and promising that the school will follow up. This alone has resulted in rapid academic advance, increases in I.Q., and less truancy.)

My hunch is that the occasional spectacular success occurs not because of the "accepting" method, but because the youth worker does not really belong to the world of the Youth Board either, and his acceptance is bona fide. For whatever motive, he confronts the young people as real. He may be a covert accomplice with the same inner dilemma as his gang, and can pass on a more practical worldly wisdom. He may be emotionally involved with some of them, so they are in fact important. He may be so deeply compassionate or so inspired a teacher that he creates new interests and values altogether, *not* the meant world of the Youth Board which is, after all, just what had proved unsatisfactory to begin with.

6.

Our society has evolved a social plan, a city plan, an economy and a physical plant, of which this delinquent youth is an organic part. The problem is *not* to get them to belong to society, for they belong a priori by being the next generation. The burden of proof and performance is quite the other way: for the system of society to accommodate itself to all its constituent members. But can it be denied that by and large the official practice is to write these boys off as useless and unwanted and to try to cajole or baffle them into harmlessness?

Suppose we look at it the other way. Like any other constitutional group, they exert an annoying pressure, but they are inarticulate. In some dumb way they are surely right, but what the devil do they want? Has much effort been made to ask them and help them find words? We can guess that they want two broad classes of things: changes in the insulting and depriving circumstances that have made them ornery, spiteful, vengeful, conceited, ignorant, and callous—unable to grow; and objective opportunities in which to grow.

Let us go back to the Governor. On the same occasion mentioned above, he issued to the press the following formal statement:

> The problem of juvenile delinquency has no easy remedy. There is no quick or overnight solution. It is compounded of neglect by parents, broken homes, poor living conditions, unhealthy background, economic deprivation, mental disturbance, and lack of religious training.

This is not a bad list of background conditions; it satisfies every popular and scientific theory of etiology. The question is, does the Governor seriously not understand how organic these conditions are in our society? They cannot be remedied by gimmicks or the busy kind of social work that offers no new vision or opportunity. He speaks of broken homes; has he some plan to improve the institution of modern marriage, especially among folk for whom it is hardly an institution? The present-day urban poor are largely Negro and Spanish, they are excluded from many unions, they often earn less than the minimum wage, they are unschooled; naturally there is economic deprivation, poor living conditions. How is their religion relevant if it is irrelevant to the basic community functions of vocation and war, and wrong on sex? There is no community and not even a community plan; naturally there is unhealthy background.

What great concerted effort is being led by the Governor to remedy these conditions, not overnight, but in the next five, ten, or twenty years?

Indeed, *official* policy has often worked to increase delinquency rather than remedy it. For instance, in a characteristically earnest analysis, our best authority on housing, Charles Abrams, has shown how the public-housing policy has had this effect. Slums have been torn down wholesale, disrupting established community life. By not building on vacant land and by neglecting master planning, our officials have created insoluble problems of relocation and have vastly increased the number of one-room flats, making decent family life impossible. (Suppose you were fifteen years old and returned home at 11 p.m., as the Mayor urges, to a room with Mama and Papa in one bed and two little brothers in your bed and a baby yowling; you might well stay out till four in the morning.) Also, families are ousted from public housing when their incomes increase, thus eliminating and penalizing the better models; and on the other hand, other families are expelled on irrelevant moral criteria, without thought of what becomes of them. And the original income segregation in large blocks was itself bound to increase tension, like any segregation. All of this has been *official* policy. The picture gets even grimmer if we turn to the quasi-official graft in Title I that for two- and three-year stretches has stalled either demolition or construction, while families pay rent in limbo.

The trouble with Abrams' analysis is that he, Mumford and others have been saying it aloud for twenty years, while the New York City Planning Commission has gone on manufacturing juvenile delinquency.

7.

Now finally (January 1960), the Governor's practical antidelinquency youth program is offered for legislation. Let me summarize its chief points: (1) Reduce the age of felonies to fifteen. (2) Space for 390 more in the forest camps (added to the 110 now there). (3) Admit a few older to these camps. (4) Establish "Youth Opportunity Centers"—residences for youths "on the verge of delinquency." (5) Provide "halfway houses" for those in transition from institutions to freedom. (6) Certified boarding houses to which the court can direct youngsters. (7) Ease compulsory continuation school. (8) Permit after-school work from fourteen to sixteen. (9) Encourage work-and-study programs "to keep potential drop-outs in school long enough to prepare for employment." (10) Centralize probation services. (11) Increase probation staff.

Of these eleven points, eight seem to be aimed primarily at punishment or control: the boys are really unwanted, the problem is to render them harmless. Only two (8 and 9) envisage, very unimpressively, any substantive change whatever. What on earth has happened to the program of "constantly devising new ways to challenge these young folks"? But let me call attention to the forest work-camps (2 and 3). There is good evidence that these are excellent and have provided a rewarding experience. But then certainly they should be made available not for convicted delinquents as such, but for all kids who want to work there a year. Naturally, however, there is no money—not even for more than five hundred delinquent boys altogether. The question is whether or not such a program of camps for many thousand boys is less important than one of the Park Commissioner's new highways to Westchester. Until they will face that question, our public officials are not serious.

8.

Positively, the delinquent behavior seems to speak clearly enough. It asks for what we can't give, but it is in *this* direction we must go. It asks for manly opportunities to work, make a little money, and have self-esteem; to have some space to bang around in, that is not always somebody's property; to have better schools to open for them horizons of interest; to have more and better sex without fear or shame; to share somehow in the symbolic goods (like the cars) that are made so much of; to have a community and a country to be loyal to; to claim attention and have a voice. These are not outlandish demands. Certainly they cannot be satisfied directly in our present system; they are baffling. That is why the problem is baffling, and the final recourse is to a curfew, to ordinances against carrying knives, to threatening the parents, to reformatories with newfangled names, and to 1,100 more police on the street.

III. CLASS STRUCTURE

I.

IN OUR economy of abundance it is still subject to discussion whether or not there is as much poverty as there was in the Thirties when "one-third of a nation was ill housed, ill clothed, ill fed." Some say 20 per cent are poverty-stricken, some as many as 40 per cent. Census, 1958: 31 per cent.

(But it is hard to determine a criterion of poverty. E.g., a Negro family in the rich county of Westchester, New York, might have an income of $4000, yet have to pay so much rent for substandard housing that it can't make both ends meet. In New York City novice Puerto Ricans are fleeced four times as much for a quarter of the space that experienced citizens manage to find in the same neighborhood.)

Nevertheless, all students would agree on two propositions: (1) The composition of the poor has changed immensely; it now consists mainly of racial and cultural minorities, including migrant farm labor. (2) And the economic relation of the poor to the system has importantly changed: simply, the earlier minorities, Irish, Jews, Italians, Slavs, poured into an expanding economy that needed people; the new come into an expanding economy that does not need people. I would add another important difference: (3) The relation of the other classes to the poor has changed. For instance, many readers are no doubt surprised that there are so many poor and, reading about it, feel that it is a mere lag, a matter of mopping up, in our general productive advance. Everything looks pretty streamlined.

The income pyramid has changed in shape. It used to be that the most were the poor at the bottom and then, *evenly*, fewer and fewer at each level up to a few at the top. But the meaning of the economy of abundance is that there are now very many, perhaps even a bulge, at the lower-middle-income level. These are the people with semi-professional and service jobs, the occupational category that has grown the most, and who get status salaries; the skilled and semi-skilled in semimonopoly factory jobs, strongly unionized; the families in which, in our artificially maintained nearly full employment, the man has two jobs or the woman also has a job; and families in newly industrialized areas in the South and Middle West. But conversely, the poorly paying unskilled jobs have diminished. It is here that simple automation (e.g., sweeping the floor in a factory) is allowed full development. Many categories are not unionized. Sometimes even the minimum wage does not apply. Migratory farm labor, mostly Negro, is not covered by social insurance. By the connivance of union and management, Negroes and the new Spanish minorities are often rejected for apprenticeship. These poor groups, behindhand to begin with, get less schooling.

That is, the economy of abundance, the bulge in the pyramid, means also that those at the bottom tend to fall out of "society" altogether.

Consider it. There is a higher standard of living, more to conform to in order to be "decent"; it is more expensive to be decently poor. Yet there is a tighter organization above that is harder to belong to, so that the standard is increasingly unattainable for the underprivileged. So far as economic and vocational causes, poverty and job uselessness, are factors—and they are mighty important factors when they add up to being "out" of society—this is a sufficient explanation for juvenile delinquency. One need go no further. For in such hopeless conditions, *any* grounds, of family hostility, unusual childhood frustration, or a gang on the street, will tip the balance. The question is whether or not this structure is organic in our present system.

(Let me say at this point, however, that many of the humble jobs of the poor are precisely *not* useless, morally. Farm labor, janitoring, messenger, serving and dish washing—these jobs resist remarkably well the imputation of uselessness made against the productive society as a whole. In the potency-ideology of teen-age delinquents, of course, such jobs are contemptible and emasculating. But we shall see that they are important for the poverty-mystique of the more thoughtful of the Beat Generation.)

2.

Recently I attended a conference (Student League for Industrial Democracy) where poverty was the theme. Eminent and earnest labor leaders spoke. As the day wore on I became eerily disturbed at the difference in tone from such discussions in the Thirties. At last I hit it: they were talking not political economy but philanthropy. Partly, maybe, this tone crept in because they were talking about our poor black and brown brothers. Mostly, however, it was because their attitude toward poverty is no longer part of their fighting economic theory. As labor economists, they do not have solidarity with *these* poor.

When poverty used to be discussed by socialists—these same men younger—the theory was that in the capitalist system labor as a whole must be at the bottom and must become poorer, because of the falling return on investment and its pressure on wages, because of the concentration of ownership and control and the increase of inequality, and the periodic crises and unemployment. Therefore the fight against poverty was solidary; it was the fight to improve the whole system in order to improve the position of labor. But now the rate of interest does not fall; the system cushions its crises; there is high employment (with significant exceptions) or insurance. There is certainly a concentration of monopolistic control, but either inequality is less (that is debatable) or, certainly, workers on a fairly high standard don't much bother who has millions. Thus, nostalgic solidarity with poverty turns into philanthropy—and even into exclusion, on issues where the poor are unassimilable into the abundant system.

One of the speakers, a portly labor leader, was asked whether the new income pyramid did not resemble a middle-aged gentleman with a bulge beneath the middle.

I did not once hear the word "proletariat," and that made sense. For the word had been used, bitterly and nobly, in a different theory: "producers of offspring" paid by the iron law of wages just enough to reproduce labor. Our present poor are more like the ancient Roman proletariat, producers of offspring kept on the dole for political reasons. It was clear, too, why the word "do-gooder" has fallen into mild disrepute. It used to refer, like "muck-raking," to quixotic attempts to reform the system; now it is diminishing suffering, accepting the system. (Muck-raking, in turn, has become the protest of Angry Young Men. My own tone in this book sounds like an Angry Middle-Aged Man, disappointed but not resigned.)

3.

For those excluded from the high standard and its organization, it is becoming harder to maintain any American standard at all. It is characteristic of systems geared to high pay that it is hard to work for low pay. There are fewer such jobs; those there are subject to grueling exploitation without benefit of union. Low pay generally means harder work under worse conditions. Prices are, of course, geared to the high standard; and the use of any commodity tends to be increasingly tied up with the use of many other commodities and services that cost money.

For instance, it is very grim to be poor and run a jalopy. The insurance costs three times as much as the car. The old car, which is safe at 50 m.p.h., is effectually barred from parkways made for cars at 65 m.p.h. The price of gasoline pays for the parkways. The price of repairs is geared to the new cars.

It costs money to have any job at all, but transportation and lunches, presentable clothes and laundry, are priced for good wages.

Unless he is capable of a different, inventive or community

culture altogether, a poor person can afford little recreation. The popular culture is high priced and he gets the dregs of it. His poverty tends to degenerate into stupidity. He cannot afford presentable shoes for the kids to go to school; they are ashamed and won't go. Thus, in Péguy's phrase, poverty becomes misery, and the poor belong to society less and less.

4.

There is little agreement in the sociology of delinquency. (As I shall discuss later, this is because the concept itself is confused and so leads to confusing statistics.) But one correlation that is generally agreed on is that: Juvenile delinquency, unlike adult crime, is more frequent in years of economic prosperity than in years of depression. Now, this would seem to contradict the other, and rather *prima facie*, theory of poverty as the important condition. The paradox is softened by pointing out that in prosperity there is more employment of women, more divorce, more money to buy liquor and drugs. These factors make sense, but let me raise some further considerations.

First, there is the possibility that the prosperous well-paying jobs do not filter down evenly to the poorest groups, who tend much more to be unemployable. This certainly seems to be our situation today. Second, in a high-standard economy, there is a vast difference between having a little extra money and being accustomed to the well-paid standard. As our Manchester forefathers used to say, you do a disservice to the undeserving poor by giving them money, because they will get into trouble. Consider the concrete situation: Even if the parents are suddenly getting better pay, the young are getting merely a little extra spending money, and this, in a society in which there is suddenly a lot of money, must work out as follows: (1) The underprivileged kids get around more and are exposed to the expensive glamour, but (2) this is precisely not attainable by them unless they take short cuts. (3) Meantime, those who have the new money are more careless with it: they leave their cars unlocked, buy sex, drink too much. And (4) the spiteful feeling is increased, that those who are better off are squares, enemies, and fair victims of the gang. In boom time, that is, there is effectually *more* exclusion than ordinarily.

During depression, contrariwise, there is more community because many others are in the same boat. The street is occupied by kids used to other mores, to whom the gang values are pointless. This leads to friction, but also to other friendships and other "things to do." But above all, as everybody knows who was unemployed during the Great Depression, it is easier to be decently poor when prices are low and the pressure to maintain appearances is diminished. Things get nearer to a human scale and life makes more sense. Likewise, at such times political activity is more common, an education that increases self-esteem in a worth-while way.

This whole picture would be quite different if the underprivileged and somewhat unemployable families had a pretty good secure income over a long period. They would then be members of society at least as consumers, and would eventually become as employable as the average. Such a condition would at once diminish certain kinds of underprivileged delinquency, e.g., thefts, malicious mischief, certain spiteful assaults, and maybe truancy. Simply to subsidize the poor might be the cheapest way of coping with their juvenile delinquency. To re-establish in general what he calls the social balance, J. K. Galbraith proposes such a high long-time subsidy for all unemployed. He assures us that this would not be inflationary, and as the one-time director of price controls for the OPA he should know.

The popular bright idea to diminish delinquency is to penalize the parents; and perhaps the effective method would be, rather, to give them money to spend, a kind of prize!

5.

At present, however, our society is settling for the first time in its history into a rigid class system. (Somewhere we missed out on equality, and this is now threatening our flexibility and stability.) It is not that individuals may not move from grade to grade—there is perhaps even more individual mobility than ever. But the statuses themselves are more rigid; there is less easy gradation, and there is less opportunity to make one's unique "classless" place. One is more definitely in or out, and in a more definite rank.

At the bottom are the poor, "outside" of society. Next are those groups who are *in* the organized system of production: (1) Those who are "in" but couldn't care less about the production and distribution, like the factory operatives mentioned in the first chapter. These are paid the lower-middle-income wages, say $4,000 to $6,000. They buy on credit and have to keep on the job to make both ends meet. If the work week is shortened to thirty hours, without a commensurate loss of income, there is evidence that they get other, part-time, jobs to buy still more refrigerators. (2) The next status who are "in" are the Organization Men proper, whose hours, thoughts, families, play, and peace of mind are dedicated to maintaining their positions in their particular firms and pushing upward there or in some other firms. Salary $7,500 to $20,000. It is this group—the junior executives, for instance—that we have compared to the juvenile delinquents for their safe conformity and competitive individuality. We shall see that another important trait in common is having no real activity, but living by role playing.

(W. H. Whyte, Jr., the Hesiod of this tribe, pleads for individuality to offset the conformity of organization life. He, rather cynically, fails to see that such polar "individuality" is the conformity by which a man advances; it is one-upping. The only offset to the organization is nature or worth-while objects; but the necessary, useful, and pleasant, and the good, true, and beautiful are not much mentioned in his book.) (3) At the top, finally, are the nine hundred managers—figure from *Fortune* magazine—whose task is to minimize risk and maximize production and sales. Also the fifty governors, the federal staff, heads of foundations, etc.

It will be seen that these three statuses in the organized system (which includes bigger business, organized labor, entertainment, government, bigger education, etc.) are engaged primarily in keeping the system itself running and slowly expanding. The most self-aware of its members are the middle-status intellectuals, among the advertising men, salesmen, and junior executives; and they describe the system as the Rat Race. So W. H. Whyte, Jr. J. K. Galbraith, however, describes it differently: "Among the many models of the good society, no one has urged the squirrel wheel." It is interesting to contrast the different species of imagined rodents between those who are running the race and the scholar who is contemplating it with wonder.

But there is another large class: those who do not properly belong to the system and are not yet submerged into the poor "outside" of society: this is the vast herd of the old-fashioned, the eccentric, the criminal, the gifted, the serious, the men and women, the *rentiers*, the freelances, the infants, and so forth. This motley collection has, of course, no style or culture, unlike the organization that has our familiar American style and popular culture. Its fragmented members hover about the organization in multifarious ways—running specialty shops, trying to teach or to give other professional services, robbing banks, landscape gardening, and so forth—but they find it hard to get along, for they do not know the approved techniques of promoting, getting foundation grants, protecting themselves by official unions, legally embezzling, and not blurting out the truth or weeping or laughing out of turn. They have no style at all, and it is understandable that neither they nor their usually rather irrelevant enterprises make much headway in the market, the universities, entertainment, politics, or labor. Besides, they often speak a minority language, English.

This is roughly the class structure of America in the middle of the twentieth century. It seems most functional to speak of three *classes*, the Poor, the Organization, and the Independents; and of three *statuses* within the dominant class, the Organization. Viz.:

I. Organized System:
  1. Workers
  2. Organization Men

    3. Managers
  II. Poor
  III. Independents

6.

Let us return now to our alert young man of average to good attainments and imagine him growing up in and *into* this arena. Most likely he will go to work for an Organization, in a factory or service job, manual or clerical, with the corresponding job attitude and way of life. But if he has been to college, he will likely be in the second status of the organized system, in business management, communications, sales or technology, with *its* job attitude and way of life.

After a few years, many such young men will perceive that they are in a Rat Race. The young workers will perceive it as the work speeds up, when they get married, as their installment payments fall due. The Organization Man will perceive it as competition, company pressure to conform, etc. Of these, most will race on, but a few will balk and stop running. Now what becomes of these few?

They are *not* likely to choose the other, motley, alternative of trying to remain in society independent of the organization. For their experience has been disillusioning. They have become hip. (We shall see later that this is a profoundly organizational attitude.) They *know* that the independent unorganized are up against it; for they have learned techniques of promotion and they don't think much, or much think, of other methods and kinds of results. But to be hip and cynical are not attitudes that prompt one to make a go on one's own. It is not surprising then that many of those who balk in the Rat Race will voluntarily choose the other remaining possibility, poverty "outside" society (whether they choose it, or fall into it, comes to the same thing). These, not boys, but early disillusioned, hip, and resigned young men, are the Beat Generation. The organization they have quit may be the armed forces or a university that they cannot compound with; these tend to be more naïve. Those who have had experience of working for a firm and making a pretty good living tend to be more cynical.

Naturally this cataclysmic transition, between being in and being "outside" society, does not occur without strong accompanying emotional moments: betrayals in love, binges, blow-ups at the boss, addiction to forbidden haunts and vices. But at this point let us stick to the social structure of it.

7.

It is relevant to introduce the Beat Generation in this context of present-day poverty because the present-day composition of the poor in America—Negroes, Puerto Ricans and Mexicans, migrant farm labor, with large urban juvenile delinquency—has been fateful for the particular culture of these young folks. Let us try to analyze the accidental and essential influences, as an interesting example of acculturation.

Artists and bohemians have always gravitated to the bottom of the income pyramid. It is cheaper there. There is less timetable. Life is simpler and more factual. These factors operate somewhat today too, but less so, because in some ways it now costs more to be poor than modestly lower-middle; and in many of their tastes, e.g., clothes, cars, recreation, and even food, the poor are even more idiotic than the average. So let us see what is particular in the cultural effect of present-day poverty on present-day bohemians.

(1) The Afro-Negro and Spanish, and a part of the migrant and delinquent, influence on Beat culture is inevitable but accidental. Resigning, the Beats have chosen to be outside, and the present poor happen to be those who, as unorganized minorities, *are* outside when they arrive. The poor might have been Chinese; the narcotics might have been different, or there might have been some kick other than narcotics; the music might have been something other than Negro jazz; the jargon might not have had a Negro base; and perhaps there might be less going on the road—though this ants-in-the-pants

moving about is pervasive in American society. (See Appendix E.) What I am saying here will be defined by the Beats themselves, for to them every aspect of their scene is equally relevant and precious. But if these aspects of their culture were not accidental, such bright and inventive fellows would by now have made more out of them. As they practice them, the bongo drums and jazz are childish, in the light of their knowledge and abilities. The jazz-and-poetry is feeble compared even to the TV commercial jingles that they have turned away from. The jive language embarrasses their poetry. The style of the particular drugs remains crude and experimental. Much of the delinquency rouses in them guilt and fear, instead of defiant approval or calm righteousness (contrast the style and depth of Jean Genet with similar material).

(2) On the other hand, the *structural* characteristics of present-day poor society—those that did not especially belong to the poor of older bohemias—*are* essential in the culture of those who gravitate to these poor, for they too do not "belong." These include: Outcastness and being objects of prejudice. Giving up trying to explain to those who, often literally, do not speak the same language. Protective exclusiveness and in-group loyalty. Fear of the cops. Economic and job uselessness. Courageously taking up, or remaining with, substitutes for community, rather than sinking in mere resignation (but this courage is common to many kinds of poor). Exotic, or at least not-standard-American, arts and folkways.

These structural characteristics of the present-day poor are essential in Beat culture. As, contrariwise, are the organizational characteristics of being hip and convinced that society is a Rat Race. This combination, we shall see, mesmerizes them into behaving as though they were trapped in a Closed Room and must live on their own guts, without available environment.

(3) But finally, there are essential traits of Beat culture that go counter to the social traits of the poor whom they have chosen. These comprise the essential morality, and morals are acculturated least. One striking trait is nonconformism and tolerance in sexual and racial questions and behavior. The poor Negroes or Puerto Ri-

cans may be estranged from the standard customs and prejudices, but they are all the more narrow about their own. In the case of the delinquents, of course, this narrow conformity is so extravagant as to be dangerous: they cannot inwardly tolerate anything that hints that their own image of perfection is questionable. It is hard to be sure, but my impression is that the poor of other times, at the bottom but *in* society, were among the most tolerant. Hard knocks had taught them to live and let live; and they did not need to protect their repressions so much as the outcast poor. In this respect the Beats are more like the old-fashioned poor, and this of course makes it easier and more profitable for them to be poor.

This brings us to another striking difference. Despite having minority traditions of their own, our present poor are absolute sheep and suckers for the popular culture which they cannot afford, the movies, sharp clothes, and up to Cadillacs. Indeed, it is likely that the popular culture is aimed somewhat at them, as the lowest common denominator. I do not mean that this is not a reasonable compensation, like the Englishman's liquor and the Irishman's betting on the horses. Everybody has got to have something, and so poor people show off and feel big by means of the standard of living. But in these circumstances it is immensely admirable that the Beat Generation has contrived a pattern of culture that, turning against the standard culture, costs very little and gives livelier satisfaction. It is a culture communally shared, in small groups. Much of it is handmade, not canned. Some of it is communally improvised. We shall speak later about the limitations of this procedure and the weakness of its products; but the *fact* of it, of a culture that is communal and tending toward the creative, is so capital that it must have a future, and it is worth while to study its grounding and economy.

8.

Beat economics underline human difficulties peculiar to the modern-American-standard economy. The Beats have a mystique of

Voluntary Poverty. But how to get along at all in a high-standard economy if one has dropped "outside" and has no incentive to work and "make good"?

In our times, the distinction between Case Poverty, due to illness, accidents, or personality defects, and Class Poverty, due to social underprivilege, doesn't amount to much. Personal and social play into each other. For it could be asked: Why wasn't the accident insured? What social conditions formed such a careless personality? Or, conversely, Doesn't the poor class have, economically, a personality defect? (Just as in the Protestant Ethic the poor had a theological defect; but of course it is also persistently true that "only the poor are saved.") Likewise, the old monastic concept of voluntary poverty is no longer much distinguishable from either case poverty or class poverty, for it happens that a person *cannot* continue the Rat Race, it makes him sick; and he chooses out, to survive. Another man would like to be rich and famous and he works hard; but he *cannot* work otherwise than the work demands, but such work might not be marketable; so he could be said to "choose" poverty. In an organized system, all poor tend to be the same poor. (The same blurring of distinctions has occurred between "political" and "common" criminals. As society becomes more close-knit and total, a criminal act may well be a dumb political gesture, and political protest is certainly taken as criminal. So the anarchist philosopher refused to distinguish between these and said, "As long as one of these is in jail, I am not free.")

It makes little difference, then, whether a young fellow chooses his lot or is cast among the poor; especially if, being there, he soon takes on habits which make it difficult for him, or unattractive to him, to belong to the system.

Suppose, then, that with pretty good awareness our scarred young man is now confirmed poor. He must still face the problem of vocation and money. On these points the writers on the Beat Generation are confused. For one thing, they have a false notion that the kind of artistic activity that proliferates among the Beats is art, and gives the justification of art as a vocation. It is not art but something else, and they do not behave as if they were justified by it. (We shall return to this later at length.)

The problem of money, again, seems simple, but is not. In voluntary poverty the problem is to get enough to subsist. (Money is called "bread.") But how? In his book *The Holy Barbarians*, Lawrence Lipton gives a considerable list of jobs that Beats take, generally temporarily. The principle is that anything will do. A fellow might work in the organized system, e.g., dressing a window at Macy's; but, it is argued, he would not thereby be in the Rat Race, because he just wants "bread" and will quit. Naturally Macy's didn't know this when they hired him, so he's using them, not they him. This might come to pretending to conform rather elaborately, for the system is total; e.g., a fellow will get the job if he shaves off his beard. Work is no different from shoplifting. One plays roles and is hip. (Money is now called "loot.")

What is not understood in this form of reasoning is that playing roles and being hip in this way is very nearly the same as being an Organization Man, for *he* doesn't mean it either. Obviously the Holy Barbarian is here on shaky ground. Getting his "loot," he is an exploiter of labor, but only a little bit. (The integral aim of useful man's-work is not mentioned by Lipton.)

Let me make a close analogy—so close that it is probably an identity—between the job in voluntary poverty and the service in wartime that a pacifist can agree to perform. Nearly any civilian job that a man does advances the war. If he picks beans he replaces a farmer for the war factory. Pacifists have commonly accepted such a job as attendant in a hospital, which is understaffed anyway. This is not a petty problem, for when the evil, as they see it, is general and close-knit, it is necessary to preserve one's personal integrity if only to influence the future when the emergency is past. Anyone who does not understand this and the hairsplitting involved, will not understand ingenuous youth. During the last great war many a young fellow went to a conscientious-objector's camp in order to avoid war work, and then left the camp in disgust and went to jail because the camp work was boondoggling.

Among some of the Beats, such a principle of integrity is clearly operating in the choice of job. To recapitulate an earlier paragraph in this chapter: Many of the humble jobs of the poor are precisely not useless (or exploiting). Farm labor, hauling boxes, janitoring, serving and dish washing, messenger—these jobs resist the imputation of uselessness (or exploitation) made against the productive society as a whole. These *are* preferred Beat jobs. For one thing, in them no questions are asked and no beards have to be shaved. Nor is this an accidental connection. Personal freedom goes with unquestioned moral utility of the job, for at the level of simple physical effort or personal service, the fraudulent conformity of the organized system sometimes does not yet operate; the job speaks for itself.

But on the other hand, such jobs, being hard and useful, are the most miserably exploited. E.g., hospital workers who struck for a union in 1959 in New York City were getting $34 a week—the minimum wage not applying because they were in eleemosynary institutions! Migratory farmers average less than $900 a year and are not welcome in the neighborhood. The big money is *in* the system. So unorganized wages are low. Yet the price of subsistence at the market is standard high. Taking such a job, a man loses his freedom, he never stops working. He is used and made a fool of by the system, and this is in itself dishonorable. This is the dilemma of voluntary poverty in our society: either to compromise one's integrity (but then why bother?), or to be abused and made a fool of.

(As one way out, let me recommend Scheme III of *Communitas*, by my brother and myself. We suggest dividing the economy into two parts: the subsistence economy and the high-standard economy. In the subsistence part, run absolutely for use, everybody will work less than one year in seven and be guaranteed his subsistence for life. The rest of the time he can work in the high-standard economy for high wages, or do nothing at all, as he pleases. This plan would seem exactly to meet the need of voluntary poverty: to work with perfect integrity at the absolutely necessary, and to have the maximum of freedom for noneconomical activity.)

9.

To sum up: In these first chapters our youth is already fairly grown-up (fifteen to twenty-five years old), and confronting the external and definite problems of jobs and money. We have seen what kinds of opportunities are open to him, either in or out of the organized system, and what kind of public attention he can expect if he makes a nuisance of himself.

My emphasis so far has been on underprivileged conditions, because we have been discussing "problematic" cases "outside" of society. In the following chapters, however, when we turn to the earlier and character-molding factors that impede growth, we shall see that they apply even more particularly to "unproblematic" youth, whether growing up in the middle class or the working class. (I do not mention the upper class simply because its numbers are few and it stands for nothing. All ideology and culture in America at present springs from the middle status of the organized system.)

My thought is that the average adjusted boy is, if anything, more humanly wasted than the disaffected. So let us go on to discuss his stupidity, his lack of patriotism, his sexual confusion, and his lack of faith.

IV. APTITUDE

I.

OUR SUBJECT is the present waste of human resources. Yet this waste is nothing new. Considering our wonderful faculties and powers, people on the average have never accomplished much. Regarded just as machines of virtue, pleasure, wisdom, battle, or friendship, we have always operated at a tiny fraction of capacity. This is evident if we contrast how people usually hang around with how people come across in emergencies, or when they are enthusiastic, or when they are calmly absorbed. Children find the average inactivity very painful and they nag, "What can I do? Tell me something to do." Adolescents are restive hanging around, and they think up ways to make trouble. Adults are inured to it, and Schopenhauer claimed that boredom is a metaphysical attribute of the World as Will.

Psychologically, we define boredom as the pain a person feels when he's doing nothing or something irrelevant, instead of something that he wants to do but won't, can't, or doesn't dare. Boredom is acute when he knows the other thing and inhibits his action, e.g., out of politeness, embarrassment, fear of punishment or shame. Boredom is chronic if he has repressed the thought of it and no longer is aware of it. A large part of stupidity is just this chronic boredom, for a person can't learn, or be intelligent about, what he's not interested in, when his repressed thoughts are elsewhere. (Another large part of stupidity is stubbornness, unconsciously saying, "I won't, you can't make me.")

Certainly a large part of our common wasteful inactivity is this

neurosis of chronic boredom. Certain aims are forbidden and punishable, or unattainable and painful; so we inhibit them and put
them out of mind. In a vicious circle, the repression then makes the
idea of the aims seem threatening: the aims are now rejected also in
ourselves. So we are bored and inactive. We see how boredom easily
turns into apathy, the lack of incentive. (The next chapter, on Patriotism, will try to show that it is hard to grow up when the community
lacks big incentives.)

At first this Sunday-afternoon neurosis, of lively children brought
to a pause, is worse among the middle class than among the poor, for
the middle class is less permissive, it has stricter standards to maintain and more expensive furniture to protect. But by adolescence it
is generally evident in all classes of the young, hanging around, reading comic books, or watching TV. It is evident in their notion of
what is acceptable behavior in their groups, in their sexual paranoia,
in their inability to think up anything interesting. Their hearts are
elsewhere and they don't remember where. Many boys are afraid to
be alone with themselves, because they might masturbate, which in
itself may be an activity of boredom.

All this has long been with us, and formerly perhaps it was worse
than it is now, for now there is more permissiveness for small children and more rationality about sexuality. In this chapter, however,
I want to discuss another factor altogether: *ineptitude*, not knowing
how; the situation in which, even if they know their aims, children
don't know the means or can't manage the means. I propose that in
this respect our present system is uniquely bad and getting worse.
For ironically, just in our times, when science and technology are so
advanced, this factor of ineptitude also increases, and children become practically more stupid.

2.

It is notorious that the physical plant and social environment
have grown out of human scale. To achieve simple goods it is often

necessary to set in motion immense masses. In scarcity, where the means are unavailable, we wistfully renounce the ends. In an abundant economy, there is a plethora of means of what a person doesn't really want. Middle-class parents know from bitter experience that billions of dollars are spent annually for children's toys and teen-age junk that are not really wanted and lie idle. But furthermore, even if the end is desirable, the means often become so complicated that one is discouraged from starting out. For instance, it's too complicated on a hot day to travel two hot hours to get to a cool place when so many others have had the same idea that it's hot there too. To adults, such complicated means are irritating and take the joy out of life. To children growing up, they are disastrous because they make it impossible to learn by doing. The sense of causality is lost. Initiative is lost. And one ends with the idea that nothing can be changed.

We must remember that to children the city plan and social plan we present them with are like inevitable facts of nature. Unless they have architects or builders in the family, they cannot realize that the buildings were drawn by somebody on a piece of paper and could have been different. Unless their parents teach them otherwise, they believe that compulsory school attendance is a divine creation and it is a sin to be absent.

It is, of course, very difficult to judge the environment concretely from the child's point of view. Thus, living in a big city does not as such make a child inept, though any city has very complicated means. The city is short on farm work, swimming holes, and animals to trap; but it has docks, freight-car yards, labyrinthine basements, pavements to chalk up, and subway trains to play tag on. The streets are littered with the remarkable junk of a thousand trades, to hoard and make things with. The ingenuity of New York ball games adapted to various improbable fields and obstacles is a model of rule making and rational debate that any senate might emulate: it sizes up the situation, argues, decides, and gets things done that work. The *London Street Games* compiled by Norman Douglas is no contemptible manual of traditional culture. History teaches that cities have made people smart because of their mixed peoples, mixed manners, and mixed learning. On the whole, cities have probably trained more intelligent children than the country. But we must remember, too, that until recently cities have been continually replenished from the country. City people had country cousins, and drew on both influences. There could be a powerful educative effect if a country boy came to the city and was exposed to bewildering new ways, or if a city boy visited the country and was exposed to space, woods, and cows.

3.

There is probably a point of complexity at which, cut off from the country, the city ceases to advance beyond country backwardness; it becomes impractical and begins to induce its own kind of stupefaction and ineptness. The endless city-spread of suburbs makes the real farming and open country unavailable. The city becomes the only world, getting duller as one leaves the center, through first the inner ring of blight and then the deadly dormitories and suburbs.

Within the big metropolises at present, industry and commerce are shut off and concealed. The freight yards go underground. Manufacture is in great walled plants on the outskirts. In New York, even the Hudson River and its ships are cut off by impassable through-highways, and stupid planning has provided a mile of child-useless landscaping, so that few kids get down to the river any more to fish. The newer high dwellings make the streets inaccessible to small children. The automobiles make the streets dangerous.

Also the streets are strange, because there is a loss of neighborhood. This is due not only to bad planning but to the greatly increased mobility of families. Children are torn from their school chums and this destroys culture. For instance, the street games and game songs that I remember, in New York 1911–1921, were the ancient London (Dublin?) games; and this tradition has now considerably faded. But it is not easily that a new child-tradition could develop, especially among minorities of various cultures. Quite the contrary, history and bad social planning have conspired to create in New York huge income and cultural ghettos—it makes no difference whether low-income or high-income; children of all classes are equally deprived of the human community. Whereas mixing sharpens intelligence, any segregated differences create prejudice and make people stupid.

The very space has been crushingly pre-empted. The cars in New York seem finally to have discouraged many of the ball games; we see boys going a mile to find a Sunday-deserted parking lot to play stick-ball which previously they played on their own street with the small children chosen in. With increasing traffic, the policing is more strict. In Los Angeles 40 per cent of the area will be swallowed up by the cloverleaves and express highways so that people can drive bumper to bumper in and out of Los Angeles! This is certainly out of human scale and is a dead loss for skating and bicycles. In Northern cities, the snow is never allowed to pile up; city sleighing is finished. The streamlined functional architecture is bare of useful stoops.

In brief, concealed technology, family mobility, loss of the country, loss of neighborhood tradition, and eating up of the play space have taken away the real environment. The city, under inevitable modern conditions, can no longer be dealt with practically by children.

Consider the dehumanizing complexity of the city just as a problem in municipal administration. In New York City in charge of housing are many agencies, some for housing the poor, some for housing generally, some agents of the city, but others agents of the state and federal governments. They are, in part, the Housing Authority, the Mayor's Commission on Slum Clearance and Urban Renewal, the Comptroller's Office, the Board of Estimate, the Bureau of Real Estate, the Department of Buildings, and the State and Federal Housing Agencies. Meantime, unco-ordinated with these, there are agencies in charge of location of schools (Board of Education), and playgrounds and parks (Parks). Transportation by rail falls to the Transit Authority, but if it is automotive it may fall to the Port Authority (for cer-

*tain highways, tunnels, and bridges) or the Triborough Author-
ity (for other highways, etc.). When cars are moving or parked in
the streets they belong to the Traffic Department, and safety in
general belongs to the Police. Nobody as such attends to the specific relation of workers and their particular industries, the cause
of all this commuting, but there are zoning laws for broad kinds
of occupancy, under the City Planning Commission. Neighborhood quarrels, family disruption, delinquency, etc., might be
handled by the Police and various social agencies. Other departments, too, have a hand in the community planning of New
York, e.g., Public Works; Gas, Water and Electricity; etc.*

   *It seems reasonable to ask if the integration of these functions
is not relevant? but nobody is in charge of that. To give a partial
list: housing, slum clearance, location of industries, adequate
schools and teachers, transportation, clear streets, traffic control,
social work, racial harmony, master planning, recreation. The
list could be long extended, not to speak of a beautiful city and
local pride. Apart from such a unified view, the solution of this
or that isolated problem inevitably leads to disruption elsewhere.
Escape thoroughfares must aggravate central traffic. Slum clearance as an isolated policy must aggravate class stratification and
delinquency. New subways aggravate conurbation. "Housing"
makes for double-shift and overcrowded classrooms. No master
plan guarantees foolishness like the Lincoln Square project.
These consequent evils produce new evils among them....*

                                (Communitas, Appendix D.)

Even so, confusing as these factors are and much as they cut down
the available child-games and child-objects, it is hard to know what
things look like from the child's-eye view. For instance, the new
public housing seems after a few years to swarm like any old-fashioned slum and is perhaps developing its own worth-while child culture. At first, active boys shunned the official playgrounds, but now,
driven by necessity, they have agreed to take them over and turn
them to their own uses, games, adventure, necking, and battle.

4.

My guess is that, in city, suburb, and small town, the chief unambiguously retarding influence of the complicated technology acts on the children through the ineptitude of the grownups—just as the stultifying effect of the movies is *not* that the children see them but that their parents do, as if Hollywood provided a plausible adult recreation to grow up into.

People use machines that they do not understand and cannot repair. For instance, the electric motors: one cannot imagine anything more beautiful and educative than such motors, yet there may be three or four in a house, cased and out of sight; and when they blow they are taken away to be repaired. Their influence is then retarding, for what the child sees is that competence does not exist in ordinary people, but in the system of interlocking specialties. This is unavailable to the child, it is too abstract. Children go shopping with Mama; but supermarket shopping for cellophane packages is less knowledgeable and bargainable than the older shopping, as well as providing tasteless Texas fruit and vegetables bred for nonperishability and appearance rather than for eating. Cooking is more prefabricated. Few clothes are sewn. Fire and heat are not made. Among poor people there used to be more sweated domestic industry, which didn't do the adults any good but taught something to small children. Now, on the contrary, the man and perhaps the woman of the house work in distant offices and factories, increasingly on parts and processes that don't mean anything to a child. A child might not even know what work his daddy does. Shop talk will be, almost invariably, griping about interpersonal relations. If the kid has less confidence that he can make or fix anything, his parents can't either; and what they do work at is beyond his grasp.

Parents, especially fathers, feel that this way of life offers too little to their children, especially the sons. They tend to blame it on the city—just as many dog lovers will not keep dogs in the city. Some guiltily give the kids more money to go to the movies. Others choose the suburbs, where they can putter and fix, even though they thereby limit their own lives in other ways. We must return to the meaning of this fateful move.

5.

Let me give a dismal illustration of the case at its worst. At an underprivileged school in Harlem, they used to test the intelligence of all the children at two-year intervals. They found that every two years each advancing class came out ten points lower in "native intelligence." That is, the combined efforts of home influencing and school education, a powerful combination, succeeded in making the children significantly stupider year by year; if they had a few more years of compulsory home ties and compulsory education, all would end up as gibbering idiots. In this same school a new principal, with a better staff, more personal attention to the kids, and more progressive methods—and also willing to give his own time for social work among the parents—has reversed the trend. One method to remedy stupidity that he swears by is to invite the free expression of criticism and hostility, e.g., "Write a composition telling why you hate your father—why you hate school—why you hate me."

6.

It was just to this deepening crisis of boredom, lack of personal engagement, cultural irrelevance, and ineptitude, in conditions of mass industry and mass education, that the movement called progressive education addressed itself. It is now moribund, but it can be revived. Its history in our century, however, is immensely instructive.

The pragmatism, instrumentalism, and technologism of James, Dewey, and Veblen were leveled against the abuses and ideals of the then dominant class: the Four Hundred and the Robber Barons—academic culture, caste morals and formal religion, unsocial greed.

The philosophers were concerned about abundant production, social harmony, practical virtues, and more honest perception and feeling, which would presumably pertain to the rising group of technicians, social-scientific administrators, and organized labor. (As a symbol of the "leisure-class culture" that they were attacking, they chose the "classical" culture of Greece, founded on slavery.) In that early turn of the century, these philosophers failed to predict that precisely with the success of the managers, technicians, and organized labor, the "achieved" values of efficient abundant production, social harmony, and one popular culture would produce even more devastatingly the things they did not want: an abstract and inhuman physical environment, a useless economy, a caste system, a dangerous conformity, a trivial and sensational leisure. (So that now we tend to think of the Greek polis as an "integral community," making a public use of leisure and having a perfected education of the whole man, whereas we have fragments.)

Yet midway in this transition from the old tycoon-and-clergyman culture to the new managerial organization, there was crystallized a practical method of education with the defects of neither extreme (and in many ways strangely like Greek education); and it was given a sounding board especially by the daring Twenties. Progressive education drew on every radical idea since the middle of the eighteenth century, in pedagogy, politics, socialist and communitarian theory, epistemology, esthetics, anthropology, and psychiatry. It was as if progressive education resolved that *in the education of the children there should be no missed revolutions and no unfinished situations.*

In its heyday, progressive education was not sectarian. Different schools laid the emphasis in different places—Dewey was more experimental, Russell more rational, Neill more sex-reformist, the people around Goddard and Antioch more communitarian, Berea more "handicrafts," Black Mountain more "creative," Muste and Fincke more political-economical, and so forth. But I think that almost all schools would have accepted, in varying degrees, all of the following positions:

To learn theory by experiment and doing.

To learn belonging by participation and self-rule.

Permissiveness in all animal behavior and interpersonal expression.

Emphasis on individual differences.

Unblocking and training feeling by plastic arts, eurhythmics and dramatics.

Tolerance of races, classes, and cultures.

Group therapy as a means of solidarity, in the staff meeting and community meeting.

Taking youth seriously as an age in itself.

Community of youth and adults, minimizing "authority."

Educational use of the actual physical plant (buildings and farms) and the culture of the school community.

Emphasis in the curriculum on real problems of wider society, its geography and history, with actual participation in the neighboring community (village or city).

Trying for functional interrelation of activities.

This is not a perfect educational program. It lacks grandeur and explosive playfulness. It lacks religious quiet. And it is weak in the models of the humanities. But there cannot be a "perfect" educational system, for each system must meet its social situation. In a period like ours, of transition, uprootedness, inhuman scale, technical abstractness, affectlessness, and conformity, *no lesser program is seriously conservative of human resources*. Our official public educators are not serious in their concern for human resources, or they would use this program.

There has always been one criticism of progressive education that must be answered, namely, that it is weak in curriculum, in cultural and scientific content. I think this is a misunderstanding. There *is* only one curriculum, no matter what the method of education: what is basic and universal in human experience and practice, the underlying structure of culture. (Cf. Appendix D, page 231.) This philosophic content fans out as speech, as finding where you are in space and time, as measuring and structuring, and being a social animal. It may be called English, geography and history, arithmetic, music and physical training; or Greek, history, logic, and Rugby; or trivium and quadrivium (plus games); or literature, social studies, science, and eurhythmics. It is the same basic curriculum; the differences are in method, and they concern how to teach the curriculum and make it second nature to the students, unblocking rather than encumbering, and bringing out the best. The curriculum is only superficially what "a man ought to know"; it is more fundamentally how to become a man-in-the-world. The method must vary with what good or bad habits and powers the young have come with in various situations. The curriculum certainly cannot vary with what is temporarily convenient for a bad society (the definition of a bad society being one that is not educational). Not to teach the whole curriculum is to give up on the whole man.

For instance, in our present Cold War debate about teaching science, Dr. Kvaraceus, the National Education Association's expert on delinquency, warns us that geometry is "too hard" for most, and that to insist on it for all will produce failure and truancy. But this is not the progressive educator's way of looking at it. Is it that geometry is too hard, or that the aim of teaching is not bona fide, being rapid technical know-how rather than humane understanding? Is it that the method is irrelevant to the aptitude and ineptitude that the children have come with? What dismays me in thinking like that of Dr. Kvaraceus is that it disregards our duty to geometry as such as a worth-while human object, our duty to Euclid, Kepler, and Einstein. The result of his attitude is that these champions will not be champions for all men. We are in a sad dilemma if, as is the case, kids don't learn because it is not humanly worth while to learn, they have no deep motivation; and then, to keep them in school we have to cut down on the few subjects that are humanly worth while. The question cannot be whether to teach science or to whom, for what is man without science? but how to teach it in various circumstances.

At the other pole from Dr. Kvaraceus, the recent public alarm about Sputnik has led to Dr. Conant's quasi-official and vastly circulated reports on the high schools. But *because* the concern is not serious but is simply fear of the Russians, the reports show such little pedagogic imagination that they are a minor national disaster. Dr. Conant's philosophy is expressed in the sentence:

Attention has been centered for so long on the unfolding of individuality of each child that [educators] automatically resist any idea that a new national concern [defense against Russia] might be an important factor in planning a high school program. [From *The Child, the Parent, and the State*.]

What an extraordinary thought, that there could be a conflict between the unfolding individuality and the achievement of habits of science! When Dr. Conant proposes that the bright upper fraction of the students be somehow induced to take hard programs—for everywhere large percentages of the brightest shirk the hard courses or quit school—he does not ask what is *at present* lacking in their motivation. He objects to treating education in a vacuum, but he treats our national needs in a vacuum. Will the incentive to fight an atomic war, or a Cold War, match the social apathy and cynicism of these boys? More important, Dr. Conant does not seem to wonder why there are so few (15 per cent) who are "academically talented." Does he think that the general dullness of the high school population has occurred in a void? Contrast a remark on the same subject by the Dean of Teachers College, John Fischer: "I have a strong suspicion that we have learned little about the abilities of human beings. I suspect they are greater than most people assume." If one is concerned about conserving human resources, this would seem to be the obvious first approach: to find why most are so inept and to invent techniques to unblock them, to increase the pool of the "academically talented." Perhaps the conventional school itself is not such a good idea, especially if the "national need" is for creative scientists; for at the point in their careers at which these boys are tested (say ages twelve to fifteen), the "brightness" of the 15 per cent might or might not indicate a profound feeling for the causes of things; it is largely verbal and symbol-manipulating, and is almost certainly partly an obsessional device *not* to know and touch risky matter, just as Freud long ago pointed out that the nagging questions of small children are a substitute for asking the forbidden questions.

If these are the important kinds of issues—motivation, unblocking ability, deep-rootedness of learning—a little *more* attention to the individuality of the child, and some more progressive education, might suit the national need. It might even speed up the invention of rockets.

(The nadir of the recent pedagogic wisdom is, I suppose, the logic of our fierce Dr. Edward Teller of Berkeley. If the Russians continue to outpace us, he informs us, they will land on the moon first, they will control weather, perfect irresistible weapons, lead the world in everything, and "then freedom will be lost here and everywhere." Yet a couple of paragraphs later we learn that "in science anybody's success is your success... scientific people can, and do, co-operate no matter what their nationalities are," they speak an international language, and they belong to an international community "who practice the brotherhood of man." "A healthy sign," rejoices Dr. Teller, "is that salaries for scientists are edging upward"; the universities, private research laboratories, industrial concerns and the government "assure to scientists a comfortable, secure life." "Not," however, "that money should be a factor in deciding on a scientific career," for the Professor's concluding theme is that "science is fun." The essay, "Should You Be a Scientist?" appeared as a public service advertisement in the *Saturday Evening Post, Ladies' Home Journal, Life*, and *Scholastic* magazines.)

7.

The revolutionary program of progressive education missed out, or I should not be writing this gloomy book. The most vocal and superficial objections to it came from the conservatives who said that it flouted the Western Tradition, the Judaeo-Christian Tradition, the

Three R's, Moral Decency, Patriotism, and the Respect for Authority. But the damaging, and indeed fatal, blows to progressive education have come from those timid within the movement itself, who feared that the training did not provide an easy adjustment to life, meaning by "life" taking one's role in the organized system. This opinion has gradually prevailed, and now the doctrines of progressive education that have made headway in the public schools are precisely learning to get along with people, tolerance, and "real life problems" such as auto driving and social dancing. They are not those that pertain to passionately testing the environment rather that "adjusting" to it. What would one expect? There is nothing special about the failure of progressive education to make its way; it has suffered the same compromises as twenty other revolutions that I shall list in this book. The dominant class in society sees to it that it gets likewise the "progressive education" that suits.

8.

Let us return to the thread of our argument. Besides the out-of-scale physical environment and its complicated techniques, the social environment too is baffling and produces ineptitude and loss of the sense of causality.

Think of a child trying to cope with Property Rights, a most abstract notion. There is no problem when it is a case of something being used by somebody else, when Jack tries to take Bobby's shovel out of his hand and Bobby clouts him over the head with it or complains to authority in no uncertain terms. The puzzlement comes when the shovel is idle and Mama says, "You mustn't use that shovel, it's Bobby's." What impresses the child is no precise idea, but the grownup's tone of conviction. The child "believes," though there is no evidence of his senses. It is the beginning of what Marx called the fetishism of commodities. What is sickening is that it is just this kind of influencing that is wanted by priests, mayors, and tavern philosophers who declare that more home influence is the remedy for our troubles of youth.

But the social relationships of the grownups themselves are out of human scale, for in the corporate system of organization the puzzling has become altogether mysterious. It is disturbing to a child to sense that his mother is under the unseen thumb of religion or his father of the boss. But the top managers in our semimonopolies are quite anonymous. This is part of the new managerial code, as described by *Fortune* itself. A child cannot use them as model heroes, for they are invisible. This is why Jackie Robinson's proposal to import the TV personalities as ersatz models is so unfortunate, for these visible "heroes" are puppets. With the increasing concentration of management and control, as A. A. Berle has pointed out, there is less relation even to Property Rights.

Consider it. If one is put upon or abused, with whom shall he be angry? One cannot vent rage against an abstract system. But there is no need to vent feeling, for it is a matter of the grievance committee and other regular channels. In the Middle Status, the heart of the organized system, the situation is not the same as in a bureaucracy, with which it is usually compared; for a bureaucracy has a written code and a definite pecking-order; but the organization protects everybody's personal dignity, and its subtle interpersonal feuding and competition cannot be codified, for it is without any objective utility to give a principle. Even that mighty system the State is more material: it has banners, soldiers, elections, postmen, police. In a child it rouses awe and fear. But the organized system exists only in the bland front of its brand-name products and advertising. There is no knowing how it is run or who determines.

It is in these circumstances that young persons grow up convinced that everything is done with mirrors, by "influence." Not even the personal influence of nepotism, but something more like the astrological influence of the planets. The sense of initiative, causality, skill has been discouraged. Merit is a trait of "personality." Learning is the possession of a Diploma. Usefulness is a Union Card. Justification is Belonging.

9.

We are now in a position to understand the Hipster as Role Player.

The Role Player is the fellow who, without any real aptitude or training to do anything, and without a commitment to any goal, can skillfully fit the expectations that people have of him, and give typical performances to prove that he can do the job. The Roles of society are the capitalized nouns in *Time* style, e.g., Philosopher Russell or Very Important Person. There are great advantages in being a hipster in this sense. First, it is a way of getting by. If a man feels that he *is* not anything, he is at least taken for something, and he belongs. Then he can feel contempt for the others because they are fools, they are taken in; and so he satisfies his spite. And he can feel more confident that the so-called worth-while aims are empty because he can give a token performance, and this calms his own gnawing feelings of frustration and worthlessness. Finally, Role Playing protects a deep conceit of one's abstract powers: one "could" if one wanted, but in fact is never tested. The hipster in this sense must be distinguished from the industrious confidence man who wants to get the swag and vanish, and does not thrive on publicity. The hipster will often boast: he knows the score, he is ahead of the game.

This cool attitude of the hipster is endemic in the organized system. But on the other hand, the committed Organization Man also *really* belongs, he has status and salary and must protect them. Therefore the junior executive is in a terrible contradiction. He is cynical about the aims of the firm, yet he fears that his own ineptitude will be found out. He has no recourse to concrete performance, for there is little contact with unambiguous material and there are no objective standards. How to meet a purely subjective demand? In pain (even ulcers) he has to get by by role playing, interpersonal relations abstracted from both animal desire or tangible achievement. He meets expectations, he conforms, he one-ups, he proves he must know how by attaining a higher status.

"The trainee," says William H. Whyte, Jr., "believes managing is an end in itself—technique is more vital than content." Compare the identical remark in a memorandum of the Liberal Project in Congress: The past few years "have given rise to a particular brand of politician. He is completely method-oriented. The substance of a bill is not important, it is rather the *process* of passing the bill that is paramount." The new-type salesman does not sell the product but the man: by the expense account he proves that *he* is a right guy and he confirms the buyer's image of himself, whatever that happens to be.

For many bright young fellows, I think, the Organization has taken the place that the Communist Party had in the Thirties. At that time young men who were frustrated in their creative lives, perhaps because unable to stand the gaff, took out their self-hatred on the capitalist system, and often with sublime self-contempt accepted jobs with high salaries. In our decade, the young men believe they belong to the governing board, and their resentment has turned to cynicism. The standard of human integrity is equivalent.

The type situation of Role Playing is the Air Force questionnaire asking who is Giotto or Vivaldi: if the candidate gives the *right* answer, he is disqualified, he will not belong. The Role Player has no difficulty.

I was recently at another convention (National Recreation Congress, 1959), and striking was the difference between the working stiffs, the actual directors of play and group activities, and the administrators. The actual directors were human beings, often enthusiastic and proud of happy improvisations and strokes of good judgment that they wanted to report. But the administrators were concerned about standards, certificates, avoiding complaints and offending, and proving their dedicated service; it was clear that they wanted above all to diminish the factor of risk for themselves and create a front to get bigger appropriations. At the same time they kept asking how to recruit Leaders; but it was evident that the more strictly they applied their standards, the more surely they would eliminate the leaders.

We must contrast the concept of Role, meeting expectations by playing it cool and knowing the technique for a token performance, with the concept of Identity that Harold Rosenberg so well describes in *The Tradition of the New*. One discovers, fights for, appoints oneself to one's Identity. Identity is defined by its task, mission, product; role depends on the interpersonal expectation of the others.

Naturally, statesmen and public spokesmen are the role players, hipsters, *par excellence*. They exist by Front and giving symbolic satisfaction, so it is not to be hoped that their speech be serious, relevant to what objectively exists. But it is dismaying to find the same symbolic relations in enterprises of production and the distribution of goods. One cannot help distrusting the goods, thinking they are only packages and brand names. And so, becoming disaffected from these enterprises, the Beat Generation sometimes comes to despise real goods. It takes goods to be *merely* commodities that must be spurned: this is the fetishism of commodities in reverse.

Let us sum up. The factory operatives who couldn't care less about their jobs are not much aware of what they produce; causality is built into the machinery. The junior executives, advertising men, salesmen are role players and have little causal relation to the products. Presumably the technicians and top managers know something about and produce the products, since the products do come to exist. And the evidence is that the top managers do work very hard on production and sales; they work a sixty-hour week and are proud of their work. But even they have to devote an increasing majority of their time to interpersonal games of no productive use—90 per cent, says one, mentioned by W. H. Whyte, Jr.

(Let me give a typical illustration. There is a well-known monthly magazine that five editors used to put out with a week's work. It was pretty good. Unfortunately it made a reputation for itself and its wealthy sponsors hired a staff of ten secretaries and assistants to the editors. Soon the editors found themselves working all month, and quit. The magazine lost all its spark.)

Considering the technical possibilities, we must say that our physical environment changes very slowly. This is not surprising, for so little thought is given to it.

10.

We have in America a mystique of "production" and a man engaged in "production" is highly esteemed. In *The Affluent Society*, J. K. Galbraith shows that this attitude is entirely specious. Of five ways in which production can be increased: (1) except in wartime we do not try to increase the labor supply; (2) we do not try to encourage new enterprises; (3) in most industries, we do not try for technological innovation. All the stress is laid on (4) full employment, and (5) efficient use of present capital.

But this economist does not even bother to mention the factor of productivity that concerns us here: (6) to increase the aptitude and skill of each lad. Indeed, as we have tried to show, rather than encouraged it is systematically retarded. It would not today be said, as it used to be, that the Americans are born mechanics. Among the model heroes of the young we do not think of Edison, Burbank, Ford, Steinmetz, and so forth. It is anachronistic to mention their names.

The juvenile literary and pictorial image of the inventor and scientist has correspondingly changed. Two generations ago it was a kindly bumbling old fool, unkempt but stubborn and brave, and with a light of divine truth in his eyes. A generation ago science began to be altogether strange and the scientist began to be a surgeon with rubber gloves or a cold maniac with diabolic power in his eyes. But this stereotype is forbidden today, for strategic reasons, and the scientist is now a young, neatly dressed, co-operative Organization Man holding up some apparatus that proves his role, but nothing in his eyes at all, at all. But he *is* having fun.

The claim of the organized system is that research and invention are in their nature increasingly corporative and anonymous, and this produces great results. That is debatable. I doubt that very much is corporatively invented which is not pretty directly dictated by managerial need and policy, whereas the essence of invention is to be hitherto-unthought-of—though, of course, there occurs the rich comedy of administrators anxiously waiting for mathematicians to turn up with something "useful," and never knowing what goes on behind those spectacles. (I have a mathematician friend who bills his firm for overtime because he tends to think of things in bed about 2 A.M. and his attitude is that they can take it or leave it.) Certainly the following example is not *un*typical: A gifted food chemist puts in six months developing a formula; he is successful and the product is going to be pushed with a million-dollar campaign; it is, in his opinion, *identical* with —— Mayonnaise, the popular brand. (In this case the scientist suddenly decided to quit and to set himself up as an independent consultant, hoping that people would come in with real problems.)

Proof on this kind of issue is difficult. On the one side, the corporations, having pre-empted much of the talent, point proudly to inventions made under their auspices, as if they might not have been made anyway. On the other side, their opponents argue from inventions-that-have-not-been-made, a peculiar metaphysical category, e.g., "If all the capital and research had not gone into internal combustion engines, by now we should have much superior steam or electric cars." It may be said definitely that research entailing million-dollar equipment and vast samplings of the populace cannot be carried on without corporative or state sponsorship; yet many would deny that this style of research, and expense of social wealth, is so fruitful as the old American shoestring operator or the seventeenth-century gentleman-philosopher with his dumb-bunny apparatus and towering intellect. We certainly have at present the dismal situation that the most imaginative men are directed by a group, the top managers, who are among the least, hard-working though they may be. Also, inventions made outside the organization are notoriously bought up and withheld or otherwise sabotaged by the organization. (To my conscience, this practice, of keeping basic new ideas in limbo until it is profitable to exploit them, is immoral and disruptive of the community of mankind far more than rigged quiz shows, but it comes from the same box, whose label is Intellect Bought.)

So we return to the President of Merck and Company, who, hauled before a Senate investigation on charges that Merck and its semimonopolistic "competitors" were criminally overpricing drugs, *warned* the Senators that they might "upset the delicate balance we have been able to develop over the years between the quest for scientific knowledge on the one hand and the drive for financial success on the other."!! *Quo usque tandem.*

The situation of a young fellow is ironical. If he has reached college age and has technical aptitude, the most desperate attempts are made to get him for this or that firm. They pay for his schooling and guarantee him a job. Meantime, the systematic behavior of those firms has been to baffle aptitude in the young and to limit it where it has survived.

It is in this context that we must listen to Dr. Conant's recommendations for the high school: the selection of the academically talented, the top 15 per cent, to major in a program of mathematics and sciences. No effort is made to increase the pool of ability; and the public schools are, effectually, to be used as apprentice training grounds for the monopolies and the armed forces.

V. PATRIOTISM

IN 1783 Washington sent a circular letter to the States, describing the situation of the new nation as he saw it. "We have equal occasion to felicitate ourselves," he said, "on the lot which Providence has assigned to us, whether we view it in a natural, a political, or moral point of light." He pointed to the natural resources of the new nation, its independence and freedom, the Age of Reason during which it had come of age, an age of "the free cultivation of letters, the unbounded extension of commerce, the progressive refinement of manners, the growing liberality of sentiment, and above all the pure and benign light of Revelation.... If these citizens," he concluded, "should not be completely free and happy, the fault will be certainly their own. Such is our situation and such are our prospects."

It is hard to read these sentences without agitation and tears, for they are simply true and simply patriotic.

In the next generations, almost to our own times, patriotic rhetoric did not cease to sound, more pompously and falsely, but never without a core of truth. There was always something special in the American destiny to be proud of. In 1825 it was the broad democracy. In 1850 it was the magnificent spread and settlement from coast to coast. In 1875, the material progress, the cable and the Pacific railroad, the building of modern industrialism. In 1900, America was the melting pot, the asylum of the poor and the oppressed.

In our century, the patriotic rhetoric began to be unbelievable—not by accident, for foreign wars (1898 and 1917) are incompatible with reasonable rhetoric. In recent decades there has been almost a surcease of such speech. Even references to the American Way, free enterprise, high production, and the economy of abundance have finally died out, because they call up the idea of tail fins and TV commercials. Highbrow journalists mention the American Way with scorn.

Our case is astounding. For the first time in recorded history, the mention of country, community, place has lost its power to animate. Nobody but a scoundrel even tries it. Our rejection of false patriotism is, of course, itself a badge of honor. But the positive loss is tragic and I cannot resign myself to it. A man has only one life and if during it he has no great environment, no community, he has been irreparably robbed of a human right. This loss is damaging especially in growing up, for it deprives outgoing growth, which begins with weaning from Mother and walking out of the house, of the chance of entering upon a great and honorable scene to develop in.

Culture is, first of all, city and patriotic culture. I shall try to show that patriotism is the culture of childhood and adolescence. Without this first culture, we come with a fatal emptiness to the humane culture of science, art, humanity and God; and this emptiness results in the best people *not* turning back, like Plato's philosopher who has emerged from the cave, to serve their country. Many of the best Americans have a strong philanthropic and local community zeal, yet it would seem odd for somebody nowadays to put himself to a big and hard task just to serve his country, to make her better, and be proud of that. Young people aspire mightily to appearances on televisions and other kinds of notoriety, but I doubt that many now think of being honored by a statue in the park and winning "immortal" fame, the fame of big culture.

Let me make the same point by analyzing a remarkable proposition of Otto Jespersen, the grammarian. He shows that, contrary to expectation, a child does not learn his mother tongue at home from his mother and immediate family, he does not pick up their accent. The accent, vocabulary, syntax, and style that form his speech are learned from his first peer groups, outside the home. Jespersen does not explain it, but the psychology seems evident. Speech occurs at the stage of the developing of the "I," it is a forming of the image of the self, it is a self-appointment to one's ideal and putting on its uniform. Changes occur as we appoint ourselves to one peer group after another. At a certain stage a lad appoints himself or commits himself to a band of friends and puts on its jargon, jacket, tattoo, and masculine ring on the fourth finger of the left hand. If he is insecure and disturbed, this conformity is a cowering protection and the band is a delinquent gang, but in every case it is also, we see by the blazon, an achievement. And one way in which the Governor of New York does not take the juveniles seriously, when he speaks of giving them a sense of belonging, is that he does not offer an ideal that promises equal manliness. He has none to offer.

It is tragic when there is no great adult peer group to meet growth. Consider the case of an artist, my own case. To have simple and sounding language, rather than merely the lovely colloquialism of Sherwood Anderson or William Carlos Williams, it is necessary to believe in the great national culture of one's people. Our popular culture does not warrant the belief, even to make the sacrifice that Virgil made when he sadly gave up his best vision because strife-torn Rome needed a national poet. True, an artist can then jump to the international and universal, for mankind and God do not let him down (mankind is the fellow on one's own block), but this is at the loss of pomp and glitter, of the glancing present. Without a patriotic peer group, it is impossible to have the brilliance of Handel, the material grandeur of Venice. With us the style of the big bright sensation belongs to cheap musical dramas on Broadway.

2.

The area of patriotism is intermediate between childhood and adulthood. We must delimit it carefully or we play into the hands of fools and rogues who have done our country plenty of damage.

To what can we correctly attach the adjective "American"? There is no "American" animal, sexual, or primary family life. The idea of American child-rearing or American medicine is idiotic, and the thought of an "American family" is abominable. At the further extreme, there is no "American" university, "American" science, religion, or peace. In only an equivocal sense is there an "American" art: the subject matter may be American, but the art is international and the aim is universal.

In between, however, there *is* an American landscape, an American primary and secondary education, an American classlessness, an American Constitution, an Anglo-American language, and an American kind of enterprising. That is, just where a child ventures from home and grows up through adolescence, the great environment becomes his scene, and this is American, a characteristic geography and history, place and community. It is just in growing up, which is the subject of this book, that a patriotic opportunity is essential. It is just this opportunity that, for ingenuous youth, is corrupted. And so it is hard to grow up.

Let us be quite clear what this American landscape and community is. I quote from a recent issue of *Life:*

> [Teen-agers] own 10 million phonographs, over a million TV sets, 13 million cameras. Counting only what is spent to satisfy their special teen-age demands, the youngsters and their parents will shell out about $10 billion this year, a billion more than the total sales of GM. Until recently businessmen have largely ignored the teen-age market. But now they are spending millions on advertising and razzle-dazzle promotional stunts. If parents have any idea of organized revolt, it is already too late. Teen-age spending is so important that such action would send quivers through the entire national economy.

This is a description of the landscape, and the prose of *Life* is part of the landscape.

3.

Equal to our businessmen, our government and public spokesmen have a knack for debasing the noble and making the excellent trivial. The current disease is to make Cold War capital out of everything, no matter what. We cannot dedicate a building of Frank Lloyd Wright's in New York without our Ambassador to the United Nations pointing out that such an architect could not have flourished in Russia. This is tasteless; the matter becomes serious when our freedoms are involved.

Not long ago there was a great to-do about the Russian censorship of Pasternak's *Dr. Zhivago*. The editorials and the rhetoric of organized friends of culture kept repeating freedom of speech, freedom of culture. (You would think that we did not have our own means of censoring, by commercial selection and by swamping.) But the outcry about Pasternak was not sincere, it was propaganda in the Cold War. In the same year, for instance, the Archbishop of Dublin effectually banned the spring theater festival because of plays of O'Casey and Joyce. (He refused to say the festival Mass if those plays were to be given. The director then canceled the plays. But the actors manfully struck and would not play at all, and this resulted in an important loss of tourist revenue. Such admirable behavior is inconceivable in my country.) On this theme, the *New York Times* ran no editorials, no, nor the New York *Herald Tribune*. For we are not at cold war with the Catholic hierarchy. (I wrote a letter to the *Times* asking that this and *Zhivago* be coupled for mention, but no one was interested.) But such behavior is patriotically disastrous; it teaches that our spokesmen are not earnest; they pick and choose when to stand up for freedom of thought. How then can a boy be proud? (But to be sure, we have little such freedom, compared with the British, for our *mass* media are not, like theirs, open to fundamental controversy. It is not surprising, therefore, that for English Angry Young Men an important topic is their outraged patriotism, whereas our Beats do not care about that.)

4.

Consider the behavior of our professors and universities during the Dies, McCarthy and Feinberg Law investigations. It is hard to say which set the worse example to the students during those hearings: the Communist professors fearful for their jobs, or the colleges that —with magnificent exceptions, like Harvard—supinely received the investigators. A monumental blunder was being made—which did us desperate damage among thoughtful Europeans—and our professors shivered in their boots and our "radicals" hid like roaches. (Cf. Appendix D.) The important thing is not which group betrays the ideal in any particular case, but that young people become cynical about political action and resigned about the possibility of making a change. Following a party line, Communist teachers, e.g., at New York's City College, denied their membership. This was a disastrous betrayal of the students. Not that it is wrong to avoid insolent force with fraud, but that young students can grow only by politically affirming themselves. With the young, honor is more important than tactics or even than prudence. Leaders of youth must be knightly—a grisly identity, but there it is.

We have now passed through a decade in which the students in our colleges showed a political apathy probably unexampled in student history. Several causes have conspired to it. First, simple shell shock: the war and the atom bomb aroused such deep anxiety that the only defense against it was conventionality. (I remember lecturing on Kafka in 1948 to a hall of collegians consisting largely of veterans on the G.I. bill, and they frantically protested that Kafka was psychotic and should be paid no attention, he had no relation to reality—they who had lived through some of the Trial and were even then roaming under the Castle!)

Secondly, the students have been seduced by business firms, which tempt and reward them for conformity; but as W. H. Whyte, Jr. points out, they are eager to conform even before they are paid. Correspondingly, in its appeal to lower-class boys, the Army has found it wise to accept the stirring slogan, "Retire at 37." If you question a boy draftee who has re-enlisted, he will explain that it is a "good deal." That is, the Army has become the IBM of the poor boy.

But finally, is there any doubt that an important cause of the present political apathy of the young is the dishonorable radical leadership that they had in the Thirties and Forties? They now believe that *all* political thinking is a sell—just as those bright Catholic lads who stop believing the superstitions of scholasticism now believe that all philosophy is an intricate fraud, including the truths of scholasticism.

This hipster skepticism is pervasive. It is partly, of course, resignation that a revolution has failed and the way is too thorny; but students are usually more resilient. I think that a more important factor is disgust that the radicals were not bona fide; the students were had. But also, I fear, it is cynical superiority, an identification with either the fraudulent or the powerful.

I referred above to the similarity between some of the Communists and young Organization Men today, in their lust for control apart from any objective good and, more deeply, in their use of an organized power-system in order to make the ingenuous and worthy not exist. In the Thirties it came about that Communists had high status in Hollywood and somewhat in publishing, so the two kinds of organized systems worked in the same offices—nor do I doubt that many of the refinements of present-day organization life were learned during this cohabitation. But it has remained for our own decade to enjoy the brutal comedy of McCarthy and the FBI investigating the Communists in Hollywood, so we had on one stage the three most cynical tribes in the country.

But let us go back to more simple ignobility.

5.

Certainly the most thrilling and romantic happening of these years is the adventure in space, surpassing in promise the voyages of the fifteenth and sixteenth centuries. This adventure makes life worth the trouble again. When the Russians beat us out, we are miffed but we can be proud that these exploits have been performed by men and man is great; Copernicus was a Pole, Galileo an Italian, Kepler a German, Newton an Englishman—and the rockets were Chinese; and we hope that we shall win the next round, for it belongs to America to achieve first in this kind of enterprise. The experiments are expensive, but it seems mean-spirited to question the appropriations and few have done so. So far, grand. But now we have corrupted even the exploration of space into the Cold War. Against an agreement of the International Geophysical Year, we, like the Russians, withheld the wave length of a satellite for strategic reasons. (I was ashamed and again I wrote dutifully to the *New York Times*, but they again had no space for such an odd way of viewing the news.) Next, we carried out a secret nuclear experiment in the ionosphere, and this one was kept secret not from the Russians for military reasons, but from the American people, because of possible objections to the fallout. The *Times* kept the secret till the Russians were about to publish it, explaining (March 19, 1959), that "it had learned of the plans for Project Argus last summer, some weeks before it took place. Nevertheless, scientists associated with the government said they feared that prior announcement of the experiment might lead to protests that would force its cancellation." A. J. Muste, an editor of *Liberation* magazine, asked them for an apology for this unexampled betrayal of journalistic responsibility, and got the astounding reply:

> It seems to me that you are suggesting that the *Times* enter the propaganda field and, in effect, set its judgment above that of military men and scientists as to what can be published.... After all, the *Times* is a responsible newspaper. [!!] [Robert Garst, Assistant Managing Editor. In *Liberation*, May 1959.]

But what is the effect on our people when we are told that our chief newspaper does not print the news? Constitutionally, for instance, *how in a democracy do they then deserve their mailing privileges, to circulate their official press releases and advertisements for department stores?* [The purpose of second-class mail is to circulate information.] When Muste wrote a letter for publication about the *Times'* handling of the story, the *Times* found no space for that letter.

But to my mind, even more important is the effect of cutting people off from the adventure of science, no matter what the risks. What an illiberal and dishonorable policy to pursue! Our government cannot see that noble things must not be made base, romance must not be turned into disillusion, or what will become of the young people? Take another example. This glorious enterprise of space! And now we have chosen seven astronauts for special training. But the nemesis of the organized system haunts us. All prove to be white Protestant, in their early or middle thirties, married, with small children, and coming from small towns—in brief, models of salesmen or junior executives for International Business Machines. And these seven have now made a solemn pact, reported in the press, that whichever one goes aloft will split evenly with the others his take from syndicated stories and TV appearances. Concerning them, Dr. George Ruff, the Air Force psychiatrist who tested them, has explained, "Knowing the qualities that made them this way, and working hard at applying those qualities in your daily life, can help you [too] to come closer to achieving what they have become: comfortable, mature, and well-integrated individuals. It's a worth-while goal."

Of course, by this writing (June 1960), it is commonly accepted that our new Midas satellite has the *function* of espionage. But it has remained for a proper scientist to hit the bottom: the professor who has advised us *not* to reply to any signals we might receive from outer space, because the astral beings are likely to be technically more advanced than we and they will come down and eat us up. This projection of the Cold War into the starry vault was favorably reported by the science editor of the *Herald Tribune*.

6.

In the time of Washington, the public men—Adams, Jefferson, Madison, Marshall, Henry, Franklin, Hamilton, Jay—were a fair sampling of the good spirits in the country, humane, literate, brave, not self-seeking. (There is a remarkable letter of Jefferson's to David Rittenhouse, urging him to waste no more time in mere politics, for the world needed him more in his capacity as a scientist.) By and large, it could not be said of our presidents and governors at present, the symbols of the country, that they are a fair sampling of the best of us. It would not be difficult to make a list of a hundred, or two hundred, who are superior to them in every relevant way, in whom a boy could feel pride and trust.

Of course this is not a new trouble among us. Just as the European writers of the eighteenth century idolized our statesmen as if they were demigods, so in the nineteenth they spoke of their inferiority. This is the consequence of another missed revolution, the democratic revolution. A man of sense obviously cannot waste his life learning to sue to an ignorant electorate and coming up through political ranks in which disinterestedness and pure convictions are not the most handy virtues. Yet the fault is not with democracy, but that we have failed to have enough of it. For instance, if our emphasis had been on perfecting the town meeting and the neighborhood commune, there would not be ignorant electors and they would choose great officers. If people had the opportunity to initiate community actions, they would be political; they would know that finally the way to accomplish something great is to get together with the like-minded and directly do it.

But the men in power do not think politically either. For instance, this year we have had the usual spectacle of politicians going about the country looking for nominators for the Presidency, presumably (why else?) because they have important new programs to offer. But as soon as it becomes clear that the county leaders of the party do not want them, they retire from the race and rally to elect whomever. What becomes of the programs? Since this is what political responsibility means to a politician, why should the electorate respect politics, and how could an honest boy be inspired to enter on such a career?

In a recent essay, the historian Henry Steele Commager asks how it is possible that we have an absolute dearth of statesmen at present in America (he cannot think of one). Characteristically, we have an immense amount of formal training in flourishing institutes for public administration at Harvard, Princeton, Syracuse, Tufts, etc., as if we could get the thing by learning the role. Commager sensibly concludes that that training does not begin early enough and it lacks the content of actual experience. The environment does not encourage public service, it does not esteem public goods. Few fathers give much thought to the distant generations of posterity, and children do not take fire in reading about the great men of history and thinking "Why not I?" as a plausible purpose. And finally, says Commager, the narrow chauvinism and energetic hostility to subversive ideas that are now the test of our politicians are precisely disastrous to patriotism, for that must be spacious, disinterested, and broad-based, otherwise it is intolerable foolishness. Let me quote a fine passage:

> The men who won our independence and laid the foundations of the American nation were devoted patriots but they were, too, men of the world. They were children of the enlightenment. Reason taught them that all men were brothers, that purely national distinctions were artificial, that there existed a great community of arts and letters and philosophy and science cutting across and transcending mere national boundaries.... The nationalism of the eighteenth century did not rest on a narrow base but on a broad one. It did not find nourishment in fear and suspicion but in faith and confidence. Perhaps one reason for the decline in statesmanship is that we have hemmed our potential statesmen in, we have denied them tolerant and spacious ideas.

As it is, what must be the effect on a boy when he comes to realize that the public spokesman up there is not even speaking his own words, but repeating, like a performer, something written for him by a staff from Madison Avenue? The boy must learn to shout, "Shame! make your own speech at least!"

Our present President (Mr. Eisenhower) is an unusually uncultivated man. It is said that he has invited no real writer, no artist, no
philosopher to the White House. Presumably he has no intellectual
friends; that is his privilege. But recently he invited the chief of the
Russian government to a banquet and musicale. And the formal music of that musicale was provided by a Fred Waring band playing
"Oh, What a Beautiful Morning" and such other numbers. This is
disgraceful.

7.

The American landscape has been badly corrupted. European writers no longer even notice the natural wonder of it, they are so put off
by the ugliness and conformity of the towns. But worse than the
ugliness and conformity is the neglect that baffles pride of place.
Our poets try to move themselves by nostalgically repeating the
names of towns: "Biloxi and Natchez, Pascagoula and Opelousas"—
but beware of paying a visit.

The Americans disesteem public goods, and improving the landscape is a big expense. Historically, the neglect of appearance and
plan of our scores of thousands of villages and small towns, especially in the Middle West and South—the diner, the Woolworth's,
and two filling stations—can be analogized to the neglect of the
present-day poor. In the tide of expansion, appearance was disregarded as not essential; later, the matter would be mopped up. But
the neglect rigidifies, it is a hard core not easy to change.

Instead, the present tendency is to impose on the countryside a
new corporation style altogether, in the form of shopping centers
(=national chain supermarkets) on the highway. This works out disastrously for the communities, for these "centers" are not centers of
villages, and there cease to be villages at all, simply scattered family
houses. This is the end of a long process of disruption, for in any case
the industry is gone, the men work in plants thirty miles away. It is
possible to travel many miles even in New England and not see a

single activity a man could make a living at, except automobile agencies and filling stations; not even a food store. The schools too are large and centralized. The families tend to move away frequently, but even while they are put, they are driving around. This does not make much community to grow up in.

In more primitive societies, a chief community activity is working together, thatching a roof, net fishing. But with us, precisely this co-operative labor, for instance the work in a factory, is removed from its community setting and emptied, by the relations of production, of any community spirit.

Places that have no shape have no face-to-face functioning, for the shape *is* the functioning community. The loveliness of so many hamlets in Europe is that they have shape and are built of local materials by local craft. Perhaps the people had to cluster to attend early masses. In Ireland, where they farm out the back door, the rows of thatched houses line both sides of a little street. In France, where men go off to their farms, there may be a square. In our own early New England villages, where congregational and political spirit was strong, there was a common green with public buildings, though the families lived scattered on the farms they worked. There was the shape of a community, with its economy, its crafts, and its ideas. The advantage of growing up in such a community in one's early years is evident. It is not family supervision, on which the physicians of juvenile delinquency are now laying such stress; quite the contrary! it is that the family does *not* have to bear the burden of teaching the culture. In a community, everybody knows the child face to face. There is an easy grading of overlapping ages, right up to the adults who are going about their business in a going concern, and not paying too much attention to children. A good city neighborhood works in the same way.

From this point of view, the swarm of kids in a city housing project form a better community than present-day country boys or the kids on Park Avenue. *Therefore* they have more local patriotism. The bother with this community chain, however, is that it terminates abruptly before it reaches the adults, who belong to a different world; so the kids are a gang and the local community spirit turns into loyalty to a Code; it does not eventuate in anything socially cohesive and culturally worth while. And such a gang is prone to be delinquent because, as we shall see, in such conditions it is the forbidden that best cements loyalty.

Politically, a delinquent gang is not lawless and not in the state of nature. Balked in its growth, the local loyalty turns on itself and simply reinvents the feud-code of Alfred the Great, marking out safe territories and making provision for special classes of revenge. On this view, if one teen-age gang, pursuing its vendetta, falls on another and murders a kid, it would not be our business to interfere in the law of that differently constituted society. Also, like Danes or Vikings of Alfred's time, they regard our larger society merely as a field of sport and plunder; they have not yet reinvented International Law. But we, of course, cannot view it so, for we live in an advanced state of politics and law: they are members of our community. We are not children but more experienced and somewhat wiser, and therefore responsible, so we cannot simply annihilate them like pirates (they are small in size, few in numbers, and armed with primitive weapons); and we cannot let them hurt themselves.

(I think it is wise sometimes to regard disaffected groups as if there *were* plausibly these two viewpoints, rival patriotisms. It is better humanity and it might make better law. The advantage is that it takes the disaffected seriously as disaffected, rather than merely pathological; it keeps in the foreground the question of allegiance. We must *deserve* allegiance.)

8.

But they are children. Let us consider rather the peculiar patriotic problem of an older disaffected group, the Beat young men, for then we can see that it *is* a patriotic problem.

Here too, I think, there has often been a strong community influence of growing up together. For instance, fellows who went to

Black Mountain College, which was oriented to community and creative arts—a powerful, and powerfully disaffecting, combination—are pillars of Beat society. Other fellows were buddies in the armed services. However it was, as Beat their community spirit is strong. They barge in to sleep, they share property, they share a culture. Now think of this community, disaffected from America, as engaged in a pathetic quest for some other big patriotism, an adult peer group.

We saw how, appointing themselves outcast, they affirm the accidental symbols of other outcast groups: Negro, Puerto Rican, and criminal. But this is pretty thin gruel for intellectual young men, many of whom have been to college. On the other hand, they are unable to make the jump to the great international humanist community because, simply, they don't know anything, neither literature nor politics. (I once taught at Black Mountain College, and to my astonishment I found that the students had never read the Bible, Milton, Dryden, Gibbon, etc., etc., nor did they feel—as a lack—that such things existed. But they knew odd facts about Mayan hieroglyphics which their teacher had been interested in.)

What then? Since it is necessary for grown fellows to have some major allegiance or other, they have latched on to the dead Japanese masters of Zen Buddhism. (This is a late effect of the early-century discovery of Japan by Fenollosa, Frank Lloyd Wright, the Misses Lowell and Ayscough, and Ezra Pound, suddenly reinforced by the postwar occupation under General MacArthur.) Now, as we shall see, Zen is *not* irrelevant to these young men's needs, for it is a theology and style of immediate experience. But the pathos is that Zen was the flower of an intensely loyal feudal system that fed, protected, and honored its masters, and to which the Zen masters in turn had fealty. For example, it is said that the haiku was invented by a poet as a public service when he was suicidally despondent because his Emperor had died. But Zen without farmers and servants is an airy business; and the young men, as we have seen, are betrayed into dubious devices to keep body and soul together, nor do they have a flag to salute.

9.

I have tried broadly to paint some of the background conditions that discourage patriotism: the lack of bona fides about our liberties, the dishonorable politics in the universities, the irresponsible press, the disillusioning handling of the adventure in space, the inferior and place-seeking high officers of the State, the shameful neglect of our landscape and the disregard of community; later I shall speak of our trivial leisure which has no community meaning. But besides these not usually mentioned background conditions, there are of course the persistent immediate uglinesses that everybody talks about and every child sees: the cases of graft, social injustice, stupid law, and injustice to persons. Yet in an important sense, these scandals do not discourage patriotism, so long as there is the feeling of a persistent effort against them. My guess is that more pride of country is engendered by one good decision, or even a good powerful dissenting opinion, of the at least traditional Supreme Court, than by billions of repetitions of the pledge of allegiance.

Racial segregation and prejudice destroy community by definition, and we need not discuss them. Here again the revolution commenced in Jefferson's time and recommended by the abolitionists, went unfinished; and we have inherited the consequences.

But it is perhaps useful to point out again that, when there is prejudice, the community of the dominant class is equally destroyed. The whites in the South, for instance, used to talk a blatant patriotism and a specious regionalism grounded in nothing but keeping the blacks under. The result is that flag and cross have become contemptible in their own eyes. (Real regionalism, that finds its culture and satisfaction in its own geography and economy and can withstand the temptations of the national cash-nexus, has long ago succumbed to Madison Avenue, Hollywood, and Wall Street.) Now that law and religion side against them, the Southerners are maniac with wounded conceit and sexual fear; their behavior on integration should be referred not to the Attorney General but to the Public Health Service. All this has come banging down on the children as the battleground. Yet, paradoxically, among all young people it is perhaps just the young people in the South, whites and Negroes both, who most find life worth living these days, because something real is happening. During the Montgomery bus boycott against Jim Crow, there was little delinquency among the Negro boys.

(In Northern cities and towns, also, the children are thrown into a central position in the community crisis of exclusion and prejudice, but sometimes as peacemakers. Let me give an interesting architectural example. It has become common to use the new centralized school building as the community building for meetings and recreation. One reason is economy. But another reason that is given is that the school is the one community function that brings together the otherwise discordant elements in the neighborhood, so maybe the adults can get together in the school. It is a curious situation when the grownups have to rely on the children to make sense for them, and when the school building is the chief community building. But it is better than nothing.)

10.

Deep in the organized system itself there has been an important new effort toward community. The postwar boom in young marriages and the sensational rise in the urban birth rate that for the first time promises to surpass the rural birth rate, have been accompanied by the moving of affluent workmen to suburban projects and of the middle status to ranch houses. These new settlements devote time and energy to common interests. Do they do anything for local patriotism?

They are communities for small children, one to five, and for women as the mothers of small children. These are the groups in society unequivocally benefited by high production, full employment, and the high standard of living. They thrive on animal security. Labor-saving devices make the world of the infants much pleasanter. Morally and vocationally, there is no question that having and caring for the children is justified work for the mothers, necessary, honored, and using good human capacities. Nearly forty years ago, H. L. Mencken pointed out in his book on women that women had real jobs, whereas men were likely to be certified public accountants or politicians. Today, when so many work in the Rat Race, few would deny that he was right. So now men too try earnestly to devote themselves to the small ones as a secondary but real career. This is called the New Fatherhood.

The child world, in the suburbs and surrounding country, and somewhat less in the city, is the best that small children have had in modern times. The new psychology of belonging is feeble stuff, but the new psychology of infant care has been radical: no toilet training, permissive thumb sucking and pregenital sexuality, free crying and movement, exposure to the grownups' nakedness, honest answers to questions. The new medicine gets them quickly over the usual diseases (though there is debate about the later consequences). The school system as a whole is poor, but the nursery schools are often first-rate, progressive, and have intelligent and dedicated young teachers. It is said that children's toys and games are excellent, practical and imaginative, up to the age of six, when the commercial criteria of the eleven-billion-dollar market begin to operate.

For the adults, the improvement of this child's world results in genuine community participation, committee meetings and lectures on psychology, concern for traffic and zoning, and even extension courses in cultural subjects to create the proper atmosphere for growing up. It seems astonishing, given so much active participation, that these community activities have not much developed into other important political and social action. But courage gives out at the political issues relevant to age six. The sponsorship and control of the organized system are everywhere apparent.

(For instance, in a recent agitation that has prevented Negroes from moving into Deerfield, a suburb of Chicago—average income $9,000–10,000—an "attractive young married couple" explained that most of their friends had most of their money tied up in their houses: "We don't expect to live in them very long. Some of the junior execs expect to become seniors and move to the real North Shore, and a lot of us will be transferred all over the United States. When this happens, we want to be sure our houses have resale value." [Reported in the *New York Times*, April 17, 1960.] The spiritedness of this speaks for itself.)

Unfortunately, when the adults devote themselves thus to the child's world, there isn't much world for the child to grow up into in the next stage. For Father to guide his growing son, it is necessary for him to have a community of his own and be more of a man. In the circumstances this is difficult. But if there is no big environment, there are no grounds for patriotism.

The corporations, however, have now entered into this arena too, to organize the next stage of growing up. This is the meaning, surely, of the publicity that has been trumped up for the Little League, the baseball teams of subteen-agers sponsored and underwritten by various business firms. What value the Little League has as play, I don't know, I haven't watched games. The high-pressure advertising has been violently denounced by the older sports writers as giving kids an unsportsmanlike taste for publicity. As a school of rule making, responsibility, and impersonality, the Little League certainly cannot compare with the free games of the street, but we saw that these have been passing away. Economically, however, the function of the Little League is clear-cut: it is child labor, analogous to ten-year-olds picking hemp in the factory a century ago: it keeps idle hands out of mischief; it is not profitable as production, but it provides valuable training in attitude and work habits.

Viewed so, the suburban and exurban trends are the formation of a new proletariat, producers of offspring.

II.

Naturally the Public Relations have been unable to restrain themselves from invading the public schools. The classes are flooded with pamphlets and documentary films on electronics and the introduction of cows into New Zealand, put out by Consolidated Edison, Ford, Shell, Westinghouse, the National Dairy Council, Union Carbide, Bell, etc., and even Merrill Lynch. These proclaim their sponsorship with more or less discreet plugs.

In the ninth grade, however, at a New York City school I know well, they have spent class time with an item called *The Educational ABC's of Industry*, a collection of advertisements interlarded with reading matter; and the class was actually required, by a teacher distracted by overwork, to copy out jingles in which C stands for Orange-*Crush*, "taste it and see," and F for the *Ford* Motor Company, "where the first car grew." I would gladly share this literature with the reader, but its publisher has not given me permission.

VI. SOCIAL ANIMAL

1.

LET US next talk about marriage and so-called "animal" functions of the social animal.

Everyone agrees that an important condition for the troubles of growing up is the troubles between the parents at home, brutal quarrels and drunkenness, coldness, one or the other or both parents getting away as often as possible and being withdrawn while present, and marriages breaking up. The most common popular, and mayoral, prescription for delinquency is "more parental supervision." In the usual circumstances this would likely *increase* the tension and the trouble, but be that as it may: the question remains, how? how to have reasonable supervision when the marriages themselves are no good? for presumably the good marriages don't have the problem children. (The frequent recommendation to fine or jail the parents is a lulu.)

I do not think the public spokesmen are serious. For powerful and well-known modern reasons, some of them inevitable, the institution of marriage itself, as we have known it for several hundred years, cannot work simply any longer, and is very often the direct cause of intense suffering. Urbanism, the economic independence of women, contraception, relaxing the inhibitions against unmarried and extramarital sexuality, these are inevitable. A dispassionate observer of modern marriage might sensibly propose, Forget it; think up some other form of mating and child care. The pastor of a large church in an ordinary Midwestern town told me that, in his observation, not one marriage in twenty was worth while; many were positively damaging to the children. If very many marriages could simply let themselves dissolve after a few years, the partners would suddenly become brighter, rosier, and younger. But of course, in this field there are no dispassionate observers. We are all in the toils of jealousy of our own Oedipus complexes, and few of us can tolerate loneliness and the feeling of being abandoned. Nor do we *have* any other formula for secure sex, companionship, and bringing up children.

This is not a newsy story. Is it kept in mind by the Mayor of New York whose canned voice says every night on the radio that parents who are not affectionately supervising the children are failing in responsibility? Has the Mayor not seen an harassed mother hysterically and unmercifully whacking a three-year-old in the sand pile? Does he think it is some different parent he is now appealing to? (I heard one mother scream, "I ask you only one simple thing, to obey me!")

"Most of the children we see [in King's County Domestic Relations Court] have been so seriously damaged by their environment that they need 24-hour-a-day corrective treatment. I'll say unequivocally that most of the children we see should be separated from their parents for their own health and welfare." (Dr. J. M. Fries.)

2.

Consider some incidents of sex and marriage in a more "privileged" and a more "underprivileged" situation. For the first, we can return to the remarkable boom in early marriages and child bearing that we mentioned in the last chapter, occurring especially among the economically privileged who previously would have married late. No doubt this has been partly due to the war and Cold War, clinging to life and clutching to something safe in an era of anxiety. But it seems to be also partly a strong reaction to the drift toward formlessness which these young persons could observe in their own parents.

These young-marrying, contemporaries or juniors of the Beat Generation, have often expressed themselves as follows: "My highest aim in life is to achieve a normal healthy marriage and raise healthy [non-neurotic] children." On the face of it, this remark is preposterous. What was always taken as a usual and advantageous life-condition for work in the world and the service of God, is now regarded as an heroic goal to be striven for. Yet we see that it *is* a hard goal to achieve against the modern obstacles. Also it is a *real* goal, with objective problems that a man can work at personally, and take responsibility for, and make decisions about—unlike the interpersonal relations of the corporation, or the routine of the factory job for which the worker couldn't care less.

But now, suppose the young man is achieving this goal: he has the wife, the small kids, the suburban home, and labor-saving domestic devices. How is it that it is the same man who uniformly asserts that he is in a Rat Race? Either the goal does not justify itself, or indeed he is not really achieving it. Perhaps the truth is, if marriage and children are the *goal*, a man cannot really achieve it. It is not easy to conceive of a strong husband and father who does not feel justified in his work and independent in the world. Correspondingly, his wife feels justified in the small children, but does she have a man, do the children have a father, if he is running a Rat Race? Into what world do the small children grow up in such a home?

It is advantageous to the smooth functioning of the organized system if its personnel are married and have home responsibilities. (E.g., it's much harder for them to act up and quit.) But the smooth functioning of the organized system may not be advantageous to the quality of the marriage and the fatherhood. It is a troubling picture. On the one hand, early marriage is excellent and promising, especially in the probable case that both the young people have had sexual experiences and could have others, and they have chosen the marriage as a reasonably steady and jealousy-free alternative. And having the children early is admirable, rather than delaying for the empty reasons that middle-class people used to give. On the other hand, to take on such early responsibilities indicates an early resignation: the marriage seems partly to be *instead of* looking ambitiously for a worth-while career.

If the highest aim in life is to achieve a normal marriage and raise healthy children, we can understand the preoccupation with Psychology, for the parents do not have much activity of their own to give rules to the family life. The thousand manuals of sex technique and happy marriage, then, have the touching dignity of evangelical tracts, as is indeed their tone; they teach how to be saved, and there is no other way to be saved.

On the children is lavished an avalanche of attention. They cannot possibly reward so much attention, and the young father, at least, soon gets pretty bored and retires to his Do-It-Yourself. Now it used to be said that middle-class parents frustrate the children more, to meet high standards, but the frustration is acceptable because it leads to an improved status, esteemed by the children; the lower classes, on the contrary, are more permissive; nor would the discipline be accepted, because the father is disesteemed. What then is the effect, in the ranch houses, if the discipline is maintained, because the standard is high, but the status is disesteemed, first by the father himself, who talks cynically about it; then by the mother, who does not respect it; then by the growing children? *Is it possible to maintain and pass on a middle-class standard without belief in its productive and cultural mission?*

I wonder if we are not here describing the specific genesis of a Beat Generation: young men who (1) cannot break away from the father who has been good to them, but who (2) simply cannot affirm father's values; and (3) there are no other dominant social values to compensate. If this is the case, where now there are thousands of these young men, there will be hundreds of thousands. *The organized system is the breeding ground of a Beat Generation.*

3.

Among poor young men, quitting school early and perhaps meeting discrimination in the better unions, or other obstacles to making something of themselves, the more permitted and widely stimulated sexuality can work as a deadly trap. For there is desire and sexual opportunity at the same time as the older adolescent's sense of personal worth is diminishing. He must act the man when he does not feel like a man. This may come to the impotence of the unemployed or the self-disapproving alcoholic. It is not helped, either, if the desirable women seem to choose "successful" fellows, or if a young man has the convention that dating costs money. The contrary alternative is that sex itself become a proof of manly worth, a form of conquest without lust or love, or not even conquest, but simply potency proving potency. For instance, young Navy sailors who on the ship are griping but docile children, on shore regard the women as their "pigs" and do not let themselves get "involved." Among the Spanish poor, too, the tradition of *macho*, masculinity, that they have brought with them, seems to be especially a means of proof that a young man is not a contemptible boy.

On either alternative, his sexual need can get a fellow into plenty of trouble. To get the money and be a success, he may steal. If he proves himself by sex, brutality or promiscuity will get him into sexual scrapes. If sex gets him into too much trouble or if his doubt of potency is too strong, he may withdraw altogether, into gambling or being a tough guy, or passively into narcotics.

4.

There are class differences; but through all classes, it is hard to grow up when the general social attitude toward sexuality is inconsistent and unpredictable. (It is hard to exist as an adult too.) In this respect our society is uniquely problematical. Broadly speaking, there are three universally widespread and incompatible attitudes toward sexual behavior, and two of these are inconsistent in themselves.

In the ideal theory and practice, sexuality is one of the most important natural functions and the attitude toward it ranges from permissive to enthusiastic. This is the position of all Thinking, of public spokesmen and women's magazines, and of the Supreme

Court in its decisions on classics of literature; and it is somewhat put into practice by psychological parents, mental hygienists, nursery schools, and bands of adolescents and adults. Yet there are puzzling inconsistencies. What applies to brother does not apply to sister, though every girl is somebody's sister. What is affirmed and tacitly condoned, must still not be done overtly. For instance, although all Serious Thought is agreed on the simple natural function and there are colorful little abstract treatises for children, it is inconceivable for a publisher to print a sober little juvenile story about, say, playing doctor or the surprising discovery of masturbation. A character in a juvenile (or adult) adventure story may not incidentally get an erection as he may wolf a sandwich or get sleepy. It seems obvious that, here as everywhere else, the only antidote for the sadistic-sexual comic books that are objected to, is the presentation of factual truth and a matter-of-fact tone; whereas what we have, permissiveness combined with withdrawal from real contact, precisely produces the sadistic-sexual need. This is the bread-and-butter of psychological theory; why is it not said in the annual investigations of the comic books? Again, although most public spokesmen are for a "healthy frankness," the public schools are run quite otherwise. Let me recall a typical incident recently in California (spring of '59). A high school science teacher employed the bright-idea project of tabulating the class's sexual habits as an exercise in fact finding. This got him into terrible hot water, and the School Board carefully explained, "What we teach is human reproduction, much as we discuss the functions of the human eye or ear," that is, without mentioning light or sound, color or harmony, or any other act or relation.

(I am writing this equably and satirically, but the stupidity of these people is outrageous.)

The treatment of sexuality in the popular culture and the commodities and advertising is less puzzling: it is to maximize sales. Existing lust is exploited and as far as possible there is created an artificial stimulation, with the justified confidence that the kind of partial satisfactions obtainable will involve buying something: cosmetics, sharp clothes, art magazines, dating entertainment. And since, for very many people, lust is at present accompanied by embarrassment, shame, and punishment, these too are exploited as much as possible. I do not think there is here any inconsistency. One simply goes along with the widespread melodramatic fantasy of lust and punishment. E.g., the public sentiment for Caryl Chessman's execution, 70 per cent, expressed itself with terrifying frequency in sadistic, pornographic, and vindictive language: the plays of Tennessee Williams are the deep poetry of these people. It would be inconsistent if the popular culture tried to be factual, analytic, or compassionate. But there is an absolute incompatibility between this sexuality of popular culture and the ideal theory and practice of the "simple natural function."

If we ask, however, what is acceptable public behavior in the neighborhoods or with the neighbors, the confusion is baffling. There are islands of contradictory practice, even though these may have the identical Culture and almost the same Thought. Kids masturbating may be smiled on or ignored, or they may be barred from one's home, or they may be arrested as delinquent. Among the boys themselves, up to the age of thirteen mutual masturbation is a wicked thrill, but after thirteen it is queer and absolutely to be inhibited. Adolescent couples must pet or it is felt that something is wrong with them; but "how far?" Sometimes they may copulate, if they can get away with it; or they absolutely must not. You may admire and speak to strange girls on the street, it is flattering and shows spirit; or you may not, it is rude and threatening. But if you whistle at them while you huddle in your own group, that's bully. You may pet in public like the French; you may not pet in public, it's disgusting; you may on the beach but not on the grass. Among the boys, to boast of actual or invented prowess is acceptable, but to speak soberly of a love affair or a sexual problem in order to be understood is strictly taboo; it is more acceptable among girls. It is assumed that older teen-agers are experienced and sophisticated, but they are legal minors who must not be corrupted. More important, any relation between an older teen-aged girl and a man even in his twenties, or between an older teen-aged boy and an experienced woman, is shocking or ludicrous, though this is the staple of sexual education among the civilized.

In this tangle of incompatible and inconsistent standards, one strand is sure and predictable: that the law will judge by the most out-of-date, senseless, and unpsychological convention, even though it is against the consensus of almost every family in the neighborhood and the confessional attitude of the parish priest. They will arrest you for nude bathing a mile away on a lonely beach. (But this tendency to maintain the moral-obsolete is, of course, inevitable in our kind of democracy. A legislator may believe what he pleases, but how can he publicly propose the repeal of a statute against sin?)

I am describing again an interrupted revolution, the so-called Sexual Revolution. We see again how the organized system of production and sales manages to profit by the confusion of the interruption, whereas a finished revolution would be economically a dead loss, since good sexual satisfaction costs nothing, it needs only health and affection.

5.

Special mention must be given to male homosexuality, which preoccupies adolescents and young men of every class from bottom to top. The preoccupation appears either as gnawing doubts that oneself might be a "latent homosexual," or as reactive contempt and ridicule, or hostility and even paranoia. Among young people every kind of nonconformism in a contemporary tends to be thought of as homosexual, whether it be a passion for music or a passion for social justice.

Inevitably in the stimulating and hectic sexual atmosphere, including overtly expressed homosexuality, repressed homosexual thoughts also begin to break through. Remnants of unfinished normal homosexual situations reappear, and one is sharply aware of new temptations in the culture. The shared narcissism of dandy hair-do's is astonishingly prevalent; the affectionate body-contact of buddies is obsessionally inhibited or immediately commented on and "interpreted"; and one sees queers everywhere.

The question must be asked why the breakthrough into awareness seems to balk and circle at just this point on just this issue? why, in the present, do just the homosexual temptations and threats loom so large? One important answer, I think, is the theme I have been developing in this book. The fellows are interrupted in growing up as men; their homosexuality threatens them as immaturity. They are afraid of going backward to boyhood status, admiring the model penises and powers of their seniors and adults. Or they regress further to a safe narcissism and would want their own penises and bodies to be loved as their personal worth, but this reversion to infantilism is fiercely resisted.

In the difficulty of growing up, the young man psychologically regresses to an earlier stage because it is easier, he cannot take on the responsibilities of heterosexual love and masculine conflict. But then, doubting his potency and to avoid ridicule and danger, he becomes obsessionally heterosexual and competitive; or alternatively, he may become apathetic and sexually not there.

6.

Other "animal" expressions, besides the sexual, are also problematical. Let us sum them up by some more philosophical considerations.

As our organized system perfects itself, there is less "open" environment. It is hard for a social animal to grow when there is not an open margin to grow in: some open space, some open economy, some open mores, some activity free from regulation and *cartes d'identité*. I am referring not to a war between the "individual" and society, or to a wild animal that has to be acculturated—for there is no such individual or animal—but to a deepening sociological flaw in the modern system itself. A society cannot have decided all possibilities beforehand and have structured them. If society becomes too tightly integrated and pre-empts all the available space, materials, and methods, then it is failing to provide for just the margin of formlessness, real risk, novelty, spontaneity, that makes growth possible. This almost formal cause importantly drives young people out of the organized system altogether and makes creative adults loath to co-operate with it. When time, clothes, opinions, and goals become so regulated that people feel they cannot be "themselves" or create something new, they bolt and look for fringes and margins, loopholes, holes in the wall, or they just run.

Our society pre-empts literally too much of the space. For instance, it is impossible in the Eastern United States to pitch a tent and camp for the night without registering with the National Parks and its list of regulations. You cannot go off somewhere for a sexual bout without paying rent. Almost any stone that a kid picks up and any target that he throws it at, is property. People hygienically adopt a permissive attitude toward the boisterousness and hyperkinesis of children, and meantime we design efficient minimum housing. Under modern urban conditions, it is impossible for an old woman to be a harmless lunatic, as was commonplace in country places; she would hurt herself, get lost among strangers, disrupt traffic, stop the subway. She must be institutionalized. If you roam the street late at night doing nothing, and looking for something to do, the cop who is protecting you and everybody else doesn't want you to be going nowhere and to have nothing to do; and you ask him, Does he have any suggestions?

7.

There is something attractive in the forbidden as such. I think that the theme of this chapter explains this puzzling attraction.

On the usual psychological theory, to do the forbidden is to attack the forbidding authority, ultimately the oedipal father. This explains the obvious fear of punishment, and also the stronger, often quite irrational, fear of transgressing the due order of things. (E.g., "Are we allowed to climb up there on that ladder?" "Naw! of course not!" "Then we'd better not"—*even though* there is nobody to catch them at it. But they then climb up anyway.) On this theory, what would the attraction be? The forbidden object itself, resonant with the other repressed things forbidden by the oedipal authority; and secondly, more subtly, a *teasing* of the authority, to win his personal attention, for he is so impersonal. I think there is a good deal to this second point, for it has somewhat the feel of the attraction of the forbidden. (E.g., "Will the watchman wake up?"—hoping that he will thrillingly wake up, even if he bites.)

But I should like to suggest still a third fundamental attraction in doing the forbidden: the animal need to transgress the limit *in order to finish the situation*. Consider. People are continually stimulated and set in motion, but they come up against limits and cannot fully go or let go. Typically, because of inhibitions and circumstances, the orgasm is not total and not altogether without "self-consciousness." The spontaneous acceleration toward an unlimited goal seems evident in the way one forbidden achievement emboldens the next, until the process comes to a natural end, rather than an imposed limit. The freedom that beckons in the forbidden attraction is not, negatively, merely a freedom from constraint, but a relief of internal pressure as one arrives and finishes the experience. There is a quiet satisfaction even if there is not much satisfaction in the forbidden object achieved. (E.g., there is nothing up on the roof and the kids soon climb down and go home.) But there is no disappointment, because the action has reached its natural end: you have climbed to the top of the mountain and that's the furthest you want to go.

This spontaneous acceleration to the goal is not the same as "raising the ante" characteristic in purely delinquent behavior. Raising the ante has a fragmented and desperate tone that comes from finding that each daring act has not paid off, and therefore the next time one must stab more wildly. The end of raising the ante is clearly self-destruction, to be "extreme"; it is not to finish a process. *Doing the forbidden is a normal function of growth;* raising the ante is a sign that a person is not in contact with his real needs.

The same twelve-year-olds I have been describing returned to the same building the next week—a pleasant spot overlooking the Hudson where they came to smoke forbidden cigarettes. They directly climbed onto the roof, for it was now the established routine, and they came down. But there was a new boy with them whose behavior was different. He promptly dared the others to jump off the roof—a ten-foot drop to a concrete pavement, guaranteed to break both ankles. He himself climbed over the ledge and hung by his hands and said he was going to drop. He would have let go, too, except that we men intervened, shouting. The other kids were indignant and disgusted at his senselessness; they did *not* seem challenged. One of the men said to him. "That wasn't smart." He, grinning: "Aw, I thought youse'd think it was smart."!! Had he been playing, after all, for *our* attention? He got it.

VII. FAITH

1.

LET US exaggerate the conditions that we have been describing. Conceive that the man-made environment is now *out* of human scale. Business, government, and real property have closed up *all* the space there is. There is no behavior unregulated by the firm or the police. Unless the entire economic machine is operating, it is impossible to produce and buy bread. Public speech quite disregards human facts. There is a rigid caste system in which every one has a slot and the upper group stands for nothing culturally. The university has become merely a training ground for technicians and applied-anthropologists. Sexuality is divorced from manly independence and achievement. The FBI has a file card of all the lies and truths about everybody. And so forth. If we sum up these imagined conditions, there would arise a formidable question: Is it possible, being a human being, to exist? Is it possible, having a human nature, to grow up? There would be a kind of metaphysical crisis.

Or put it another way. These conditions are absurd, they don't make sense; and yet millions, who to all appearances are human beings, behave as though they were the normal course of things. For instance, we encourage economic lunacy by watching TV; we gossip about the new cars though they will make our cities unlivable; we answer impertinent questions of investigators about our friends; we attend conventions, listen to public spokesmen, and smile a lot and shake hands. A man is put into doubt about his own sanity. Do they have the right of it, that there is nothing absurd? Then what kind of animal is oneself? Automatically one begins to use their words and think their thoughts, although one *knows* that they are absurd. One feels depersonalized.

It then becomes necessary to stop short and make a choice: Either/Or. Either one drifts with their absurd system of ideas, believing that this is the human community. Or one dissents totally from their system of ideas and stands as a lonely human being. (But luckily one notices that others are in the same crisis and making the same choice.)

The picture is an exaggeration. In important ways the American system is not inhuman but human-all-too-human. The tone of dependency, for instance, is not servile but, like the diet of hamburgers and malted milk, a regression to childhood. The Americans can make fun of themselves. The top managers and the president are not calculating monsters, but ignorant and willful human beings. Sympathy with suffering and the feeling for social justice are quite genuine in our country. We are empirical and experimental. Although the official spokesmen and the mass media present an impenetrable front, the speakers are confused persons and quickly betray it under personal questioning. For all the foolishness we are bombarded with, the Americans are not stupid; we have a saving sense built in, just like other peoples. And there are carelessly swept corners full of Long-haired Professors, Beat Generations, Winos, and other assorted fry who are officially conceded to exist. This does not add up to a metaphysical crisis. It is not even hard to see the economic and psychological causes of many of the existing absurdities and to think up expedients. But the difficulties *are* arduous; to persist as a man *does* require unusual moral character, intellect, or animal spirits.

For many young people, however, the difficulties of growing up have been so great that they do think that they are faced with the critical choice: Either/Or. They have this picture of themselves and of the world. And then unfortunately, whichever way they choose tends to create in fact the very metaphysical crisis that they have imagined. If they choose to conform to the organized system, reaping its rewards, they do so with a crash, working at it, marrying it, raising their standard of living, and feeling cynical about what they are doing. If they choose totally to dissent, they don't work at changing the institutions as radical youth used to, but they stop washing their faces, take to drugs, and become punch-drunk or slap-happy. Either way they lose the objective changeable world. They have early resigned.

2.

When these disaffected find one another and form a subculture, they tend to see their choice, fraught with crisis, as a religious movement. One of the favorite spokesmen of the Beat Generation announces:

> For the crucifix I speak out, for the Star of Israel I speak out, for the divinest man who ever lived who was a German (Bach) I speak out, for sweet Mohammed I speak out, for Buddha I speak out, for Lao-tse and Chuang-tse I speak out, for D. T. Suzuki I speak out.

This is typical public speaking; like an address by Eisenhower it includes all voting creeds and betrays a similar lack of acquaintance. (The bother is that the speaker is in his late thirties and ought to know better.) But as we shall see, this formless ultimate experience is not irrelevant to the plight of being resigned, for there is no available world to give experience a form.

But let me at once give a similar strain of rhetoric of a seasoned public spokesman in the organized system itself. I quote from an address to the National Recreation Congress of 1957 by Dr. Paul Douglass. He is concerned with the terrifying Problem of Leisure, namely that with a shorter work week and automation many millions of adults might simply goof off and get into mischief.

> The assimilation of leisure into the folkway tomorrow makes essential the reconstruction of the goals and values of life, the

evolution of a new ethics, and the definition of an esthetic suitable for the upreaching of taste, the deeper comprehension and enjoyment of beauty in its many forms, and a more meaningful existence.

Of course this is not serious. A "new ethics" would, presumably, be the work of an Isaiah or Ezekiel or at least Socrates. It would be convenient for us if someone's lips were touched with fire and he got himself rejected by us and swept our children in his wake; it would solve other problems than our leisure time.—The Beat spokesman, surprisingly, seemed to be satisfied with the ethics that we have inherited.

(As an artist I find this kind of public speech vaguely insulting. Do we need an esthetic? I cannot cope with the artistic tradition that we have, especially its modern triumphs, so that my own work is both unclassical and dated according to standards right on my bookshelf. Does Dr. Douglass mean a popular esthetic? Is it news to him that the popular taste is systematically debauched by Hollywood, Broadway, Madison Avenue? that by the unanimity of publishers, producers, and broadcasters, aided by the censorship, it is almost impossible to get an honest or vivid word to the public? and that if something slips by it is swamped by trash and singled out for neglect by ignorant critics?)

Dr. Douglass cannot mean what he says, yet he does mean something. Under what conditions do public spokesmen use this kind of language, asking for new ethics and a meaning for existence, when there are concrete tasks glaring them in the face?

The conditions are disappointment in oneself according to a lofty ethics, and resignation about doing anything. Not early resignation, but after the profound disappointment of experience. The buoyant abstractions, spoken as if miracles were for the asking, ward off pain and uneasy conscience when one is no longer going to try to do anything practical. (The crisis will occur "tomorrow.") The tone, if not the content, fits the American style, optimistic about expedients. And the disappointment is more profound because the American promise was so bright. Achieving most of what we set out to get, we are surprised to find that it's useless, and worse. For after the century of progress, the folk who are wealthy and pretty healthy are not only not happy or wise, but they are uneasy. Their own writers hold them in contempt. Foreigners keep saying that the atom bombs were dropped for no good reason. The beautiful American classlessness is freezing into statuses. People ask for a stop to immigration.

In the modern world, we Americans are the old inhabitants. We first had political freedom, high industrial production, an economy of abundance. Naturally we are the first to be disappointed. Europeans, when they ape and envy us, are like children.

Disappointed and resigned, adults do not see a future for their own children, for they do not know the Way themselves. Immigrants of the first generation wanted their children to make good and have careers; in the third generation they just "want their children to be happy."

3.

This public spokesman, then, asks for new inspiration to give us a "more meaningful existence." But other public spokesmen say that the juvenile delinquents get that way because they don't attend the churches we have. One explanation of this contradiction, of course, is that *we* are human and have new problems, but the boys are hardly human and ought to be better socialized to the appropriate institutions. This is not serious.

What is the *actual* religious plight of a young man growing up in our society? Let us discuss it theologically, though I am aware that this vocabulary is at present puzzling.

If a person asks "How am I justified? What is the meaning of my life?" he will surely find no rational answer. The bother is that the question has arisen and begun to plague him. If the *question* arises, as an important question, something is wrong; he will feel unworthy and damned, and wasted. Historically, appeal has then been had to psychological techniques of revivalism or physical techniques of sacramental magic. (Dr. Douglass' intellectual approach cannot work.)

But it is possible to avoid the imputation of being damned if the question, as that question, never gets to be asked—if the matter is mentioned, if at all, as a moment of reflection in an ongoing process of life. This non-asking can happen in two ways. First, if certain life behavior is *necessary*, no questions are asked. (We shall return to this first alternative.) But secondly, if a man's developing needs and purposes do indeed keep meeting with real opportunities and duties, no "final" questions are asked. As Rabbi Tarfon said, "You do not need to *finish* the task, and neither are you free to leave it off." The opportunities need not be such as to satisfy a man and make him happy—that would be paradise; the duties must not be such that he must succeed in performing them—that would be hell; it is sufficient if there are simply *possible* ways for his activity and achievement, so that he knows the world is a world for him, if he is earnest. This condition of meeting the world is called being in a state of grace. In such a case the questions that are really asked are practical and specific to the task in hand. The question, "How am I justified? what is the meaning of my life?" is answered by naming the enterprise that one is engaged in, and by the *fact* that it is going on. As Kafka said, "The fact of our living is in itself inexhaustible in its proof of faith."

(By analogy, if a young couple has had good sex without external or internal interruptions, they don't feel guilty and are fortified against adult criticism. The behavior justifies itself. But if the sex has worked out badly, they are disappointed, resentful of one another, and vulnerable to being made guilty by the others.)

The sense that life is going on and the confidence that the world will continue to support the next step of it, is called Faith.

It is hard to grow up without Faith. For then one is subject to these nagging unanswerable questions: Am I worthless? How can I prove myself? What chance is there for me? Did I ever have a chance? (These will be recognized as "questions of a juvenile delinquent to his soul.") Children, if we observe them, seem normally to be abounding in simple faith. They rush headlong and there is ground underfoot. They ask for information and are told. They cry for something and get it or are refused, but they are not disregarded. They go exploring and see something interesting. It is the evil genius of our society to blight, more or less disastrously, this faith of its young as they grow up; for our society does *not*, for most, continue to provide enough worth-while opportunities and relevant duties, and soon it ceases to take them seriously as existing.

Desperately, then, people may try to fill the void of worthlessness-and-abandonment by seeking money or status, or by busy work, or by self-proving exploits, both to silence critics and to silence own doubts. They substitute role playing, conforming, and belonging for the grace of meeting objective opportunity. But there is no justification in such "works," for they are not really the man's own works, nor God's providence for him. As the theologians have said, Real works are the natural products of faith taking its next step. Or alternately, people may spurn the false roles that are available and try for formless mystical experiences. This seems to be the aim of the Beat Generation, which is a kind of brotherhood of Quietism plus stimulants. Or alternately, again, where the despair of abandonment is acute, as with many juveniles, they rush fatalistically to punishment, to have it over with and be received back.

Finding a new ethics or esthetics, as Dr. Douglass asks, will not put us in a state of grace. Existence is not given meaning by importing into it a revelation from outside. The meaning is *there*, in more closely contacting the actual situation, the only situation that there is, whatever it is. As our situation is, closely contacting it would surely result in plenty of trouble and perhaps in terrible social conflicts, terrible opportunities and duties, during which we might learn something and at the *end* of which we might know something, even a new ethics; for it is in such conflicts that new ethics are discovered. But it is just these conflicts that we do not observe happening. Everybody talks nice. At most there is some unruliness and dumb protest, and some withdrawal.

So urging the juveniles to go to church is not serious, for *how* will the church give them faith? What opportunity will it open?

4.

The early Protestants made a profoundly happy connection between Justification and a man's Calling or Vocation in worldly society. Max Weber famously drew attention to this, in his book on the Protestant Ethic, as an explanation of the acceptance of ascetic self-righteous capitalist enterprise and the modern rationalized "specialized division of labor" which he equated with calling. I think that he missed the simple meaning of the connection and has thereby taken sociologists off on a wrong track. (Modern sociology can hardly stand much poor theology since it has so little at all.)

In the Bible, there are two kinds of prescription about callings. First, the simple proverbial wisdom: "Modestly attend to your business and you'll do all right." Second, the apocalyptic gospel advice that a man should carry on in his station in a damned world for the few years till the Second Coming, because he would be lacking in faith to make long plans. But the point of the Protestant connection was that, in a religious community, the various occupations *in fact* justify by giving people the right ongoing activity. This idea was accompanied by a whole spectrum of radical and sometimes violent programs to make the community religious, from anarchies and communities of love, to congregational churches, to puritanical theocracies. (A modern enterprise with the identical philosophy is the Zionist *kibbutz*. There is no need of a particular "supernatural" sanction.)

Vocation *is* the way a man recognizes himself as belonging, or appoints himself, in the community life and work. We saw, in Jespersen, how a child takes on the languages of the peer groups that he chooses because they are his ideals as he grows up. So his occupations. A good community has, for the most part, positions and callings that facilitate a man's activity and achievement. It is a world for *him*.

A man might *have* the vocation, know it, in various ways: by childhood and family traditions; through his chosen peers; by interest and aptitude; through a teacher who brings him out; by inspiration; or even by recognizing that a certain job must be done and responsibly accepting the necessity as his own, because it is his community and various jobs may be equivalent to him (his real vocation is being a citizen). A man may do a job because he can, *noblesse oblige*. Sometimes the community does not offer the needed opportunity, but has to make a place for it when it is wrested by the man: this is the case of original creative persons who appoint themselves to an ideal new for the community, a vocation not provided by the community, but that finally the community accepts. A good community tries to provide every youth with his right calling, understanding, however, that its providence is not Providence.

Vocation, therefore, is a solid means of finding one's opportunities, things worth while, useful, and honorable to do and be justified by. As such, vocations are neither traditional nor rationalistic in some system, but whatever happens to be the ongoing work of the particular community of human interests. The religious point is that a man can work hard, as every man wants to do; can do it boldly and "lose himself," because his community supports him; and he can thereby miraculously satisfy the stringent demands of conscience. Such a man *is* in a state of grace. On this interpretation, the "Protestant Ethic" is correct; and when our society now turns against it, it is admitting that it has lost a saving grace.

I don't know if this is what Luther had in mind when he spoke of "callings"; presumably he was referring mainly to farmers and guild craftsmen, who did have a community in their unquestionable callings, and the knights who were essential in the world as he saw it. Such callings are earnest; I fail to see why they should be ascetic, self-denying or self-abasing, though hopefully they are self-transcending. But by the time (1905) that Max Weber came to write, the notion of a human-centered community had so faded into the modern system of alienated production and distribution that he could think of calling only as an imposed discipline, more mild in the "traditional" Luther, more severe in the "rationalistic" Calvin. The irony is that in our decades, the combination of rationalism, asceticism, and individualism (the so-called Protestant Ethic) has produced precisely the system of boondoggling, luxury-consumption, and statuses (and rejection of the Protestant Ethic)!

5.

To give up the religious community of work is a great loss. But even more terrible is that our society weakens the growing youth's conviction that there is a Creation of the Six Days, a real world rather than a system of social rules that indeed are often arbitrary. Many things conspire to weaken this conviction. The trouble occurs, for instance, when city life turns into Urbanism; and when the use of our machines is submerged in the Industrial System.

Airplanes and their engines are beautiful, but consider how the ancient dream of man to fly among the stars and go through clouds and look down on the lands and seas has degenerated in its realization to the socialized and apathetic behavior of passengers who hardly look out the windows. City life is one of the great human conditions, but in Urbanism, no one gives birth, or is gravely ill, or dies. Seasons are only weather, for in the Supermarket there is no sequence of food and flowers. We have seen how just with the maturity of the Industrial System, children cease to learn mechanical aptitudes. When the sciences are supreme, average people lose their feeling of causality. And all different timbres of music come from one loud-speaker (an earnest musician, therefore, resignedly composes with the tapes).

But this same socialized weakening of the sense that there is a nature of things corrupts the social nature itself. For instance, in the newspapers you will rarely read the words envy, spite, generosity, service, embarrassment, confusion, recklessness, timidity, compassion, etc.—the actual motives of life. They might occur, typically, in little items of "human interest," as if the doings of politicians and financiers happened otherwise. But the doings of financiers, etc., *do* happen otherwise, by rational accommodations in the system; there is little room for "motives" in making decisions. The question is, What is occurring with the social animals who are, with other hats, the agents of the rational accommodations? This fascinating question used to be the great realistic subject of Balzac, Zola, Dreiser. Later it came to be treated "weirdly" by Kafka and Musil; and then not at all.

The big stories of crime and divorce are treated in stereotypes of "passions," as if people were characters in movies. But nature soon imitates art, and people imitate the stereotypes and produce further big stories.

So with the workaday occupations of people. There are standards and categories of employment, certificates and union cards, that may have little relation to the concrete tasks and capacities required; but they do make it easier for the tabulators, and they more or less guarantee that the ones chosen to fill the Roles will not be the ones peculiarly able to do the jobs; and they will initiate nothing. The work is determined not by the nature of the task but by the role, the rules, the status and salary; and these are, then, what a man *is*. Typically, a man can't accept a position at a lower salary and status, even though he may want that task and doesn't care about money; it would give an altogether wrong notion of him and jeopardize his whole career. Or again: A well-known magazine asks a man how they should refer to him, as Psychologist X, as Author X? He suggests man of letters, for that is what he is, in the eighteenth-century meaning. But they can't buy that because the word does not exist in *Time*-style; he *cannot* be that, and presumably the old function of letters cannot exist. But *Time*-style, alas, exists.

An organization has High Standards if its members have diplomas and "accreditation." A piece of research is important if it is sponsored or carried out by an Institute with a Regents license. In such cases these organizations and enterprises can get substantial tax-dodge Foundation grants and perhaps public money. But often these licenses have no relation to reality whatever. E.g., can you imagine that a chap who at thirty-five would make a splendid leader of youth or adult recreation, experienced in life and having decided to serve in this field, could possibly have majored at twenty in physical education? Freud pointed out long ago, in his *Problem of Lay-Analysis*, that it is extremely unlikely that a young man who would throw the best years of his life into the cloistered drudgery of getting an M.D. degree, could possibly make a good psychoanalyst; so he preferred to look for analysts among the writers, the lawyers, the mothers of families, those who had chosen human contacts. But in their economic wisdom, the Psychoanalytic Institute of Vienna (and New York) overruled him.

The notion that colleges are the right sponsors for creative research is quite disastrous. It both corrupts the right function of the school, to teach, and it guarantees that the research will be incestuously staffed by academics. The cynical pork-barreling of these "projects" is a scandal; but the damage is not that the worthless make a good thing of it, but that those who have been absorbed in real nature and creative thought, and therefore out of *this* world, are the least likely to know the arts or have the connections to get any support at all. They cannot possibly be "safe"—how could they be? They will rarely have a smoothly continuous career résumé; years at a stretch might be lacking, or there might be a couple of years of working as a house painter, a taxi driver, a piano tuner—all wrong. (Let me mention an episode that made me see red when I heard of it: A young fellow, needing to eat, applied for a job as stock boy at a self-reputed and very successful Advance-Guard publisher in New York. He was hired and told to report; but the president, seeing his name, said, "Isn't that the poet whose book we rejected last year? We can't have a literary man as a stock boy, it wouldn't be fitting. Phone and tell him not to come in."!!)

There *is*, of course, a real and hard question: how to find these creative people and give them means and encouragement? But *that* is the task, and not processing certified and affidavited applications. In order to make good bets on the best leader and the inspired research, somebody has got to take the risk of making concrete untabulated judgments, and perhaps even using his legs. But it is the essence of the organized system to sit on its behind and take no risks, and let the tabulator do the work, and strengthen its own position by incestuously staffing itself, and *then* fostering the lie that outside of the system nothing exists.

We are so out of touch with the real work in the field that, in America, a dean is superior to a professor and a board of trustees or regents is superior to a faculty. The editor knows better than the author what should be in a book, and the publisher knows better than either. Naturally everything sounds alike. And top managers and generals map out the lines of basic research.

Think of it. If the university is controlled by its board of trustees, the student, the pick of the youth in the final period of his training, is left high and dry with no contact with responsible men.

Or think of this: an important executive of a *very* large publishing house has carefully explained to me that the criterion of their printing books, and of the books they choose to print, is the need to keep their several huge printing-presses occupied. That is, will the book promise enough sales (200,000) to warrant setting one of these presses going? and on the other hand, they must manufacture some books or other to keep all their presses going. As an author, I think this example is remarkable; one can turn it like a beryl and examine its prismatic lights.

In the elementary schools, children are tested by yes-and-no and multiple-choice questions because these are convenient to tabulate; then there is complaint later that they do not know how to articulate their thoughts. Now Dr. Skinner of Harvard has invented us a machine that does away with the creative relation of pupil, teacher, and developing subject matter. It feeds the child questions "at his own pace" to teach him to add, read, write, and "other factual tasks," so that the teacher can apply himself to teaching "the refinements of education, the social aspects of learning, the philosophy of it, and advance thinking." But who, then, will watch the puzzlement on a child's face and suddenly guess what it is that he *really* doesn't understand, that has apparently nothing to do with the present problem, nor even the present subject matter? and who will notice the light in his eyes and seize the opportunity to spread glorious clarity over the whole range of knowledge; for instance, the nature of succession and series, or what grammar really *is*: the insightful moments that are worth years of ordinary teaching. I wonder how Dr.

Skinner's machine would compare in efficiency with the method of Socrates in the *Meno?* Dr. Skinner proposes to organize the collections of "facts" by big-idea lectures of the type of the New School for Social Research. This appallingly fails to understand that philosophy and science occur in scrutinizing the concrete.

But the worst effect of losing the created world is that a young man no longer knows that he is a creature, and so are his friends creatures. This has three fatal consequences. He feels that the social roles are *entirely* learned and artificial; he cannot *begin* to belong and play a part just being himself and following the promptings of nature and ordinary human associations. Conversely, his own creaturely feelings then seem to him to be private and freakish. Instead of being a source of strength, they become a cause of guilt and of feeling worthless and excluded. Most important of all, not being a creature, with its awe and humility, he does not dare to be open to the creator spirit, to become himself on occasion a creator. If, by exception, he does create something, he is conceited about it and contemptuous of the others, as if it were his; and conversely, he is gnawed by fear that he will lose the power, as if it were something he had. A society that so discourages its young has nothing to recommend it.

6.

Nor does our present society foster the noble need of Honor.

One striking characteristic of modern education is the unanimous disapproval of exploiting the powerful feeling of shame, the hot blush and wanting to sink into the ground out of sight. It is claimed that this injures personal dignity and either makes a child vengeful and not belonging, or breaks his spirit. Youth workers with delinquents make a fetish of protecting self-esteem, as contrasted with the cops' "You young Punk!" Yet in ancient education, e.g., in the Socratic dialogues, this very arousal of shame is a chief device; the teacher greets the hot flush as a capital sign that the youth is educable, he has noble aims. Such a youth has dignity in his very shame.

The difference seems to be that we cannot offer available opportunities of honor, we do not have them; and therefore we must protect what shreds of dignity the youth has. Since he has no future, if we make him ashamed of his past and present, he is reduced to nothing. In other ages, the community had plenty of chances of honor, and to belong to the community itself was honor. (Let me make an analogy from psychotherapeutic practice: when a patient is schizoid, you give reassurance, protect the weak ego; when he is neurotic and can take care of himself, you attack the character resistances.)

Now shame is the only direct attack on conceit, the defensive image of oneself. Conceit is the common denominator of the Organization Man, the hipster, and the juvenile delinquent—this is why I have been lumping them together. The conceited image of the self is usually not quite conscious, but it is instantly woundable; and people protect it with a conformity to their peers (oneself is superior). But the conceited groups differ in their methods of confirming and enhancing conceit: the juvenile delinquent by surly and mischievous destructiveness of the insulting privileged outgroup; the hipster by making fools of them with token performances; the Organization Man by status and salary. To this inner idol, they sacrifice the ingenuous exhibition and self-expression that could make them great, effective, or loved in the world; but that can also be shamed if it is mistaken, out of place, or disproportionate.

Being ashamed ought to mean that a youth gives up some cherished error or conceited image of himself, and goes on, without loss of dignity, to achieve an ideal that is real; this is honor. Only the community can bestow honor, on those who enhance the community, who follow the useful callings, or bring new culture.

In New York, those who have kept out of jail for a generation are not made much of by a grateful and admiring citizenry. It is a hard achievement but, like other public goods, it is not esteemed.

Among cities, Venice had magnificence; but it is Florence that knew how to pay honor to her sons. She made it hard for them, with neglect and exile, to be themselves and serve her; but when nevertheless they achieved their ideals, her praise was loud.

Boys today hardly aspire to immortal honor, the honor of self-fulfilling achievement. It is highly disapproved of in the code of the organized system. Instead, they devote themselves to protecting their "personal honor" against insults; and conversely they dream of the transient notoriety which will prove that they are "somebody," which they doubt. The personal honor that they protect does not include truthfulness, honesty, public usefulness, integrity, independence, or virtues like that. A reputation for these things does not win respect, it has no publicity value; it's believed to be phony anyway, and if it's true, the person is hard to get along with. A British disaffected young man, an Angry Young Man, can make his protest by simply being a Cad, like Osborne's George Dillon; but that would not much distinguish him on this side of the sea. A *bad* reputation naturally makes people prudent in their personal dealings, but it generally doesn't do much harm in the press or on TV, even to a public official, for the plug is more important than the content of it. On the other hand, any official bad mark that gets on an IBM card, like being arrested and fingerprinted—no matter what the charge and even if he was exonerated of it—can be disastrous to a young man, for his name can thereby drop out of the system. Nobody, but nobody, may disesteem a man for something, or he may even get wished-for notoriety for something, that at the same time makes him unemployable. Just try to imagine nowadays the administrator of old-fashioned juvenile fiction who says, "Young man, I don't care what Personnel reports, you have an honest face and we'll give you a chance!" Rather, a good man will be asked to resign for the sake of Public Relations. And correspondingly, suburban "good families" increasingly shun "bad families" that have had troubles, such as divorces or delinquency or even death of a parent(!), for that makes the family untypical.

(A few years ago an editorial in *Life* complained that our novels always contain alcoholics, jailbirds, addicts, crazy people, perverts, etc., and do not portray average families who have none such. James Farrell, pointing out that the combined numbers of these deviants come to much more than the number of families, drily offered that the editor of *Life* probably did not have a material family, a very abnormal case.)

There is an organized system of reputations that is calculated statistically to minimize risk and eliminate the unsafe; likely it succeeds in this. It may make the enterprise as a whole *less* efficient, for it guarantees excluding the best, but be that as it may; the important thing is that there has ceased to be *any relation whatever* between "personal honor" and community or vocational service.

Conversely, the way in which our society does do honor to its indubitably great and serviceable men—say, Gandhi, Schweitzer, Einstein, Picasso, Buber—is a study in immunizing people against their virus; it would be a remarkable and melancholy subject for a sociologist. They are transformed into striking images and personalities, and we assign to them the Role of being great men. We pay respectful attention to their birthday sayings. They are the menagerie of Very Important People who exist only for ceremonial occasions and to sponsor funds and drives for enterprises in which they will have no further function.

This effectually prevents the two practical uses that we could make of them. We neither take seriously the simple, direct, fearless souls that they invariably are, whether humble or arrogant, to model ourselves after them because they make more sense as human beings; nor do we have recourse to them please to help us when we have need of exceptional purity, magnanimity, profundity, or imagination, giving them a free hand on the assumption that their action is really better. Though we publicize the image, we do not behave as though we really believed that there were great men, a risky fact in the world. (They are likely to be and do the damnedest things: Picasso is a communist; Einstein sponsored the atom bomb; Gandhi was a pacifist and vegetarian and dressed so oddly; Bernard Shaw was arrogant and peculiarly sexless; Frank Lloyd Wright was wildly arrogant and sexually immoral; Bertrand Russell was a convicted pacifist and has practically advocated free love; etc. Few great men could pass Personnel.) Or alternatively, we do not behave as if we believed that the affairs of our world were significant enough for the intervention of great men.

For instance, no one would think of looking for sages to intervene in our racial troubles—that is not their "field of competence" (though we did have the sense to get some good sociology on the subject from Gunnar Myrdal). We would not officially ask a man of letters, as the British used Bernard Shaw, to criticize the penal system. When it comes to improving the high schools, we choose a well-licensed administrator, we do not try to persuade some extraordinary scholar or natural philosopher, a man who has actually learned something and therefore perhaps knows how it is done; naturally we come out with an excellent administrative report, but no ideas. John Dewey was called on, by passionately interested people, to make an impartial inquiry into the death of Trotsky; that seems a reasonable use of a judicious and incorruptible man; but we do not much imitate it. But even when there is no doubt of the field of competence, when we choose a man to beautify our towns, we do not automatically call on the major artists of the world; for instance, we now lavishly praise Frank Lloyd Wright, but we never made any community use of him, though he longed for the chance and kept badgering the country with community projects.

My belief is that one can easily put great men to work, even against their own freedom and advantage, for they allow themselves to be imposed on, *noblesse oblige;* but one must, of course, then take the consequences.

I understand that to consider powerful souls as if they were a useful public resource is quite foreign to our customs. In a small sense it is undemocratic, for it assumes that some people really know better in a way that must seem arbitrary to most. In a large sense it is certainly democratic, in that it makes the great man serve as a man. Either of these choices, to eschew them or to use them, however, is preferable to creating glamorous images with empty roles.

But let us return to our average folk.

7.

Balked, not taken seriously, deprived of great objects and available opportunities, and in an atmosphere that does not encourage service—it is hard to have faith, to feel justified, to have a calling, or win honor. But what then fills the places of these? for every experience that a human being has is a whole way-of-being-in-the-world.

First, necessity gives justification. Having something that you must do, solves the problem of having something to do. Necessary behavior may or may not be honorable. To wrest subsistence is necessary and honorable. If a young man falls in love, a temporary psychosis, his entire day is under the iron rule of necessity, foolishly and honorably; he has something to do, if only to watch under a window. When the class struggle against exploitation was lively, it was something necessary and honorable to engage in. Indeed, it is a major defect of our present organized system and the economy of abundance that, without providing great goals, it has taken away some of the important real necessities, leaving people with nothing to do.

The void is soon filled. Behavior like going into debt on the installment plan, gives an artificial but then real necessity, something to do, paying up. This *is* the Rat Race, but I doubt that it would be run if people did not need its justifying necessity, for the commodities themselves are not that attractive. Young fellows drift into narcotics, and then find that they have something they must do all day, looking for a connection and a fix, and how to get the loot. Compulsive sex-hunting is something to do. By dividing into rival gangs, as Clausewitz pointed out long ago, it is possible to create a state of uncertainty of what the enemy is up to, that keeps you constantly on your toes. This is a condition, also, apt to raise the ante, for no matter how you have planned to stay within limits, you can never be sure that the others won't take advantage. Many of the apparently pointless repeated risks that juveniles take, where there cannot be any kick left in the exploit itself, make a little sense when we learn that there is a competition: Carlos has stolen twenty-six cars, Pedro twenty-three, and each is driven by necessity not to be worsted, especially since the others come along for the rides. (But Carlos has an unfair advantage because he had gone as a punishment to a "Vocational High School" where he took auto mechanics.)

When psychologists like Lindner speak of the aimless, unconcentrated, unsequential behavior of "psychopathic personalities," I wonder whether they enough take into account that it requires a real object and an interest in it to make a good Gestalt of experience and growth. To structure the behavior of long hours and weeks requires a goal that, from some point of view at least, is pretty worth while. Our society is *not* abounding in highly worth-while goals available to average gifts and underprivileged attainments. Many goals that are busily and perseveringly pursued by some might reasonably seem not worth the trouble to others who have more animal spirits or plain sense. These really might have "nothing to do," and their aimless and sensation-seeking killing time might indicate nothing but chronic boredom. Yet they will be judged psychopathic personalities. But once they have hit on a necessitous and important activity like finding their dose of heroin or stealing twenty-six joy rides (in the teeth of two arrests), they become models of purposiveness and perseverance.

Such are the justifications and callings. The honor is to protect one's masculinity and normalcy, yet to prove by notoriety that one is superior.

8.

More interesting and likely is the religious effort of the Beat Generation, to which we shall shortly turn. They are older and are not willing to have given up one Rat Race to fall into another. Can they solve the problem of the nagging unanswerable questions of justification and vocation? Their principle is the traditional one of classical mysticism: by "experiences" (= kicks) to transcend the nagged and nagging self altogether and get out of one's skin, to where no questions are asked—nor is there any articulate speech to ask them in. Resigning from society, they form peaceful brotherhoods of pure experience, with voluntary poverty, devotional readings, and a good deal of hashish.

9.

These first seven chapters have described the "organized" economy, social plan, and moral atmosphere in which an average American boy grows up. Of course they do not constitute the whole environment; they do not constitute even a big fraction of it—or we should all have died of hunger, exposure, and boredom long ago. Mostly people go about their business more directly, produce real goods and get real satisfactions and frustrations. But the Organization does butt in everywhere, it does set the high style of how things are done. It dominates "big" enterprise, politics, popular culture; and its influence is molding enough to man the future with a new generation of dependent and conformist young men without high aims and with little sense of a natural or moral community.

In such an environment there operates an unfortunate natural selection. Since not only the rewards but also the means and opportunities of public activity belong to the organized system, a smart boy will try to get ahead in it. He will do well in school, keep out of trouble, and apply for the right jobs. It would follow from this that the organized system is sparked by a good proportion of the bright boys, and so it is. On the other hand, in sheer self-protection, smart boys who are sensitive, have strong animal spirits or great souls, *cannot* play that game. There are then two alternative possibilities: (1) Either the advantages of the organized system cause them to inhibit their powers, and they turn into the cynical pushers or obsessional specialists or timid hard workers who make up the middle status of the system. Or (2) their natural virtues and perhaps "wrong" training are too strong and they become Independents; but as such they are hard put, not so much hard put for money as for means to act;

and so they are likely to become bitter, eccentric, etc., and so much the less effective in changing the system they disapprove.

("Wrong" training can be a very innocent thing. Consider a father who allows his child to read good books. That child may soon cease to watch television or go to the movies, nor will he eventually read Book-of-the-Month Club selections, because they are ludicrous or dull. As a young man, then, he will effectually be excluded from all of Madison Avenue and Hollywood and most of publishing, because what moves him or what he creates is quite irrelevant to what is going on: it is too fine. His father has brought him up as a dodo.)

These two great groups—the bright young men wasted in the Rat Race and the bright young men increasingly unused and thwarted as Independents—*are* the vast wasted resources of our country. But they are not "problems"; they are just unhappy and unfulfilled.

The interesting groups, the Problems, are those who can neither operate in the organized system nor essentially disregard it. In the next chapter I try to define their various kinds. Then in the following chapters I choose two for special treatment: those who are qualified to run in the system but who balk, the Early Resigned; and those who are underprivileged and do not have a chance, the Early Fatalistic.

VIII. AN APPARENTLY CLOSED ROOM

GIVEN, then, this illusion of a closed world that seems so critical to young folk, let us make a new beginning and collect our sentences about their various kinds of reaction.

I have been showing that there is one prevailing system of ideas according to which our organized society behaves in all kinds of cases: whether the Governor of New York asks what to do with unruly boys, or universities embark on basic scientific research, or the press defends fundamental freedoms, or a slum block is rebuilt, or a man works in a factory, or social scientists think about human nature. Lever House, a Ford factory, and the Air Force Academy are built in the same "functional" style, for there is apparently only one function, Public Relations. (If *in fact* we lived in the World of Public Relations and America were that world, there would be no bread to eat but only colorful cellophane wrappers with brand names, and there would be no water to drink but only Public Works Sponsored by Governor X, Mayor Y, and Chief Engineer Z.)

So imagine as a model of our Organized Society: *An apparently closed room in which there is a large rat race as the dominant center of attention.* And let us consider the human relations possible in such a place. This will give us a fair survey of what disturbed youth is indeed doing: some running that race, some disqualified from running it and hanging around because there is nowhere else, some balking in the race, some attacking the machine, etc.

I.

Start with those running the race. Of these, most interesting are the middle-status Organization Men of various kinds, for they are aware that it is a rat race, their literature proclaims it. But they are afraid to jump off. Since they think it is a closed room, they think there is nowhere to go. And *in* the room, if they jump off, they fear they will be among the disqualified, they will be Bums. But besides, they are afraid *of* the disqualified, to mix with them, and this keeps them running. This important point is generally overlooked, so let us explore it.

Sociologists of class structure seem to think that the values of the middle class are not only hard to achieve and maintain, which they are, but also that they are esteemed as good by the middle class themselves. This is evidently no longer true in a status structure within a closed system; the literature is self-contemptuous. Many a junior executive would now sincerely, not romantically, praise and envy the disqualified poor: their uncompetitiveness, animality, shouting and fighting, not striving for empty rewards; but he is afraid of such things for himself because they are too disruptive of his own tightly scheduled structure. Further, the upper class and the middle class have ceased to produce any interesting culture, and the culture of the organization is phony. The underprivileged have produced at least Negro jazz; and the strongest advance-guard artists move less and less in upper- or middle-status circles, and if they do they are corrupted.

A persistent error of the sociologists has been to regard middle-class and working-class values as *co-ordinate* rival systems. Rather, they are related vertically: each is a defense against some threat of the other. Primary values are *human* values. The middle-class "values" are reaction formations to inhibit in themselves some human values still available to simpler people. Therefore, under stress of life or disillusion, such inhibitions may give way. They may give way to an ambivalent opposite, like becoming a bum; but they may also simply relax to ordinary nature and community, spontaneity, nonconformity, etc. Conversely, the working-class "values" are nothing but ignorance, resignation, and resentment of classless human values of enterprise and culture, at present available only to the middle class; and many a poor boy escapes his petty class attitudes and achieves something. In brief, it takes *effort* to make a middle class obsessional, and it takes *effort* to make a poor boy stupid.

It is inevitable that in a *closed* status structure middle-class values will become disesteemed, for such values are rewarded by upward "betterment." And more philosophically, all value requires an *open* system allowing for surprise, novelty, and growth. A closed system cannot make itself valuable, it must become routine, and devoted merely to self-perpetuation. (When a mandarin bureaucracy is valuable it is because of the vastness of the underlying population and the absence of communication: each mandarin individually embodies the emperor.)

So the rat race is run desperately by bright fellows who do not believe in it because they are afraid to stop.

(2) Not running in the race are the Disqualified. First let us consider the average nondelinquent Corner Boys (the term is William F. Whyte's, not to be confused with William H. Whyte, Jr.). The underprivileged Corner Boys have strong natural advantages over the College Boys, such as more community, a less repressive animal training, and in some ways more resourcefulness. These things happily help to disqualify them from the rat race, but the question is why they do not lead to a more honorable and productive life in some other setup. It is that the boys are in an apparently closed room; they are mesmerized by the symbols and culture of the rat race. They have seen their parents running it on the installment plan and in the usual trade-union demands, and their own schooling has urged them to nothing else. So they are reduced to hanging around, getting, with luck, enough easy-going satisfaction to keep them content. Ultimately they will take factory jobs and couldn't care less, and then find themselves trapped, like their parents, in the rat race.

(3) Indeed, the group in society that most believes in the rat race as a source of value is the other underprivileged: the ignorant and

resentful boys who form the delinquent gangs. In our model, we can conceive of them as running a rat race of their own, but not on the official treads. Now what is the style of their race?

A. K. Cohen, the author of *Delinquent Boys*, has pointed out that the *content* of the delinquent subculture has classically been a direct counteraction to the middle-class culture from which these juveniles are excluded, and toward which they are spiteful. But here again, in recent years, the likeness of the organized system and the delinquent culture has become more striking than their difference. Morally, both groups are conformist, one-upping, and cynical, to protect their "masculinity," conceal their worthlessness, and denigrate the earnest boys. Perhaps even more important, *they learn these things from one another.* Madison Avenue and Hollywood provide the heroes for the juveniles. (A member of the Connecticut Parole Board urges this as a dandy thing.) Yet these post-Hemingway heroes have in turn been drawn from tough adolescents with *cajónes* or misunderstood adolescents with wavy hair. It is hard to tell whether the jackets and hair-do's, profitable for the garment industry and the drugstores, were invented in Cherry Grove or Harlem; the flash and style is from Cherry Grove and percolates down through the good haberdashers to the popular stores; but on the other hand, the ego ideals of the homosexual designers are the young toughs who finally wear the fashions. Both groups aspire to the same publicity and glamour. There have now been numerous reported cases of criminal delinquent acts performed to get a picture in the paper, just as a young man on Madison Avenue may work hard for a year to get two five-second plugs on TV. The delinquents, perforce, take short cuts to glamour. Do they teach the junior executives to take short cuts or is it the other way? Intermediate between the two groups, remember, is the integral whole of politics-and-rackets staffed from the families of both groups. (Much evidence of this is given in the issue of the *Nation* called "The Shame of New York.") This is, then, a powerful defensive alliance of the organized system and the delinquents against the good boys who naïvely try to make something of themselves.

But in the alliance, the juvenile delinquents get the short end of the stick, for they esteem the rat race though they do not get its rewards. Naturally, their esteem has the effect of making them still more contemptuous of their own backgrounds, and all the less able to get real satisfactions that are attainable. To put this another way: the eleven billion dollars of teen-age junk is not bought by these boys, but the entire pressure of the organized system is to teach everybody that only these things are worth while; therefore these boys do not emulate their hard-working fathers, and they do steal cars. I have not heard that those who ask for a Congressional investigation of comic books have asked for a Congressional investigation of *Life* and *Esquire*.

(Unless we keep in mind this context, what is the sense of the concern about the narcotics? Poor people who have neither future prospects nor lively present satisfactions will *always* gravitate to this kind of euphoria: quick satisfaction because a slower climax is in fact cut short by external difficulties and internal anxiety. A Youth Worker tells me that the "heroin, although probably physically harmless (except in overdose), prevents the full realization of the kids' powers—the people of China stagnated." Seriously, *is* the general concern for the realization of *any* of these kids' powers, or is it fear that the habit will spread to the middle class? I do not mean that the Youth Workers as such are not concerned for the kids, for they are.)

(4) In our model, there are some who used to run the rat race but have broken down and flunked out, and fallen into the dreaded and ambivalently wished-for status of Bums. (I know a young man who works on Madison Avenue who dreams of looking for his father in the municipal dormitory.) Take as typical the Winos who lead a quiet existence in their small fraternities. It is easy, on the more blighted streets of New York, to panhandle forty-eight cents for Thunderbird, and a man drinking sweet stuff doesn't get very hungry. Talking to Winos, one often gets the first impression of a wise philosophical resignation plus an informed and radical critique of society (e.g., Wobbly; it is startling to hear a twenty-five-year-old spout statistics of 1910). But soon succeeds irrational and impotent

resentment, and one realizes that these men are living in a closed room.

(5) The Beat Generation, however, are more genuinely resigned. They have more or less rationally balked in the race, or have not had the heart to start it. They therefore have some perspective and available energy to get personal satisfactions and even worth-while cultural goods. As we saw, they slip easily into the Disqualified and make something of poverty—more than the underprivileged do.

Yet the apparently closed room and the central fascination of the rat race are pervasive in Beat thinking too. They are not merely going their own way, they also feel "out," and therefore they do not use for their own purposes many parts of standard academic culture that are available to them; so their own products are doomed to be childish and parochial. And they betray their best selves by seeking for notoriety and by cynical job-attitudes. Politically, their onslaughts on the Air-Conditioned Nightmare, as Henry Miller—their John the Baptist—called it, sound very like the griping of soldiers who do not intend to mutiny. Talcott Parsons has a theory that the middle-class boy, dominated by his mother and with a weak identification with his father, is driven to prove himself by delinquent hell raising. (This is the so-called "middle-class delinquency" that, of course, rarely gets to courts or social agencies and is therefore not counted in the statistics.) But I rather think that it is these Beats who best illustrate Parsons' thesis: they have resigned the effort to cope with father at all, and they are pacific, artistic, and rather easy-going sexually.

(6) Some in the closed room direct more vigorous attacks against the machine itself and try to stop it. They are more reminiscent of old-fashioned radical youth who, however, were not fascinated by the model of the rat race but had other definite social ideals. If the energy and values that are available are restricted to those in the closed room, the machine is very tough. This seems to me to be the behavior and plight of the English Angry Young Men. Angry are not resigned, but disappointed. For instance, they complain that their elders have failed to provide them with good leadership. They

are disappointed that England has degenerated into a phony Welfare State that provides no welfare and has ceased to provide a patriotic ideal. Compare Colin MacInnes:

> In this moment, I must tell you, I'd fallen right out of love with England. And even with London, which I'd loved like my mother, in a way. As far as I was concerned, the whole dam group of islands could sink under the sea, and all I wanted was to shake my feet off of them, and take off somewhere and get naturalized, and settle.... They all looked so dam pleased to be in England at the end of their long journey, that I was heartbroken at all the disappointments that were in store for them. And I ran up to them through the water, and shouted out above the engines, "Welcome to London! Greetings from England! Meet your first teenager!"

Young Americans are old hands at modern life and too sophisticated to be disappointed in their fathers or their country. But the English, of course, are seeing from the perspective of the Battle of Britain, which must have held out enormous promise. Certainly their tone is not "angry"—attacking an obstacle to destroy it or make it see sense—but waspish and bitter; and a favorite method of attack is not to demand some good but to behave like a cad. Yet perhaps these young English can be effective, they have strong advantages. The system they are attacking is, unlike ours, very unsettled —the Empire lost, the class system relatively weakening. They are better educated than our young men, and therefore not so ready nor able to resign their culture and history. They seem to remember what it is to act like human beings, and therefore they are surprised and indignant when people fall short. (This is the point of the exemplary caddishness.) Not least, in their oddly undemonstrative way, they seem to have more sexual security.

(7) French "existentialist" youth, on the other hand, have inherited a long recent tradition of public treachery. The spirit of the Resistance is no longer much apparent, and one is astonished at the

cynical motives that seem to be taken for granted in quite standard theater like Anouilh. The tactics of youthful protest are to fraternize with the North Africans; but these are not an outcast group like our racial minorities, but haughty and conceited enemies engaged in war. Yet the tone of protest is not "social justice," as among the young in England, but disdain and self-disdain. They stand aside in the closed room and comment cuttingly on the closed room they are in. So our model seems to fit them like a glove: *Huis-Clos, No Exit*, as their official writer put it.

But one must not judge at a distance. Self-disdain is already a very lofty stance; and maybe their existentialist theory of a closed crisis is a maneuver to produce a crisis. (One must not teach the inventors of modern revolution how to be revolutionary.) Genet, their philosopher of delinquency, is probably the best writer in Europe—and nothing comes from nothing.

(8) Finally, everywhere in the closed room is the spirit of the hipster, jumping, playing every role. The closed room is a very busy yet very limited world; there is no surprising possibility in it; if anything really happened, it would be a catastrophic explosion. The hipster wards off surprise by being ahead of every game. Norman Mailer quotes Caroline Bird as saying, "The hipster contents himself with a magical omnipotence never disproved because never tested." This is a fairly psychotic state of mind, and the coolness of the hipster is a necessity in order not to "flip." (We shall see that it is the aim of the Beats precisely to flip.)

The hipster desperately stabs for some real experience; but, as Mailer describes him, in any orgasm there is the craving for some better orgasm beyond. This disappointment is inevitable if one controls the orgasm, but of course the hipster cannot afford to let go since he has no faith or support, for nothing exists, he thinks, but the rat race. Love, too, is a rat race. So alternately cool and jumping, and raising the ante, he swings with the rat race. Naturally this fantasy of "proving" pervades every other group in the closed room, the organization men, the juvenile delinquents, the existentialists, but also the Beats, for whom it is a crippling error. On the other hand, by all providing a hipster subculture for one another, they do increase the boundaries of their closed world.

Our historical situation is ironical to the point of sarcasm. There is every reason why young people growing up should be baffled and confused; and the subjective response to it is that every teenager in a pool room is hip and knows the score like an IBM tabulator or a social scientist.

2.

The model of the apparently closed room of the rat race is far from the old model of Progress. But it is also essentially different from the model of the Class Struggle. Like the rat race, the class struggle had a dominant and an underprivileged group, but the class struggle was conceived as taking place in an open field of history, in which new values were continually emerging and the locus of "human value" changing: gradually "human value" would reside in the next rising class and make it powerful against the old dominant class.

In the closed room, however, there is only one system of values, that of the rat race itself. This is shared by everybody in the room and held in contempt by everybody in the room. This does not give much motivation for a fundamental change, since there are no unambiguous motives to fight for and no uncontaminated means. It is remarkable in our society how rarely one hears, even delivered unctuously, the mention of some lofty purpose; one has to go to the Ethical Culture Society or the Reformed rabbis. Correspondingly, the most important practical objectives astoundingly go by default, for instance disarmament. "Everybody" is for disarmament, but nobody believes anybody.

Suppose our State Department sent to Europe a thousand earnest missionaries to ask in every hamlet and on every street corner if the Americans will have unanimous and enthusiastic support if we unilaterally disarm at once, as soon as the survey is over. If the popular demand is irresistible, we then do disarm—on the assumption that no enemy can withstand the united sentiment of the world. If such a proposal is made, the immediate response is: "Don't be naïve. The Russians will at once attack and the Americans will give in."

The existence of the closed room of one pervasive system of cynical values is expressed by the prevalent proposition: "There is no use of a fundamental change, for the next regime will be like this one." Then it is hard to grow up.

IX. THE EARLY RESIGNED

I.

THE BEAT Generation, in our model, are those who have resigned from the organized system of production and sales and its culture, and yet who are too hip to be attracted to independent work. They are a phenomenon of the aftermath of World War II, and even more of the Korean war. Their number is swelled by youths whose careers, hesitant at best, have been interrupted by the draft.

This group is socially important out of proportion to its numbers, and it has deservedly and undeservedly attracted attention and influenced many young people. The importance of the Beats is twofold: first, they act out a critique of the organized system that everybody in some sense agrees with. But second—and more important in the long run—they are a kind of major pilot study of the use of leisure in an economy of abundance. They are not, as such, underprivileged and disqualified for the system; nor are they, as such, emotionally disturbed or delinquent. Some young men might be driven to this position by personality disturbances, but the subculture they have formed has made sense and proved attractive to others without those disturbances, but who have the identical relation to the organized society.

In many ways the Beat subculture is *not* merely a reaction to the middle class or to the organized system. It is natural. Merging with the underprivileged, the Beats do not make a poor go of it. Their homes are often more livable than middle-class homes; they often eat better, have good records, etc. Some of their habits, like being unscheduled, sloppy, communitarian, sexually easy-going, and careless of reputation, go against the grain of the middle class, but they are motivated by good sense rather than resentment: they are probably natural ways that most people would choose if they got wise to themselves—at least so artists and peasants have always urged. Their rejection of the popular culture, Broadway theater, status commodities, bespeaks robust mental health. (It is, oddly, just these reasonable and natural ways that have won undeserved attention as outrageous. For Madison Avenue boys are miffed and fascinated that the Beats get away with it, and so they keep writing them up.)

We pointed out in Chapter Three that the Beat culture shares specific traits of the "outside" class to which they have appointed themselves. Some of these are accidental, belonging to the particular minorities who form the present-day poor—just as in France, it is the North Africans who set the tone. Others are essential, pertaining to being "outside" of society, such as being outcast and objects of prejudice; defying convention rather than just disregarding it; ingroup loyalty; fear of the cops; job uselessness.

Besides these natural traits and present-day poor traits, Beat culture is strongly suffused with the hipsterism that belongs to the middle status of the organized system. This appears in some of the Beat economic behavior that we described in Chapter Three; in a defensive ignorance of the academic culture; and in a cynicism and neglect of ethical and political goals.

Balked in their normal patriotism and religious tradition, the Beats seek pretty far afield for substitutes, in D. H. Lawrence's red Indians or feudal Zen Buddhists. (But I was delighted, the other night, to hear Allen Ginsberg, one of their best spokesmen, speak with wonder about visiting the Grand Canyon and boast of going to Walt Whitman's house. Soon, I trust, he will take the cruise up our lordly Hudson to Bear Mountain.)

As a typical genesis for a Beat Generation we have suggested (1) attachment to a middle-class home but (2) withdrawing from its values, (3) without growing into other worth-while values. They are on speaking terms with their families but dissent from all their ways. They experience the University, for instance, as a part of the worthless organized system rather than as Newton and Virgil.

Finally, we saw that the Beats regard themselves as in a metaphysical crisis: they have to choose between the system and eternal life; and therefore their more philosophic utterances are religious and strewn with references to the apocalypse and saints of yore, as when Allen Ginsberg, again, calls *Time* "the Whore of Babylon"—but indeed she *is* very like the Whore of Babylon.

This is not, on the whole, a strong position: to be resigned and still attached, and therefore to have recourse to apocalyptic means. But let us see what can be made of it, and turn first to the jargon, a variant of a Negro jargon of English, jive.

2.

In this talk there is a phrase "make it," meaning "to establish oneself in some accepted relation to something." One can make it as a writer, as a counter boy, with a girl. The word comes from the common English "make it against difficulties," as, "They kept shooting at him but he made it across the field." It is akin to "make good as a lawyer, a writer," but it is not so strong and positive. (We should not say "Make good as a counter boy.") The difficulties overcome are those that confront anyone who has dropped "out" of the ordinary social functions when he tries to establish himself as anything at all, to be a *something*, a something or other. The usage is an acceptance of withdrawal. (The notion of Norman Mailer, in *The White Negro*, that this and most other jive terms express positive energy or manliness, is quite idiotic.) Consider the series: "He wrote the book—he was a writer—he made good as a writer—he made it as a writer." Very common is the encouraging, or self-encouraging, exclamation, "You've got it made!" or "I'll have it made!" This refers almost exclusively to the future-improbable. When it is said in the past perfect, "He had it made," it refers, somewhat wistfully, to some other third person. To express a neutral or proud past fact about oneself, one says simply, "I wrote the book."

This usage, of establishing an acceptable social relation against obstacles, draws from the Role Playing that is the chief function of the middle status of the organized system (just as, in any period, a Negro would see the white society as a closed system with roles to be aped). One can say, "He made it, I made it, with IBM," indicating no specific job, for that is unimportant.

Now a more general withdrawal, from experiencing altogether, is expressed by the omnicapable word "like." E.g., "Like I'm sleepy," meaning "if I experienced anything, it would be feeling sleepy." "Like if I go to like New York, I'll look you up," indicating that in this definite and friendly promise, there is no felt purpose in that trip or any trip. Technically, "like" is here a particle expressing a tonality or attitude of utterance, like the Greek μέν, verily, or δή, now look. "Like" expresses adolescent embarrassment or diffidence. Thus, if I talk to a young fellow and give him the security of continued attention, the "like" at once vanishes and is replaced by "You know," "I mean," "you know what I mean," similarly interposed in every sentence.

The vocative expletive "Man," however, has different nuances in different groups. Among the Beats it is used diffidently and means, "We are not small children, man, and anyway like we are playing together as like grown-up." Among Negroes it is often more aggressive and means, "Man, now don't you call me boy or inferior." Among proper hipsters it means, "We are not sexually impotent." So far as I can hear, it never means acceptance of the speakers as adult males, nor does it have the ring of respect or admiration (*Mensch*), as a woman or hero worshiping boys might use it. When the interlocutor is in fact respected or feared, he would not be called "man." (Perhaps "boss"?)

"Cool," being unruffled and alert, has the same nuances. In standard English a man "keeps cool in an emergency." If there is *always* an emergency, it must imply that the danger is internal as well as external: the environment is dangerous and feeling is dangerous. As spoken and enacted by a young Beat, maintaining a mask-face and tapping his toe quietly to the jazz, it means, "I do not feel out of place, I am not abandoned and afraid, I am not going to burst into tears." In the original Negro the nuance is rather, "I'll stay unruffled and keep out of trouble around here; I won't let on what I feel, these folk are dangerous." With the hipster, the jaw is more set and the eyes more calculating, and it means, "I'm on to your game, you can't make me flip." In general, coolness and mask-face are remaining immobile in order to conceal embarrassment, temper, or uncontrollable anxiety.

To make a remark about the language as a whole as used by the Beats: Its Negro base is, I think, culturally accidental; but the paucity of its vocabulary and syntax is for the Beats essentially expressive of withdrawal from the standard civilization and its learning. On the other hand this paucity gives, instead of opportunities for thought and problem solving, considerable satisfaction in the act and energy of speaking itself, as is true of any simple adopted language, such as pig Latin. But this can have disadvantages. One learns to one's frustration that they regard talk as an end in itself, as a means of self-expression, without subject matter. In a Beat group it is bad form to assert or deny a proposition as true or false, probable or improbable, or to want to explore its meaning. The aim of conversation is for each one to be able, by speech, to know that he is existing and belonging. So among perfectly intelligent and literate young men, some movie or movie star will be discussed for an hour, giving each one a chance to project his own fantasies; but if someone, in despair, tries to assert something about the truth or worth of the movie, the others will at once sign off.

(Among all American adolescents and even fellows in their late twenties, however, there is an embarrassment about "what to say"— "I never have anything to say to a girl," or "They keep talking about painting and I have nothing to contribute." Speaking, that is, is taken as a role. They do not have confidence that if they are interested in the subject, they'll say something, and if they're not, why bother? Here too the Beats have helped formalize and make tolerable a

common difficulty; one contributes just by saying, "Like," "Cool,"
and "Man.")

3.

Let us interrupt discussing the jargon and look at the related problem of the artistic activities that are carried on in resignation. These
are multifarious and voluminous, including painting, poetry, reading to jazz, decorating the pads, and playing on drums. Everybody
engages in creative arts and is likely to carry a sketchbook, proving
what the psychologists and progressive educators have always
claimed, that every child is creative if not blocked. Resigning from
the rat race, they have removed the block.

They work at these arts honestly, with earnest absorption, and are
not too immodest about the modest products, even if they do continually subject one another and passers-by to listening to readings,
and encourage the community by exclaiming, "It's the greatest!"
Such creative activity sharpens the perceptions, releases and refines
feelings, and is a powerful community bond.

In itself it has no relation to the production of art works or the
miserable life of sacrifice that an artist leads. It is personal cultivation, not much different from finger painting. Like the conversation
just described, its aim is action and self-expression and not the creation of culture and value or making a difference in the further
world. There is, of course, no reason why it should be. All men are
creative but few are artists. Art making requires a peculiar psychotic
disposition. Let me formulate the artistic disposition as follows: it is
reacting with one's ideal to the flaw in oneself and in the world, and
somehow making that reaction formation solid enough in the medium so that it indeed becomes an improved bit of real world for
others. This is an unusual combination of psychological machinery
and talents, and those who, having it, go on to appoint themselves to
such a thankless vocation, are rarer still. These few are not themselves Beat, for they have a vocation, they are not resigned. (My ob-

servation is that if artists are blocked in their vocation, they *cannot* resign themselves to seeking other experiences, and certainly they do not do finger painting, for if they can do finger painting they can make art.)

Nevertheless, living among the Beats, there will be a disproportionate number of artists, for the same reason that artists gravitate to any bohemia. Also, some of these genuine unresigned artists will make works that *speak for* the Beat community that they live among. That is, the "Beat" artists are not themselves Beat, for they are artists; but their art works tell us about the Beat.

This situation raises interesting questions about the relation of an artist and his immediate audience, and it is worth exploring.

It is both an advantage and a disadvantage for an artist to have around him an intensely creative gang of friends who are not rival artists. They provide him an immediate audience that helps assuage the sufferings of art loneliness and art guilt. On the other hand, it is a somewhat sickening audience because it has no objective cultural standard, it is not in the stream of ancient and international tradition. So its exclamations, "It's the greatest!" or, "Go, man, go!" don't give much security. The artist finds that he is a parochial group hero, when the reassurance that he needs, if he is diffident, is that he is a culture hero for the immortal world. Let me tell a few anecdotes to illustrate this fascinating dilemma of the relation of the "Beat" artist both to the Beats and to the objective culture in which he must finally exist.

An incident at a party for Patchen. Patchen is a poet of the "previous" generation, of long-proven integrity, with an immense body of work, some of which is obviously good, and the importance of the whole of it (may much still be added!) not yet clear. The point for our anecdote is that Patchen has the respect of writers but has received no public acclaim, no money, no easy publication. Now at this party, one of the best of the "Beat" writers, a genuine young artist, came demanding that the older poet give some recognition to the tribe of Beat poets, to "give them a chance." This was ironical since, riding on the Madison Avenue notoriety that we have mentioned, they had all got far more public acclaim, invitations to universities, night-club readings, than all of us put together. But Patchen asked for the names. The Beat spokesman reeled off twenty, and Patchen unerringly pointed out the two who were worth while. This threw the younger poet into a passion, for he needed, evidently, to win artistic recognition also for his parochial *audience*, among whom he was a hero, in order to reassure himself that he was a poet, which he was and as Patchen would at once have said. So he insulted the older man. Patchen rose to his height, called him a young punk, and left. The young man was crushed, burst into tears (he was drunk), and also left. At this, a young woman who often accompanied him, came up to me and clutched me by the knees, pleading with me to help him grow up, for nobody, she said, paid him any attention.

That is, the Beat audience, having resigned, is not in the world; yet being an eager creative audience, it wins the love and loyalty of its poet who becomes its hero and spokesman. But he too, then, doubts that he is in the world and has a vocation. As a Beat spokesman he receives notoriety and the chance of the wide public that every poet wants and needs; but he cannot help feeling that he is getting it as a pawn of the organized system.

Here is a simpler illustration of the relation of the spokesman-artist to the objective culture. This fellow is a much weaker poet, more nearly Beat himself, and quite conceited. At a reading of some other poet who is not a Beat spokesman, he tries to stop the reading by shouting, "Don't listen to this crap! let's hear from X." His maneuver is to make the parochial the *only* existing culture; then, by definition, he himself is an artist.

And here is an illustration of the most elementary response. A Beat spokesman, not ungifted but probably too immature to accomplish much, gives a reading in a theater. During the intermission, he asks a rather formidable and respected critic what he thinks of a particular poem, and the critic says frankly that it's childish. At this the outraged poet, very drunk, stands in the lobby screaming, "I hope you die! I hope art dies! I hope all artists die!"

These illustrations and the analysis of Beat conversation bring out the same point: In a milieu of resignation, where the young men think of society as a closed room in which there are no values but the rejected rat race or what they can produce out of their own guts, it is extremely hard to aim at objective truth or world culture. One's own products are likely to be personal or parochial.

4.

Shared creative expression has a therapeutic effect, and so results in transference, unconscious attachment. The striking, and often amusing, example of this is the young ladies who take modern dancing, with its beautiful exercises that release tense muscles; they are all head over ears in love with Martha or Doris, and fiercely loyal and sectarian.

The same occurs among the young Beats, except that, since there is no "leader," the emerging love attaches either to the community or to each one's self-image narcissistically. This makes for a powerful warmth of life—"the warmth of assembled animal bodies," as Kafka said—but it makes it even harder to get into the world. It gives the young men a daily interpersonal excitement, more satisfactory than the empty belonging or conformity of the organization, and happier than the loneliness of art. But it does not give them "something to do."

5.

So we return to our crucial problem: What to do that is self-justifying when the great social world is pretty unavailable?

The essential Beat answer is: to heighten experience, and get out of one's usual self.

To heighten experience is a common principle of Beat, Hipster, and Delinquent, but the differences are marked. Among the Hipsters, as Mailer points out, the craving for excitement and self-transcendence is darkly colored with violence and death wish, and they therefore dread flipping, which they interpret as weakness, castration, and death. Among the younger delinquents, we shall see, it is fatalism, the wish is to get caught and be brought back into society. But for the Beats, it is a religious hope that something new will happen, a revival.

In my observation, the Beats do not seem to be self-destructive. The risks of delinquency, criminality, and injury rouse in them a normal apprehension, and they express a human amazement at the brutality and cruelty of some with whom they keep company. In taking drugs for the new experience, they largely steer clear of being hooked by an addiction. On the other hand, if the aim is to get out of this world, one can hardly play it safe. So it is not surprising if they push their stimulants, sleeplessness, and rhythmic and hallucinatory exercises to the point of having temporary psychotic fugues, or flipping. In his book, Lipton speaks touchingly of someone who goes off to the municipal psychiatric hospital as an expected and regular occurrence. Perhaps *this* is the feudal support which I have claimed to be lacking in Beat Zen Buddhism: the young sages seek enlightenment, and the city hospital succors them when they break down.

Let us now go back to the jargon. The supreme words are "crazy," "far out," "gone," "high," "gas," "sent." These mean not in this world but somewhere, not rational but something. "Flip" is generally used with enthusiastic self-deprecation.

When the crazy or far-out moment can be maintained for long enough to be considered a something and somewhere, it is "groovy," that is, one is like somebody else's phonograph record. One is "with it" or "falls in." The "it" or the understood "where" is not, of course, definite, for pure being has no genus and differentia. "Swinging with it" is the condition of passing from here and now to the heightened experience of "it."

Contrariwise, it is bad and painful to be "nowhere," to "fall out" (take an overdose), or to be "drug" (dragging).

The way of being-in-the-world, that is, is to be either cool and mask-faced, experiencing little; or to be sent far out, experiencing something. However, since the cool behavior of these usually gentle middle-class boys looks like adolescent embarrassment and awkwardness rather younger than their years, one wonders whether ordinary growth in experience would not be a more profitable enterprise and ultimately get them much further out.

A possibility that has interestingly dropped from Beat culture is the exploitation of shared athletic or wildly physical agitation, which belonged grandly to the old jazz-for-dancing and revival meetings. This is certainly an important truth in Mailer's proposition that jive is energetic, in words like "go" and "dig."

(To the jazz-for-listening one is not supposed to respond overtly by more than a quietly tapped toe. It can then be hypnotic and speak to the listener like a crystal ball or a fountain or a hearth fire. As music it is remarkably thin gruel (no doubt I am tone deaf). For the performer, of course, it provides the deepening absorption of any simple improvised variations, plus the solidarity of the group.)

I can think of two reasons why the overtly shared crazy physical rhythms are spurned. First is that this motion is in fact too much in the extremities of the body rather than in the solar plexus, it is too superficial an excitement and more fit for teen-agers. The difference is between the lostness in juvenile jitterbugging and the "central" experience of Oriental dance or Mary Wigman. Some young men have taken to the Oriental dance, but most Beats do not practice this physiological yoga either, just as their Zen is without breathing-exercises or correction of posture. So perhaps another reason for their dropping the old physical jazz and revival is just the opposite, that the display of energy would upset their coolness, it would be embarrassing and make them feel too young. I wonder if this is not the simple explanation of their disdain of social dancing as "dry" sex; for certainly one of the reasonable uses of social dancing is body contact and sometimes sexual foreplay. But these boys are embarrassed to get an erection, to betray feeling, in public, though they are more than willing to take their clothes off and exhibit themselves, or to beat a drum wildly in public as an exhibition for the others, but not as contact with them.

6.

An awkward consequence of heightening experience when one is inexperienced, of self-transcendence when one has not much world to lose, is that afterward one cannot be sure that one was somewhere or had newly experienced anything. If you aren't much in the world, how do you know you are "out of this world"? This problem has been fateful for Beat literature. (The classical mystic who loses this world knows well, on returning to it, that it is a poor thing; and also that it is pointless to try to describe the Reality in terms of this world.)

The Beat novelist does not say, "Like when we left Chicago, we went to like New York." (Samuel Beckett does, of course, do just this in principle, and mighty strange and dull his novels are.) The Beat novelist wants to say that we did leave Chicago and did go to New York. But how would one know? When there is not much structure for the experience—no cause to leave Chicago, no motive to go to New York—these things become very doubtful and it is hard to make the narrative solid. So incidents are multiplied without adding up to a plot; factual details are multiplied that do not add up to interpretation or characterization; and there are purple passages and exclamations. The point of the perseveration is to insist that *something* happened. (Cf., Appendix E of this book, a review of *On The Road*.)

(This narrative difficulty of more or less articulate grownups is important in reminding us of what might otherwise be dark about the juvenile delinquents: that in the immense multiplicity of their exploits and kicks, including even horrifying deeds, it is not necessarily the case that they experienced what they were doing. It is therefore beside the point to judge or treat them as if they were performing acts.)

Similarly the Beats make a social ritual of reminiscing and retelling. Meeting in a group, they retell exactly what happened, each one adding his details, with the aim of proving that something indeed happened, and perhaps they can recapture the experience of it, if indeed anything was experienced; just as at a later date, this meeting at which the retelling is occurring will be retold. It is like a man who dreams in exact detail of the fight he had with the boss; what could be the wish in such a dream? It is that when the event occurred he failed to get angry, but dreaming it he is angry. Except that in the Beat retelling, they are not angry this time either.

In such circumstances, it seems to me inevitable that heightened experiences too will pall, for they do not transform enough natural and social world to create experience and new experience. They do not accumulate knowledge, establish better habits, make hypotheses probable, and suggest further projects, all the things that constitute seasoned experience. A Beat will tell you a remarkable vision that he had under peyote, but you do not feel that it was a vision for *him;* it is as useless as the usual experience of extrasensory perception that is irrelevant to anybody's practical affairs. So in their creative activity young Beats compile thick notebooks of poems and drawings, but since there are no problems of art, these do not add up to a body of work. What might then occur, unfortunately, is that, when the flesh is not better nourished, the spirit fails. Since better habits are not developed, the young men simply succumb to bad ones, relying more and more on the drugs, and becoming careless about meaning anything. Then other young fellows who chose this way of life because it suited and solved a problem, quit it because of the bad company.

The word "Angry," we saw, was a misnomer for "bitter and waspish." The word "Beat," however, is exquisitely accurate, meaning "defeated and resigned." Public spokesmen of the Beats have, as the result of various visions, assured us that the word means *Beatus, blessed;* but this too soon comes to the same thing, "punchy."

7.

Lawrence Lipton tells us that the word "work" always means copulate. (A job of work is a "gig.") This is a good thought, for it means that the sex is feelingful and productive, even though effortful.

My impression is that—leaving out their artists, who have the kind of sex that artists have—Beat sexuality in general is pretty good, unlike delinquent sexuality, which seems, on the evidence, to be wretched. Animal bodies have their own rhythms and self-limits; in this, sex is completely different from taking drugs; so if inhibition is relaxed and there is the courage to seek for experience, there ought to be good natural satisfaction. One sees many pretty young Beat couples. (*I* think they are pretty; some people think they are hideous.) Since conceit and "proving" are not major factors, there is affection. Homosexuality and bisexuality are not regarded as a big deal.

But the question remains, What is in it for the women who accompany the Beats? The characteristic Beat culture, unlike the American standard of living, is essentially for men, indeed for very young men who are "searching." These young fellows are sweet, independent, free-thinking, affectionate, perhaps faithful, probably sexy—these are grand virtues, some of them not equally available among American men on the average. But Beats are not responsible husbands and fathers of children.

There are several possible sexual bonds. Let us recall the woman at the Patchen party, who pleaded for someone to help the young man. Her relation to him is maternal: she devotes herself to helping him find himself and become a man, presumably so that he can then marry her. (Typically; I do not mean actually in this case.)

Another possible relation is Muse or Model: her Beat is her poet and artist and makes her feel important. This is a satisfaction for her feminine narcissism or penis envy. But it comes, often, to ludicrously overestimating the young man's finger painting and laying on him an impossible burden to become the artist that he is not.

One sometimes sees a pathetic scene in a bar. Some decent square young workingmen are there, lonely, looking for girls or even for a friendly word. They feel that they are "nobodies"; they are not Beats, they are not artists. They have nothing to "contribute" to the conversation. The girls, meantime, give their attention only to the Beats, who are sounding off so interestingly. But these Beats will not make any life for the girls, whereas the others might make husbands and fathers. If a square fellow finally plucks up his courage to talk to a girl, she turns away insultingly.

Lipton suggests that women follow Beats as they followed roving Gypsies. But this makes no sense, for the Gypsy was an independent who moved with his tribe, his wife, his kids, his animals, and he was (in the ballads) a masterful character. A Gypsy is not a resigned young man, searching.

Finally, of course, there are the young women who are themselves Beats, disaffected from status standards. Perhaps they have left an unlucky marriage, have had an illegitimate child, have fallen in love with a Negro, and found little support or charity "in" society. They might then choose a life among those more tolerant, and find meaning in it by posing for them or typing their manuscripts.

8.

To repeat, Beat is not a strong position and it can hardly work out well. The individual young man is threatened either with retreating back to the organized system or breaking down and sinking into the *lumpen* proletariat. Nevertheless, culturally there is a lot of strength here; let us try to see where it is.

Considered directly, their politics are unimpressive. They could not be otherwise since they are so hip and sure that society cannot be different. Explicitly, they are pacifists, being especially vocal about the atom bomb. The Bomb is often mentioned by themselves and other commentators as an explanation of their religious crisis; but it's not convincing. Their own diatribes seem to be mostly polemical self-defense, as if to say: "You squares dropped the atom bombs, don't you dare criticize my smoking marijuana." In the play *The Connection* this is openly stated as a defense for heroin. On the whole one does not observe that the Beats are so concerned about nuclear weapons as many mothers of families or squares who have common sense. One of the Beat spokesmen wrote a long dithyramb about the Bomb, of which the critic George Dennison remarked:

"He seems miffed that people pay attention to the atom bomb instead of to him."

At the same time, their peacefulness is genuine and their tolerance of differences is admirable, extending also to the squares, except for loathsome class enemies like *Time*, Housing, or gouging employment agencies. Their ability to occupy themselves in poverty on a high level of cultural and animal satisfaction is remarkable, with paper-back books, odd records, and sex. Their inventing of community creativity is unique. If we consider these achievements, we see that they are factual evidence for a political proposition of capital importance: *People can go it on their own*, without resentment, hostility, delinquency, or stupidity, better than when they move in the organized system and are subject to authority. (To be sure, the Beats were not among the underprivileged to begin with; they had some useful education and their poverty is in part voluntary; but these are not circumstances unavailable to others.) They do not go far, they invite degeneration, they seem hard put to assume responsibility; but they do exist interestingly and peacefully.

In one important respect, their community culture could be made far more effective. I am referring to the jazz and drums in a community setting. They have chosen too primitive a model, e.g., Haiti. If they would ponder on the Balinese dances, they might learn something—not the Bali dances on a stage on Broadway, but as they exist in their home villages where, to the music of the gamelan, the onlookers suddenly become entranced and fall down or become possessed and would do violence to themselves, except that they are rescued one and all by their friends of the community. (Cartier-Bresson has excellent pictures of these sessions; and of course Artaud, who is becoming scriptural among the Beats, was an ardent champion of them.)

9.

Beat literature and religion are ignorant and thin, yet they have two invaluable properties. First, they are grounded in the existing situation, whatever the situation, without moralistic or invidious judgment of it. It is in this sense that Henry Miller is their literary father. Their experience is admittedly withdrawn. (Miller's too does not add up.) Their religion is unfeasible, for one cannot richly meet the glancing present, like Zen, without patriotic loyalty, long discipleship, and secure subsistence. Nevertheless, their writing has a pleasant bare surface, and it *is* experience. It is often bombastic, but on the average it is more primary than other writing we have been getting in America.

A second valuable property of the Beat style is that it tries to be an action, not a reflection or comment. We saw that, in both their conversation and heightened experience, this action doesn't amount to much, for they do not have the weight or beauty to make much difference. But their persistent effort at the effective community reading, appearing as themselves in their own clothes, and willing to offend or evoke some other live response; and also their creative playing (especially if it would become more like the Bali dances), are efforts for art and letters as living action, rather than the likeness to literature that we have been getting in the *Kenyon Review* and the *Partisan Review*.

Religiously, they are making a corrigible error. What they intend, it seems to me, is not the feudal Zen Buddhism, which is far too refined for them and for our times, but Taoism, the peasant ancestor of Zen. Tao is a faith for the voluntary poor, for it teaches us to get something from the act of wresting a living with independent integrity. It is, as Beat intends to be, individual or small-group anarchy. If the Beats would think this through, they would know how to claim their subsistence under better conditions, and perhaps they would have more world. Tao teaches, too, divine experience from the body and its breathing. In this it is like the doctrine of Wilhelm Reich, much esteemed by the Beats but not followed by them. The magic they are after is natural and group magic, and they need not be so dependent on ancient superstitions and modern drugs.

Most important, Tao teaches the blessedness of confusion. Tao is not enlightened, it does not know the score. Confusion is the state of promise, the fertile void where surprise is possible again. Confusion is in fact the state that we are in, and we should be wise to cultivate it. If young people are not floundering these days, they are not following the Way.

The sage is murky, confused. As it says, "Block the passage. Shut the door.... I droop and drift as though I belonged nowhere.... So dull am I. All men can be put to some use, I alone am intractable and boorish."

It's square to be hip.

The basic words of our jargon are "Search me," "Kid," "I couldn't give you a clue," "I'm murky." "Creator spirit, come."

X. THE EARLY FATALISTIC

I.

FROM THE subjects of our last chapter, the Beat Generation, we could learn something culturally useful. If we turn now to the big-city juvenile delinquency of the underprivileged, e.g., new immigrants economically marginal, we are dealing with uneducated children. Their legal arrests and convictions occur at average age fifteen to sixteen, but their delinquencies date from twelve and thirteen, if not earlier; and of course they attend school the least and get the least out of it. The so-called "delinquent subculture" has a few flashing and charming traits, but nothing in it is viable or imitable. On the other hand, the fight these kids put up, the record of their delinquencies, does test and explore our society.

The accounts and statistics of delinquency come mostly from social agencies, the police, and reform schools. In a sense we know about juvenile delinquency only from its failures, the lads who are most disturbed and have the least general ability—except the one important ability of getting caught. I do not believe this gives us a valid picture; so in the following discussion, I shall persistently try to distinguish Delinquent Behavior as doing-the-forbidden-and-even-defiant from Delinquent Behavior in-order-to-get-caught. (Naturally I shall often have to say, "I guess.")

2.

Thus far we have been using a fairly standard theory of delinquency, though better rounded, I think, than the usual statement of it. Let us recapitulate it: The early childhood of juvenile delinquents is "permissive" or "neglected," depending on the point of view. They play truant and quit school as soon as they can. This is not necessarily a failing in them, for the schools are poor, and the policy of keeping them there to educate them for some viable life or other in modern society, is benevolent but largely doomed.

Their escape from school proves that they are less supervised at home, and in turn it gives them more freedom, at first, to sharpen their wits on the streets. Less restricted, they probably have more elaborate early sexual experience than the middle class or the more regulated poor boys. This may get them into early and repeated trouble, and it *may*, therefore, result in repression and becoming *less* sexually adventurous than the average boy later. Such an outcome is, I think, common and when it occurs it is certainly disastrous, for repressed sexuality will drive them to more and more frantic excitement to break through.

(My guess is that the delinquent older adolescents who are active with the girls are *not* the lads who are caught and get counted. For one thing, important sexual adventure is rarely a gang activity. For another, sexual success diminishes the need to raise the ante and be punished. And it always gives "something to do." That is, my guess is that *sexual expression is compatible with, and perhaps favorable to, "delinquent acts"; but is incompatible with delinquency-in-order-to-get-caught.* This is speculation; but consider the following two statements of F. M. Thrasher: "Sex represents a decidedly secondary activity in the gang. In the adolescent group in particular it is subordinated to the primary interests of conflict and adventure." But "groups of this [sexually very active] type are probably far more common than is ordinarily supposed"—that is, such kids don't get caught and counted.)

Mostly these kids have nothing to do and *will* have nothing worth while to do. They feel worthless and guilty, and these feelings are often enhanced by unusual hostility at home, both taken and given. (The psychological mechanism is that some of the child's hostility against his parents turns against himself and is felt as guilt.) As a reaction to these feelings, they develop the characteristic conceited self-image that has to keep proving itself: proving that they are men and not boys, potent and not impotent, and that they are good as anybody else.

It is *this* syndrome, of conceit and hostility, which then meets their social situation of being underprivileged and deprived, and finds it so insulting; whereas other poor boys—in a less hostile home, more tolerant of school, and perhaps more lucky in keeping out of sexual trouble—make an easier adjustment. In the case of racial minorities, there is certainly real insult as well as fantasy insult; and there is real insult when a fresh kid is treated as a young punk. The combination of family hostility, conceit, and the insult of underprivilege now makes the kids disaffected, at war with ordinary society, and they have their sport and triumph by breaking its laws.

They appoint themselves to a gang. Positively, this gives them pride and something to belong to; negatively, it protects each one's conceit by conformity. The finding of the Gluecks and others that the delinquent juveniles are more unconventional than the average applies, of course, to their standard behavior and their disturbed personalities; but all the more they are undeviatingly conformist in their own peer groups. The gangs have highly satisfactory communal features: living and working together (e.g., a boy angry at home can sleep at his friend's), often sharing such sexuality as there is, and as careless of one another's property as they are of the world's. But it is a community, we have seen, that lacks personal affection and that stops abruptly at the adults, and therefore provides no grounds for growth. This abrupt divide is of course sharper in the usual case of first-generation immigrant parents.

In our model of the closed room and the rat race, we pointed to a clandestine alliance between juvenile delinquents and the middle status of the organized system, exchanging culture heroes, norms of cool behavior, and the values of cynicism, against the earnest boys in the middle class and working class. This view seems to me more currently realistic than A. K. Cohen's proposition that, whereas the nondelinquent "corner-boy culture temporizes with middle-class morality, the delinquent subculture does not: it permits no ambiguity in its negation of the respectable status-system, and so sets the delinquent *above* the most exemplary college boy." On the contrary. It is likely, rather, that the nondelinquent corner boy, less conceited, has not cut himself off from ordinary poor satisfactions, and therefore does not need to run in gangs and get caught; he is not "temporizing" with middle-class morality but is not much bothering about it. Conversely, it is obvious that the juvenile delinquents, like the hustlers (male prostitutes), fancy themselves as movie heroes in sports cars; and it is importantly the inner conflict between their dreams of American glamour and their own impotent resources that exacerbates their resentment. It is perhaps *only* the juvenile delinquents who take the American way of life fully earnestly. This is what is implicitly hinted at by those students, e.g., Barron, who speak of the juvenile *in* delinquent society: it is the hipster attitude of the organized system that provides the model for delinquent behavior: the short cut, the empty sensation, raising the ante, and contempt of honest effort and earnest goals.

In sum, we have a picture of early freedom, underprivileged frustration, reactive conceit, and gang conformity. If we now consult the personality picture of caught delinquents—given in, for instance, the painstaking study by Sheldon and Eleanor Glueck—we see it is quite identical with that of the young hero of our story:

He is: vivacious, extroverted, less self-controlled, more manually inclined, more aggressive, less fearful of failure and defeat, more independent, more initiating, less submissive, less amenable to conventional expectations. These are positive powers and must *therefore* be early survivals, for only physical nature has such energies. But the frustration appears in responses like "impulsive, oral, narcissistic," and the reactive conceit appears as "hostile, resentful, defiant, suspicious, destructive, socially assertive, not feeling recognized or appreciated, defensive, unco-operative." And finally he is more sociable in play in the sense of "needing supportive companionship," which we can take as both a positive and a negative trait.

3.

But these are, let us not forget, the characteristics of below-average kids in a reformatory compared with those of carefully matched nondelinquents, equally below average and underprivileged. Accordingly, they tell us very little about more gifted or favored kids either prone or not prone to delinquent behavior. In the nature of the case, such statistics are hard to collect. E.g., it is essential for the *intelligent* performance of forbidden deeds to keep them under your hat and not have too many accomplices; then how can we know how many gifted kids are performing how many misdemeanors? And middle-class delinquents don't end up in reform schools but in military academies and other schools that promise "to make a man of your boy."

From this point of view, it must be said that the essential property of *juvenile delinquency as defined* is: such personality and behavior as guarantee getting caught, punished, and tabulated. I do not think that this property is a tautology: it has important content that distinguishes the delinquency of doing-the-forbidden-and-defiant from the delinquency to-get-caught. Getting caught is guaranteed by:

(1) Compulsive repetition of a behavior because it is not really giving satisfaction. This tends to allay the alertness and prudence of the routine tries, as well as to multiply the chances of being caught. And it leads to:

(2) Raising the ante, in order to force feeling. This must result in disaster.

(3) Conversely, in place of mischief or the attraction of the forbidden or rebelliousness or even malice, the caught delinquent exhibits a profound fatalism, indicating an unconscious need to be saved from his compulsive round or not worth-while experience and

brought back into the "meaningful" structure of authority and punishment. It looks as though the caught delinquent has done the forbidden and defiant deed in order to tease and provoke the authority, to compel his attention. Psychologically, then, though he thinks and operates on his own, he is not "independent."

(Let me mention the touching case of an English boy who stole a watch and then returned it, saying he had found it, "in order that somebody should say he was a good boy." The next best thing is for somebody to say that one is a bad boy.)

(4) The gang is used as a structure for psychological support. But running with the gang also guarantees getting caught, both because it is conspicuous and because its in-group concentration and habits soon get quite out of touch with the surrounding mores. Aping his friends, a lad forgets what safe behavior is, what ought to be concealed because people are outraged by it. A lad who is infinitely secretive and suspicious gives himself away by his slouch, his clothes, and every word he utters. Also, they dare one another to excesses that each individual would avoid. Naturally this is all the worse with cultural minorities who do not know the "right" behavior to begin with; e.g., Spanish boys might be badly judged for behavior that to them is perfectly acceptable.

I propose that these four guarantees of getting caught make juvenile delinquency an interesting cultural study. For it is: *the powerless struggling for life within, not resigned from, an unacceptable world.* At first inspection this does not seem a promising lesson. But on reflection, we see that this fatalism is a deeply religious position, not far from what Dostoevski was trying to tell us. Many of his characters are adult delinquents. In our time, Genet has made of the doomed delinquent culture a powerful thought and poetry. The fatalism of juvenile delinquency is a kind of adolescent religious crisis, with a religious passion and content, whereas the conventional religion is empty. On the streets, they feel worthless-and-abandoned; in the reformatory, they are accepted back home.

This fatalism in the face of the overwhelming and unacceptable is a commentary on the poignant remark of the criminologist:

It must be confessed that it is much easier and hence more "practical" to deal with superficial symptomatic behavior or its immediately observable causes than to strive to cut the deeper roots of delinquency. When those deeper roots are made evident, however, we have to ask ourselves how deep we wish to go in the attack on crime. Are we willing, for example, to sacrifice many of our material satisfactions or to give up our racial prejudices? [Donald Taft]

4.

As ordinarily used, the term "juvenile delinquency" is thoroughly confused. First, as we have said, we must distinguish forbidden-and-defiant-acts from behavior-to-get-caught. Then, among the socially forbidden acts we must obviously distinguish those that any lad of sense and spirit will perform if he has to and whenever he can, from those that are indeed harmful to others or disruptive of good society. And again, as many authorities have pointed out, with respect to any of these acts there is an immense discrepancy in their adjudication and our information: delinquent acts of middle- and upper-class boys almost never get to courts or social agencies; white boys are dismissed or put on probation where Negro or Spanish boys are put away; the incorrigibility and sexual offenses of boys are treated lightly, of girls severely, and so forth. It is not surprising, then, if many statistics and analyses of delinquency disagree. Apart from the one factor of getting caught, there is no real concept of delinquency. Yet obviously this factor is not sufficient by itself, for getting caught does have *some* essential relation to forbidden acts.

Let us therefore take a different tack. Instead of looking for a concept of delinquency, let us expand the subject matter as a series of possible punishable relations obtaining between the boy struggling for life and trying to grow up, and the society that he cannot accept and that lacks objective opportunities for him. Roughly, we can name six importantly distinct stages in the series:

(1) Acts not antisocial if society had more sense.

(2) Acts that are innocent but destructive in their consequences and therefore need control.

(3) Acts antisocial in purpose.

(4) Behavior aimed at getting caught and punished.

(5) Gang fighting that is not delinquency yet must be controlled.

(6) Delinquency secondarily created by society itself by treating as delinquents those who were not delinquent, and by social attempts at prevention and reform.

5.

(1) Acts not antisocial that are punished are most animal expression and some spirited enterprise. These include a lot of trespassing and hell raising with annoyance and minor damage. Most sexual behavior. Running away and truancy. But even certain important "theft."

The trespassing and hell raising speak for themselves. Where everything has become property and order, it is quite impossible to be vivacious, aggressive, undeliberate, exploratory and venturesome, without being out of order and sometimes smashing things. This is generally agreed and the police are usually not unreasonable. But the bother comes when emotional heat is generated and meets incipient deeper grounds of delinquency, the exchange of insults and the need for revenge. E.g., a cop is rude and the boys get angry; or a chap foolishly drives away the kids who are diving from his cruiser, so they retaliate by boring holes in the bottom of it and sinking it.

Most sexual behavior would give more satisfaction and do lasting good, and certainly result in far less damage, if any, if it were completely ignored by the police and not subject to any social disapproval *qua* sexual. There may be grounds for debate about the harmfulness or indifference of "corrupting the morals of a minor"—many societies have managed handsomely without such notions; but all competent authority would agree that, in most cases, more damage is done by the fear and shame accompanying a sexual act than can possibly follow from the simple act itself. (Typically, "Masturbation is a habit without deleterious effects in itself, yet a source of behavior difficulties because of strong social disapproval.... [It is hard] to find a rational reason for committing mere sex delinquents to an institution. To be effective, [help for these girls] must be divorced from restraint and stigma."—Donald Taft, *Criminology*.)

In truancy, the burden of proof lies on the schools, which are demonstrably stupefying to many children, whose truancy is therefore a kind of self-preservation. Naturally, these kids get nothing from hanging around the streets either. The solution is hard but simple: decide that the kids are in the right and *make good education at whatever cost*.

The same thinking applies to vagabondage. If a kid is a lonely runaway without domicile or means of support, it takes no great wisdom to infer that he has left a cruel or drunken home or a situation of intolerable uselessness and boredom, or that he is ashamed. Then provide him with something worth while, and give him solace.

But consider the principle of the burden of the proof in even an important crime like auto theft, important *solely* because cars are expensive. (The real social danger, from wild driving, occurs with all car-crazy adolescents, not only those who steal cars.) Almost all juvenile auto theft—in 1959, 68 per cent of *all* auto theft—is for joy riding. For example, a band of Spanish kids, now mostly locked up, made it a point of their game to return the car to the identical spot, a foolhardy gesture. Now we live in a society where for all classes these cars are the chief means, and the Madison Avenue symbols, of power, manliness, freedom to go and do. Kids of other periods drove the horses at an early age; in rural places they drive cars at fourteen. In urban traffic conditions young adolescents cannot be licensed to drive. Underprivileged kids may never have the means to drive. What then? When an absurd social pattern has created an insoluble dilemma, is it the case that the kids must be the ones punished? Certainly from such a crime as auto theft I fail to see, with Bloch and Flynn's *Delinquency*, that "youthful offenders under eighteen years have become our greatest single threat to law-abiding security." But as it is, our dilemma works out as follows: "A couple and their three-year-old son were killed in Queens last night when their car hit a telephone pole after it was struck by a stolen car being chased by the police. Five shots were fired in the pursuit and two hit the car.")

(2) Auto theft takes us into the second category of "innocent acts destructive in their consequences and needing control." Of course none of these acts, except vagabondage, is innocent in the sense that the kid does not know it is forbidden, unless he is a moron. But to do the forbidden, in order to transgress limits that *seem* unnatural, is normal and innocent; and if the limits *are* unnatural it is often necessary and admirable.

But I want especially to call attention to acts whose motivation is strongly *approved* socially, but where the frustrating conditions or the boys' ignorance or ineptitude in handling the baffling means, gets them into trouble.

An obvious cause of innocent trouble is playing. Some wise authorities have compared delinquent behavior to play. So when A. K. Cohen, again, speaks of the "uselessness" of much delinquent destructiveness and thievery as a counteraction to middle-class ethics, he is surely exaggerating. All play is "useless," and since everything is property, underprivileged kids are bound to play with other people's property. This can be very serious. A band of kids decide it would be bully to remove the blocks and set a huge truck in motion downhill, resulting in $10,000 worth of damage. But of course it *is* bully. (*I* think so.)

But let us go on to a much more thorny illustration, which would not generally be viewed in the light I want to place it in: the plight of a present-day poor boy with regard to earning money and having a little money. First, let me quote an official spokesman, the Superintendent of Schools of Rochester, New York:

Many parents have long since given up the struggle to encourage youths to share in the few remaining home duties that still require physical effort. Yet, no school program can provide the discipline, the maturity, or the self-respect that comes from performing real work that is highly valued and fairly paid for by the adult world.

Well said. Now this quotation is taken from a Sunday supplement article praising newsboys and containing the joyful report that "over one half of today's newspaperboys belong to our middle- or upper-middle-income groups." This is not a surprising fact; in present conditions, it takes a good deal of arranging, and living in the suburbs, to get such a news route going. Does it not raise the question as to how the poor boys, who have not learned such expert management, will get their discipline, maturity, self-respect?

This matter is highly important; let us be clear about the usual thinking. Eugene Gilbert, the census taker of teen-age economics, says: "Within a decade the number of teen-agers holding steady jobs has doubled.... Some four and one-half million do part-time work or odd jobs throughout the year." *That* sounds promising; but he then goes on to explain that "Typical [!] of most American youngsters today are the students and graduates of the Pearl River High School in Rockland County, N. Y.," *nearly 100 per cent of whom are going on to college*, though in the country at large barely a half graduate from high school, and only 15 per cent enter college. The poor, the working-class, and even the lower-middle-class boys seem to have vanished from society; they do not contribute enough to the ten- to eleven-billion-dollar annual teen-age sales. This is *not* a promising attitude for giving serious attention to the young of America.

For a child, to get money is a major part of his notion of being grown-up and independent, for this is what all grown men do: they make money and are thereby free to act. (This has very little connection with Max Weber's version of the Protestant Ethic or middle-class ideology.) Let me give a precise, if annoying, illustration. In countries where it is not too antipathetic to the mores, young fellows will engage in homosexual activity; but they might ask for a few pennies, enough to buy five cigarettes. This sum is *not* the wages of prostitution; such a thought would outrage them, for if they did not

*

enjoy what they were doing they would not do it. It is, rather, a way of making the act legitimate, justified, not merely pleasure. The money serves exactly the same symbolic function as the wedding ring for a young woman. Earning some money affirms that a young fellow is a man. (In America, however, this youth would at once be driven to "proving" and delinquency. Having engaged in the sex, he is vulnerable to contempt and therefore may react by robbery and assault. "Rolling queers" is the ideal delinquent calling—better than auto mechanic—for it combines pleasure, profit, morality, and grounds for boasting; and it is pretty safe from follow-up by the police.)

As our system becomes more tightly organized and highly urbanized, it is the poor city kids who are squeezed out. We no longer have a neighborhood tradition of small after-school jobs—fewer shops make occasional deliveries; to deliver for the chain stores is a full-time job (except perhaps on Saturdays); messengers are hired full time; there are no lawns to mow, there is no snow to shovel; there are fewer news routes in the city; baby sitting is a middle-class business and anyway belongs to girls. An early teen-ager is caught in the following trap: he gets nothing out of school and does not do his homework; on the other hand, he is too young to get working papers. (We saw that one of the few proposals in the Governor of New York's antidelinquency program was aimed at this situation.) The youth cannot continue to beg from his parents, for the sums now come to three or four dollars and he feels degraded by being dependent. How will he get some money to prove his legitimacy and independence?

Many petty thefts and burglaries—that seem "uselesss" risks to the sociologist, and therefore he interprets them as counteraction to bourgeois values—are desperate efforts to feel grown-up. They are compelled by an objective dilemma. Naturally, subjectively, they are not innocent; they are energized by frantic excitement, cold sweat and terror, and finally the need to be caught, to escape the anxiety; but we must look at the whole picture. They are "short cuts," but maybe there is no long way round. The question is this: if these kids had socially acceptable opportunities to earn money, would they avail themselves of them? Some would. It is worth trying. They might learn discipline, maturity, self-respect.

(Consider the following by the Executive Director of the New York City Mission Society: "We have experimented for two summers with employment of 100 to 150 teenagers from high delinquency areas....Our $10-per-week employees all stayed out of trouble. [But] on the occasions we tried what were essentially 'made work' jobs, the young people understood this immediately and lost all interest.")

(3) It is with the next category, acts intentionally antisocial, that we come to the delinquents who largely fill the courts and the reformatories. Malicious destructiveness, theft and burglary for real money (often for narcotics), vengeful assaults, sexual attacks. In these, the reactive hostility of the standard delinquent syndrome has begun to operate, and it inevitably leads to getting caught. An illustration: some fifteen-year-olds hold up a crippled old man; the loot is too small and their disappointment at once triggers the deep passion: that his debility is an intolerable threat to their own glorious perfection, so they stomp him to death.

A less horrible illustration: The behavior of a pedestrian or of another motorist that happens to inconvenience the youth in the slightest degree is at once interpreted as a deliberate insult or at least as a proof that that person ought not to exist; and this may easily lead to a case of hit and run.

An absolutely typical economic illustration: If a fellow offers to walk half a mile in order to save fifteen cents carfare, his mates will at once contemptuously say that he is "cheap." Once the "proving" syndrome is present, the boys are quite out of touch with the simplest realities; and vice versa, because they are out of touch with the simplest realities, they are called on to "prove."

(4) So we come to behavior-to-get-caught: compulsive repetition, increasing negligence, raising the ante, giving way to irrational rage. We can see the fatalism on the surface.

Here is a scrap of conversation with one of the auto thieves mentioned above, not caught:

"How is it you weren't caught?"

"I got scared the other time, the time the cop pulled up and I got away. So I wouldn't go with them."

"Isn't Carlos [the leader] scared?"

"No."

"What do you mean? Isn't he scared they'll catch him?"

"No. He don't care if he gets caught."

"Is that what he says? or is that what you think?"

"That's what he said, and I think so too."

"Why did *you* go ten rides?"

"What else is there to do? I can't just hang around when they all go."

The problem, that is, is the fatalism that the one has whereas the other experiences fear and prudence. (In this particular case the fatalist is the more able boy and has a better home background.) One part of the fatalism is certainly apathy: life has no interesting prospect—e.g., there might be a sexual block. Another part is certainly the need to be caught, to get out of the anxious round of risks.

6.

(5) I doubt, despite Thrasher, that there is a nondelinquent "gang." The gang begins like the primitive fraternity of boys who live in the boys' house; but in the primitive culture this is done by social sanction, whereas the defining property of the gang, as we customarily use the term, is that it is a community *abruptly cut off* from the adults and their sanction. The full-blown gang suits its members not as a fraternity in which to learn growing up, but essentially in so far as they *are* "grown up" or have ceased to grow: it is a sharing of a common conceit. The members consider it their identity, they appoint themselves to it. But since it is only a conceit, it is vulnerable, and therefore all the more must be protected by strict conformity of behavior and opinions, it does not tolerate individual interests or wandering off by oneself. Existing *instead of* the adult society, the gang is

in principle an extraterritorial enclave in society, and therefore it has developed a feud Code. It is this extraterritorial loyalty that is powerfully cemented by the shared danger of the delinquencies: all are in the same boat of having participated in punishable deeds; anyone who would get out is tacitly or explicitly blackmailed.

But it does *not* follow from this that the gang is delinquent-to-get-caught. On the contrary. Finding one's gang is a haven from the fatalistic drive toward disaster. One is caught by the gang; the gang provides a supportive structure; it is not so necessary to provoke the old authority. (But of course, as we have seen, running with the *adolescent* gang accidentally increases the certainty of getting caught. Adult criminal gangs have learned the ropes.) It could be said that belonging to the gang diminishes the *delinquent* behavior of the members of the gang. The chief activity of the gang becomes war against other groups; it is no longer a struggle for the growth of the self by forbidden acts. And correspondingly, the persisting "delinquencies" of the gang members begin to look very much like *crime*, war against society. They are no longer merely incidents of growing up, but self-conscious acts of a responsible achieved-identity.

Some such analysis as this is necessary to explain the puzzling predominance suddenly assumed by gang fighting. Adolescent gang wars are not, as such, delinquent any more than international wars are. Gang wars are significant nowadays mainly because of the technological improvement of the weapons, which used to be mainly sticks and stones. (The same could be said of the international wars.)

If the rest of society did not exist, the gang wars would continue as the absorbing interest of these youths. Since the rest of society exists, it becomes a background for plunder—as an army lives on the land. Irate magistrates, trained in Hobbes and on *Leviathan*, are impatient at having to deal with young punks as if they were citizens of a foreign power with its war chief and other grand viziers and its territorial rights. The Youth Board, as we have seen, accepts the situation as it is and tries to win over the youth's allegiance.

In this framework of analysis, it is clear why the gangs war on one another. The entire structure, and most of the loyalty, of each gang is grounded in the vulnerable conceit of its members, now socialized and immeasurably strengthened by the gang name, uniform, and territory. So there at once begins to operate, on the gang level, what Freud beautifully called the "narcissism of small differences": that it is the *smallest* difference from one's own self-image of grandeur and perfection that is most threatening and most arouses rage. Living on the other block is quite sufficient to make an enemy. Being a slightly different color is guaranteed. We must remember that the gang has almost no real social or cultural resources to support its tight structure and intense loyalty; it has to make everything out of "points of honor," out of the formal fact that its territory has been invaded. (Thus, if it is publicly acknowledged that Joe is no longer a member of the Dragons, he can safely walk down X Street.)

Into this formal insult pours all the accumulated *real* frustration, the undischarged stimulation, the thwarted growing up, and the natural insult that is endemic in our society. In our truly remarkable and unexampled civil peace, where there are rarely fist fights; where no one is born, is gravely ill, or dies; where meat is eaten but no one sees an animal slaughtered; where scores of millions of cars, trains, elevators, and airplanes go their scheduled way and there is rarely a crash; where an immense production proceeds in orderly efficiency and the shelves are duly cleared—and *nevertheless* none of this comes to joy or tragic grief or any other final good—it is not surprising if there are explosions. They occur at the boundaries of the organized system of society: in juvenile gang fights, in prison riots, in foreign wars.

> *These conditions are almost specific for the excitement of primary masochism. There is continual stimulation and only partial release of tension, an unbearable heightening of the unaware tensions—unaware because people do not know what they want, nor how to get it. The desire for final satisfaction, for orgasm, is interpreted as the wish for total self-destruction. It is inevitable, then, that there should be a public dream of universal disaster, with vast explosions, fires, and electric shocks; and people pool their efforts to bring this apocalypse to an actuality.*

*At the same time all overt expression of destructiveness, an-
nihilation, anger, combativeness, is suppressed in the interests of
civil order. Also, the feeling of anger is inhibited and even repressed. People are sensible, tolerant, polite, and co-operative in
being pushed around. But the occasions of anger are by no means
minimized. On the contrary, when the larger movements of initiative are circumscribed in the competitive routines of offices,
bureaucracies, and factories, there is petty friction, hurt feelings,
being crossed. Small anger is continually generated, never dis-
charged; big anger, that goes with big initiative, is repressed.*

*Therefore the angry situation is projected afar. People must
find big distant causes to explain the pressure of anger that is
certainly not explicable by petty frustrations. It is necessary to
have something worthy of the hatred that is unaware felt for oneself. In brief, one is angry with the Enemy.*

(Gestalt Therapy, II, viii, 8.)

7.

(6) Last, but not least, by its own response to annoyance, society creates delinquent behavior and delinquents. If a child, who does not
know what he is, is authoritatively told that he is a delinquent, he
obediently conforms to this role too, especially when it involves exclusion from nondelinquent playmates. A spell in a "reform" school
increases the chances of returning to some other correctional institution on a more serious charge, and almost guarantees belonging to
a gang, for it deepens fatalism and throws one in with congenial
companions. For a long time philosophers have been pointing out
that if there were no jails there would, in time, be less crime; but the
popular wisdom will not buy it.

The social creation of the delinquent character is a matter of the
very highest importance and deserves a book to itself. Consider
what happens. There are a number of quite different behaviors, some
really harmful and antisocial, some indifferent and even performed

innocently, yet all forbidden. When, however, they are all tarred with the same brush, the salient fact about them all becomes their defiance, culpability, and punishability. Vice becomes "vertical": if a boy masturbates, smokes, plays truant, he *might as well* steal, joy ride, hustle, use narcotics, commit burglaries, etc. Such a boy no longer has friends, but mutually blackmailing accomplices. A spectacular example of this social creation of felony is the illegality of marijuana, which increases contact with pushers of addictive drugs; and the intransigent attitude toward heroin as a criminal rather than a socio-medical problem guarantees worse consequences still.

8.

The delinquent fatalism is the feeling of no chance in the past, no prospect for the future, no recourse in the present; whence the drive to disaster. It is a religious crisis. We spoke of the French writer Jean Genet as its literary prophet. Let us conclude this chapter by some remarks about his work.

Genet writes, sometimes explicitly but always essentially, as a *juvenile* delinquent. The criminals with whom he empathizes are not fully grown like those of Dostoevski or Shakespeare, like the Possessed or Iago and Edmund. They are not adequate, they do not have pretensions, to the independent social identities of kingship, marriage, fatherhood, politics, wealth. Genet's heroes are young hustlers, sailors dependent on the mother ship, young men in jail, soldiers of occupation. His thieves do not rob to get rich, but to get spending money or money to squander and show off. This thwarted juvenilism is the same thing as the exclusive homosexuality of his world, with its phallic proving and phallic adoration. Yet with this unpromising material, he performs a poetic miracle.

He does it by stripping away the conceit, the conformity and the one-upping. He accepts, fully and fundamentally, the true situation of degradation, humiliation, uselessness, and terror in which his fellows live. In this he is like Dostoevski. He does so with perfect awareness and even, as a writer, with deliberate calculation. For instance, he begins *Les Pompes Funèbres* as if he had asked: What is the most degrading and offensive episode possible for middle-class French readers? Yet his aim is *not* to offend, he is not defensive; it is that, like a classical playwright, he wants to establish his premises at once: that in the situation in which he finds himself, *these* are the things that work for him as an artist, that are still alive.

In a speech on delinquency (banned from the radio), he explained that if he tried to write about the bourgeois and their important doings, his pen stuck, he had nothing to say; but if he turned to these young criminals (really juvenile delinquents), his thoughts took wing, his style glowed. Therefore he *knows* they are more heroic, they are the superior people.

That is, he drops the defenses of the underprivileged boy-man and gives himself completely to his own riches as an inspired artist; and the effect is not sensational—nor even bravado—but, as the images soar and the feeling becomes more tender and anguished and the thought more profound, our normal valuation of things is indeed swept away, and is succeeded by a living confusion. Naturally, then, his book is rewarded by coming to the cataclysmic little sentence: *"T'as été malheureux, hein?"* (You been unhappy, haven't you?) This *truth* is, of course, precisely what the tough juvenile delinquent could in fact never say—but neither could most adults. We are back to total abandonment, and there is nothing to do but bawl.

When the conceit, the being cool, the mask-face, are taken away, the kids at once appear in their variety, color, lyric speech, and graceful and vigorous poses, very different from either the usual delinquent sullenness or the conventionality of the resigned Beats. Having himself not achieved independent perspective to view them from, Genet cannot, of course, treat them fully as characters in their real place in nature. But again his art does not fail them. What he presents is his own and their existent fact: how these shapes appear as fantasy-objects for himself and one another. (He is writing as an heir of Proust.) He uses as the basis of his narrative manner the evoked serial daydreams of schoolgirls and adolescent boys, that are often masturbation fantasies. This is a literary innovation.

The importance of Genet for our purposes is this: By a scrupulously honest artistic method he creates from this unpromising material a world that has interest and value. Without being phony, he makes the doings of ignorant and self-destructive kids glow with nobility and religious significance; he makes them more *worth while* than the apparently adult doings in our standard writers. Now an artist demonstrates his world. If Genet can write more beautiful books about them, then they have more love and nature in them, for nothing comes from nothing. Like Miller and the Beat writers, Genet also accepts what is, whatever it is; but in their world "whatever it is" is ashen dull, whereas at the level of Genet's disaffected juveniles, it begins to glow a little; some live embers are uncovered.

And indeed, the fatalistic self-destruction of the kids struggling for life in an environment not suited to produce great human beings, is more interesting than the successful doings of that society.

9.

It is not interesting *enough*; for they are juvenile delinquents and do not have enough world. As soon as we ask questions from the world of great culture and society, these boys begin to be, in Robert Lindner's phrase, rebels without a cause, and that is not interesting.

Here is the pathos of literary critics like Lionel Trilling who demand that our novels illuminate the manners and morals of prevailing society. Professor Trilling is right, because otherwise what use are they for *us?* But he is wrong-headed, because he does not see that the burden of proof is not on the artist but on our society. If such convenient criticism of prevalent life does not get to be written, it is likely that the prevailing society is not inspiring enough; its humanity is not great enough, it does not have enough future, to be worth the novelist's trouble.

The history of contemporary novel-writing tells the story very clearly. Hemingway, for instance, is a pretty good writer and he caught the spirit of the young men of a whole generation; but this ideal, we have seen, turns out to be the conceited "proving" of tribes of junior executives and juvenile delinquents. Faulkner is a pretty good writer but his world is resigned (this is the meaning of its parochialism), and his work turns out to be a very complicated way of being Beat. In my own *The Empire City*, I undertook the task of not giving up *any* claim of culture and humanity, but my characters then turn out to be far out of this world. Meantime there has developed a counterstream of writing that has given up the task of integrating, and depicts instead the situation as it is, whatever it is: so Céline, Miller, Genet, Burroughs. But among the many virtues of this school, conspicuously absent is edification.

XI. THE MISSING COMMUNITY

I.

THE USE of history, Benjamin Nelson used to say, is to rescue from oblivion the lost causes of the past. History is especially important when those lost causes haunt us in the present as unfinished business.

I have often spoken in this essay of the "missed revolutions that we have inherited." My idea is that it is not with impunity that fundamental social changes fail to take place at the appropriate time; the following generations are embarrassed and confused by their lack. This subject warrants a special study. Some revolutions fail to occur; most half-occur or are compromised, attaining some of their objectives and resulting in significant social changes, but giving up on others, resulting in ambiguous values in the social whole that would not have occurred if the change had been more thorough-going. For in general, a profound revolutionary program in any field projects a new workable kind of behavior, a new nature of man, a new whole society; just as the traditional society it tries to replace is a whole society that the revolutionists think is out of date. But a compromised revolution tends to disrupt the tradition without achieving a new social balance.

It is the argument of this book that *the accumulation of the missed and compromised revolutions of modern times, with their consequent ambiguities and social imbalances, has fallen, and must fall, most heavily on the young, making it hard to grow up.*

A man who has attained maturity and independence can pick and choose among the immense modern advances and somewhat wield them as his way of life. If he has a poor society, an adult cannot be very happy, he will not have simple goals nor achieve classical products, but he can fight and work anyway. But for children and adolescents it is indispensable to have a coherent, fairly simple and viable society to grow up into; otherwise they are confused, and some are squeezed out. Tradition has been broken, yet there is no new standard to affirm. Culture becomes eclectic, sensational, or phony. (Our present culture is all three.) A successful revolution establishes a new community. A missed revolution makes irrelevant the community that persists. And a compromised revolution tends to shatter the community that was, without an adequate substitute. But as we argued in a previous chapter, it is precisely for the young that the geographical and historical community and its patriotism are the important environment, as they draw away from their parents and until they can act on their own with fully developed powers.

In this chapter, let us collect the missed or compromised fundamental social changes that we have had occasion to mention; calling attention to what *was* achieved and what *failed* to be achieved, and the consequent confused situation which then actually confronts the youth growing up.

2.

Let us start with the physical environment.

Technocracy. In our own century, philosophers of the new technology, like Veblen, Geddes, or Fuller, succeeded in making efficiency and know-how the chief ethical values of the folk, creating a mystique of "production," and a kind of streamlined esthetics. But they did not succeed in wresting management from the businessmen and creating their own world of a neat and transparent physical plant and a practical economics of production and distribution. The actual results have been slums of works of engineering, confused and useless overproduction, gadgetry, and new tribes of middlemen, promoters, and advertisers.

Urbanism. As Le Corbusier and Gropius urged, we have increasingly the plan and style of functional architecture; biological standards of housing; scientific study of traffic and city services; some zoning; and the construction of large-scale projects. But nowhere is realized the ideal of over-all community planning, the open green city, or the organic relation of work, living, and play. The actual results have been increasing commutation and traffic, segregated ghettos, a "functional" style little different from packaging, and the tendency to squeeze out some basic urban functions, such as recreation or schooling, to be squeezed out altogether.

Garden City. The opposite numbers, the Garden City planners after Ebenezer Howard, have achieved some planned communities protected by greenbelts. But they did not get their integrated towns, planned for industry, local commerce, and living. The result is that actual suburbs and garden cities are dormitories with a culture centering around small children and absence of the wage earner; and such "plans" as the so-called shopping centers disrupt such village communities as there were. The movement to conserve the wilds cannot withstand the cars, so that all areas are invaded and regulated.

3.

Let us proceed to economic and social changes.

New Deal. The Keynesian economics of the New Deal has cushioned the business cycle and maintained nearly full employment. It has not achieved its ideal of social balance between public and private works. The result is an expanding production increasingly consisting of corporation boondoggling.

Syndicalism. Industrial workers have won their unions, obtained better wages and working conditions, and affirmed the dignity of labor. But they gave up their ideal of workers' management, technical education, and concern for the utility of their labor. The result is that a vast majority couldn't care less about what they make, and the "labor movement" is losing force.

Class Struggle. The working class has achieved a striking repeal of the iron law of wages; it has won a minimum wage and social security. But the goal of an equalitarian or freely mobile society has been given up, as has the solidarity of the underprivileged. The actual result is an increasing rigidity of statuses; some of the underprivileged tending to drop out of society altogether. On the other hand, the cultural equality that has been achieved has been the degradation of the one popular culture to the lowest common denominator.

Production for Use. This socialist goal has been missed, resulting in many of the other failures here listed.

Sociology. During the past century, the sociologists have achieved their aim of dealing with mankind in its natural groups or groups with common problems, rather than as isolated individuals or a faceless mass. Social science has replaced many prejudices and ideologies of vested interests. But on the whole, social scientists have given up their aim of fundamental social change and an open-experimental method determining its goals as it went along: the pragmatist ideal of society as a laboratory for freedom and self-correcting humanity. The actual result is an emphasis on "socializing" and "belonging," with the loss of nature, culture, group solidarity and group variety, and individual excellence.

4.

Next, political and constitutional reforms.

Democracy. The democratic revolution succeeded in extending formal self-government and opportunity to nearly everybody, regardless of birth, property, or education. But it gave up the ideal of the town meeting, with the initiative and personal involvement that alone could train people in self-government and give them practical knowledge of political issues. The actual result has been the formation of a class of politicians who govern, and who are themselves symbolic front figures.

The Republic. Correspondingly, the self-determination won by the American Revolution for the regional states, that should have made possible real political experimentation, soon gave way to a national conformity; nor has the nation as a whole conserved its resources and maintained its ideals. The result is a deadening centralism, with neither local patriotism nor national patriotism. The best people do not offer themselves for public office, and no one has the aim of serving the Republic.

Freedom of Speech. Typical is the fate of the hard-won Constitutional freedoms, such as freedom of speech. Editors and publishers have given up trying to give an effective voice to important but unpopular opinions. Anything can be printed, but the powerful interests have the big presses. Only the safe opinion is proclaimed and other opinion is swamped.

Liberalism. The liberal revolution succeeded in shaking off onerous government controls on enterprise, but it did not persist to its goal of real public wealth as the result of free enterprise and honestly informed choice on the market. The actual result is an economy dominated by monopolies, in which the earnest individual entrepreneur or inventor, who could perform a public service, is actively discouraged; and consumer demand is increasingly synthetic.

Agrarianism. Conversely, the Jeffersonian ideal of a proud and independent productive yeomanry, with natural family morals and a co-operative community spirit, did in fact energize settling the West and providing the basis for our abundance. But because it has failed to cope with technological changes and to withstand speculation, "farming as a way of life" has succumbed to cash-cropping dependent on distant markets, and is ridden with mortgages, tenancy, and hired labor. Yet it maintains a narrow rural morality and isolationist politics, is a sucker for the mass culture of Madison Avenue and Hollywood, and in the new cities (e.g., in California, where farmers have migrated) is a bulwark against genuine city culture.

Liberty. Constitutional safeguards of person were won. But despite the increasing concentration of state power and mass pressures, no effort was made to give to individuals and small groups new means easily to avail themselves of the safeguards. The result is that there is no longer the striking individuality of free men; even quiet nonconformity is hounded; and there is no asylum from coast to coast.

Fraternity. This short-lived ideal of the French Revolution, animating a whole people and uniting all classes as a community, soon gave way to a dangerous nationalism. The ideal somewhat revived as the solidarity of the working class, but this too has faded into either philanthropy or "belonging."

Brotherhood of Races. The Civil War won formal rights for Negroes, but failed to win social justice and factual democracy. The actual result has been segregation, and fear and ignorance for both whites and blacks.

Pacifism. This revolution has been entirely missed.

5.

Let us proceed to some more general moral premises of modern times.

Reformation. The Protestant Reformation won the possibility of living religiously in the world, freed individuals from the domination of the priest, and led, indirectly, to the toleration of private conscience. But it failed to withstand the secular power; it did not cultivate the meaning of vocation as a community function; and in most sects the spirit of the churches did not spring from their living congregations but was handed down as dogma and ascetic discipline. The final result has been secularism, individualism, the subordination of human beings to a rational economic system, and churches irrelevant to practical community life. Meantime, acting merely as a negative force, the jealous sectarian conscience has driven religion out of social thought.

Modern Science. The scientific revolution associated with the name of Galileo freed thinking of superstition and academic tradition and won attention to the observation of nature. But it failed to modify and extend its method to social and moral matters, and indeed science has gotten further and further from ordinary experience. With the dominance of science and applied science in our times, the result has been a specialist class of scientists and technicians, the increasing ineptitude of the average person, a disastrous dichotomy of "neutral" facts versus "arbitrary" values, and a superstition of scientism that has put people out of touch with nature, and also has aroused a growing hostility to science.

Enlightenment. The Enlightenment unseated age-old tyrannies of state and church and won a triumph of reason over authority. But its universalism failed to survive the rising nationalisms except in special sciences and learning, and its ideal of encyclopedic reason as the passionate guide to life degenerated to the nineteenth-century hope for progress through science and learning. And we now have an internationalism without brotherhood or peace, even concealing science as a strategic weapon; and a general sentiment that the rule of reason is infinitely impractical.

Honesty. The rebellion for honest speech that we associate with Ibsen, Flaubert, etc., and also with the muckrakers broke down the hypocrisy of Victorian prudishness and of exploiting pillars of society; it reopened discussion and renovated language; and it weakened official censorship. But it failed to insist on the close relation between honest speech and corresponding action. The result has been a weakening of the obligation to act according to speech, so that, ironically, the real motives of public and private behavior are more in the dark than ever.

Popular Culture. This ideal, that we may associate in literature with the name of Sam Johnson and the Fleet Street journalists, in the plastic arts with William Morris and Ruskin, freed culture from aristocratic and snobbish patrons. It made thought and design relevant to everyday manners. But it did not succeed in establishing an immediate relation between the writer or artist and his audience. The result is that the popular culture is controlled by hucksters and promoters as though it were a saleable commodity, and our society, inundated by cultural commodities, remains uncultivated.

6.

Finally, some reforms directly connected with children and adolescents.

No Child Labor. Children have been rescued from the exploitation and training of factories and sweat shops. But, relying on the public schools and the apprentice-training in an expanding and open economy, the reformers did not develop a philosophy of capacity and vocation. Nor, since there were many small jobs, did they face the problems of a growing boy needing to earn some money. In our days, the result is that growing youths are idle and vocationally useless, and often economically desperate; and the schools, on the contrary, become apprentice-training paid for by public money.

Compulsory Education. This gave to all children a certain equality of opportunity in an open expanding industrial society. Formal elementary discipline was sufficient when the environment was educative and provided opportunities for advancement. In our circumstances, formal literacy is less relevant, and overcrowding and official interference make individual attention and real teaching impossible; so that it could be said that the schools are as stupefying as they are educative, and compulsory education is often like jail.

Sexual Revolution. This has accomplished a freeing of animal functioning in general, has pierced repression, importantly relaxed inhibition, weakened legal and social sanctions, and diminished the strict animal-training of small children. The movement has not so much failed as that it is still in process, strongly resisted by inherited prejudices, fears, and jealousies. By and large it has not won practical freedom for older children and adolescents. The actual present result is that they are trapped by inconsistent rules, suffer because of excessive stimulation and inadequate discharge, and become preoccupied with sexual thoughts as if these were the whole of life.

Permissiveness. Children have more freedom of spontaneous behavior, and their dignity and spirit are not crushed by humiliating punishments in school and in very many homes. But this permissiveness has not extended to provide also means and conditions:

Young folk might be sexually free but have no privacy; they are free to be angry, but have no asylum to escape from home, and no way to get their own money. Besides, where upbringing is permissive, it is necessary to have strong values and esteemed behavior at home and in the community, so that the child can have worth-while goals to structure his experience; and of course it is just these that are lacking. So permissiveness often leads to anxiety and weakness instead of confidence and strength.

Progressive Education. This radical proposal, aimed at solving the dilemmas of education in the modern circumstances of industrialism and democracy, was never given a chance. It succeeded in destroying the faculty psychology in the interests of educating the whole person, and in emphasizing group experience, but failed to introduce learning-by-doing with real problems. The actual result of the gains has been to weaken the academic curriculum and foster adjustment to society as it is.

7.

Let us consider the beginning, the ending, and the middle of these little paragraphs.

The headings printed in bold type are, in their summation, a kind of program of modern man. It is evident that every one of these twenty-odd positions was invented-and-discovered as a response to specific historical conditions. The political positions were developed to oppose the absolutism of the kings who had unified the warring feudal states; the program for children and adolescents has been a response to modern industrialism and urbanism; and so forth. But it does *not* follow, as some sociologists think, that they can therefore be superseded and forgotten as conditions change.

Consider the following of C. Wright Mills: "The ideals that we Westerners associate with the classic, liberal, bourgeois period of modern culture may well be rooted in this one historical stage of this one type of society. Such ideals as personal freedom and cultural autonomy may not be inherent, necessary features of cultural life as such." This is like saying that tragic poetry or mathematics was "rooted" in the Greek way of life and is not "inherently" human. This kind of thinking is the final result of the recent social-scientific attitude that culture is added onto a featureless animal, rather than being the invention-and-discovery of human powers. This is effectually to give up the modern enterprise altogether. But we will not give it up. New conditions will be the conditions of, now, this kind of man, stubbornly insisting on the ideals that he has learned he has in him to meet.

Yet the modern positions are not even easily consistent with one another, to form a coherent program. There have been bitter conflicts between Liberty and Equality, Science and Faith, Technology and Syndicalism, and so forth. Nevertheless, we will not give up one or the other, but will arduously try to achieve them all and *make* a coherent program. And indeed, experience has taught that the failure in one of these ideals at once entails failure in others. For instance, failure in social justice weakens political freedom, and this compromises scientific and religious autonomy. "If we continue to be without a socialist movement," says Frank Marquart, "we may end up without a labor movement." The setback of progressive education makes the compulsory school system more hopeless, and this now threatens permissiveness and sexual freedom; and so forth. So we struggle to perfect all these positions, one buttressing another, if we are to fulfill our unique modern destiny.

There is no doubt, too, that in our plight new modern positions will be added to these, and these too will be compromised, aborted, their prophetic urgency bureaucratized and ironically transformed into the opposite. But there it is.

8.

If we now collect the actual, often ironical, results of so much noble struggle, we get a clear *but exaggerated* picture of our American society. It has: slums of engineering—boondoggling production—chaotic congestion—tribes of middlemen—basic city functions squeezed out—garden cities for children—indifferent workmen—underprivileged on a dole—empty "belonging" without nature or culture—front politicians—no patriotism—an empty nationalism bound for a cataclysmically disastrous finish—wise opinion swamped—enterprise sabotaged by monopoly—prejudice rising—religion otiose—the popular culture debased—science specialized—science secret—the average man inept—youth idle and truant—youth sexually suffering and sexually obsessed—youth without goals—poor schools.

This picture is not unjust, but it is, again, exaggerated. For it omits, of course, all the positive factors and the ongoing successes. We have a persisting grand culture. There is a steady advance of science, scholarship, and the fine arts. A steady improvement in health and medicine. An economy of abundance and, in many ways, a genuine civil peace and a stubborn affirming of democracy. And most of all there are the remarkable resilience and courage that belong to human beings. Also, the Americans, for all their folly and conformity, are often thrillingly sophisticated and impatient of hypocrisy.

Yet there is one grim actuality that even this exaggerated picture does not reveal, the creeping defeatism and surrender by default to the organized system of the state and semimonopolies. International Business Machines and organized psychologists, we have seen, effactually determine the method of school examinations and personnel selection. As landlords, Webb and Knapp and Metropolitan Life decide what our domestic habits should be; and, as "civic developers," they plan communities, even though their motive is simply a "long-term modest profit" on investment while millions are ill housed. The good of General Motors and the nation are inseparable, says Secretary Wilson—even though the cars are demonstrably ruinous for the cities, ruinous for the young, etc. Madison Avenue and Hollywood not only debauch their audiences, but they pre-empt the means of communication, so nothing else can exist. With only occasional flagrant breaches of legality, the increasingly interlocking police forces and the FBI make people cowed and speechless. That Americans can allow this kind of thing instead of demolishing it with a blow of the paw like a strong lion, is the psychology of missed revolutions.

9.

For our positive purposes in this book, it is the middle parts of our paragraphs that warrant study: the failures, the fallings-short, the compromises. Imagine that these modern radical positions had been more fully achieved: we should have a society where:

A premium is placed on technical improvement and on the engineering style of functional simplicity and clarity. Where the community is planned as a whole, with an organic integration of work, living, and play. Where buildings have the variety of their real functions with the uniformity of the prevailing technology. Where a lot of money is spent on public goods. Where workers are technically educated and have a say in management. Where no one drops out of society and there is an easy mobility of classes. Where production is primarily for use. Where social groups are laboratories for solving their own problems experimentally. Where democracy begins in the town meeting, and a man seeks office only because he has a program. Where regional variety is encouraged and there is pride in the Republic. And young men are free of conscription. Where all feel themselves citizens of the universal Republic of Reason. Where it is the policy to give an adequate voice to the unusual and unpopular opinion, and to give a trial and a market to new enterprise. Where people are not afraid to make friends. Where races are factually equal. Where vocation is sought out and cultivated as God-given capacity, to be conserved and embellished, and where the church is the spirit of its congregation. Where ordinary experience is habitually scientifically assayed by the average man. Where it is felt that the suggestion of reason is practical. And speech leads to the corresponding action. Where the popular culture is a daring and passionate culture. Where children can make themselves useful and earn their own money. Where their sexuality is taken for granted. Where the community carries on its important adult business and the children fall in at their own pace. And where education is concerned with fostering human powers as they develop in the growing child.

In such an utopian society, as was aimed at by modern radicals but has not eventuated, it would be very easy to grow up. There would be plenty of objective, worth-while activities for a child to observe, fall in with, do, learn, improvise on his own. That is to say, it is not the spirit of modern times that makes our society difficult for the young; it is that that spirit has not sufficiently realized itself.

In this light, the present plight of the young is not surprising. In the rapid changes, people have not kept enough in mind that the growing young also exist and the world must fit their needs. So instead, we have the present phenomena of excessive attention to the children as such, in psychology and suburbs, and coping with "juvenile delinquency" as if it were an entity. Adults fighting for some profoundly conceived fundamental change naturally give up, exhausted, when they have achieved some gain that makes life tolerable again and seems to be the substance of their demand. But to grow up, the young need a world of finished situations and society made whole again.

10.

Indeed, the bother with the above little utopian sketch is that many adults would be restive in such a stable modern world if it were achieved. They would say: It is a fine place for growing boys. I agree with this criticism.

I think the case is as follows: Every profound new proposal, of culture or institution, invents and discovers a new property of "Human Nature." Henceforth it is going to be in *these* terms that a young fellow will grow up and find his identity and his task. So if we accumulate the revolutionary proposals of modern times, we have named the *goals of modern education*. We saw that it was the aim of Progressive Education to carry this program through.

But education is not life. The existing situation of a grown man is to confront an uninvented and undiscovered present. Unfortunately, *at* present, he must also try to perfect his unfinished past: this bad inheritance is part of the existing situation, and must be stoically worked through.

II.

Let me repeat the proposition of this chapter: *It is the missed revolutions of modern times—the fallings-short and the compromises—that add up to the conditions that make it hard for the young to grow up in our society.*

The existing local community, region, and nation is the real environment of the young. Conversely, we could define community spirit and patriotism as the conviction in which it is possible to grow up. (An independent and not too defeated adult confronts a broader historical, international, and cosmic scene as his environment for action.)

Modern times have been characterized by fundamental changes occurring with unusual rapidity. These have shattered tradition but often have not succeeded in creating a new whole community. We have no recourse to going back, there is nothing to go back to. If we are to have a stable and whole community in which the young can grow to manhood, we must painfully perfect the revolutionary modern tradition we have.

This stoical resolve is, paradoxically, a *conservative* proposition, aiming at stability and social balance. For often it is not a question of making innovations, but of catching up and restoring the right proportions. But no doubt, in our runaway, one-sided way of life, the proposal to conserve human resources and develop human capacities has become a radical innovation.

Right proportion cannot be restored by adding a few new teachers formally equivalent to the growth in population. Probably we need a million new minds and more put to teaching. Even Dr. Conant says that we must nearly double our present annual expenditure on education for teaching alone, not counting plant and the central schools he wants. And this does not take into account essentially new fields such as making sense of adult leisure.

It must be understood that with the increase in population and crowding, the number and variety of human services increase disproportionately, and the laissez-faire areas, both geographical and social, decrease. Therefore the *units* of human service, such as school classes or the clientele of a physician (and even political districts?), ought to be made *smaller*, to avoid the creation of masses: mass teaching, mass medicine, mass psychotherapy, mass penology, mass politics. Yet our normal schools and medical schools cannot cope with even the arithmetic increase.

Right proportion requires reversing the goal in vocational guidance, from fitting the man to the machine and chopping him down to fit, to finding the opportunity in the economy that brings out the man, and if you can't find such an opportunity, make it. This involves encouraging new small enterprises and unblocking and perhaps underwriting invention. Again, if at present production is inhuman and stupid, it is that too few minds are put to it: this can be remedied by giving the workman more voice in production and the kind of training to make that voice wise.

Probably, right proportion involves considerable decentralizing and increasing the rural-urban ratio. Certainly it involves transforming the scores of thousands of neglected small places, hopelessly dull and same, into interesting villages that someone could be proud of. A lot of the booming production has got to go into publicly useful goods, proportionate to the apparently forgotten fact that it is on public grounds, because of public investment, and the growth of population, that private wealth is produced and enjoyed. We have to learn again, what city man always used to know, that belonging to the city, to its squares, its market, its neighborhoods, and its high culture, is a public good; it is not a field for "investment to yield a long-term modest profit." A proportionate allocation of public funds, again, is not likely to devote more money to escape roads convenient for automobiles than to improving the city center. (If I may make a pleasant suggestion, we could underwrite a handsome program for serious adult leisure by a 10 per cent luxury tax on new cars; it would yield over a billion.)

Since prosperity itself has made it more difficult for the underprivileged immigrant to get started, right proportion requires devoting all the more money and ingenuity to helping him find himself and get started. (In such cases, by the way, ingenuity and friendly aid are more important than money, as some of our settlement houses in New York have beautifully demonstrated.) And some way will have to be found, again, for a man to be decently poor, to work for a subsistence without necessarily choosing to involve himself in the total high-standard economy. One way of achieving this would be directly producing subsistence goods in distinction from the total economy.

In arts and letters, there is a right balance between the customary social standard and creative novelty, and between popular entertainment and esthetic experience. Then, to offset Hollywood and Madison Avenue, we must have hundreds of new little theaters, little magazines, and journals of dissenting opinion with means of circulation; because it is only in such that new things can develop and begin to win their way in the world.

It is essential that our democratic legislatures and public spokesmen be balanced by more learned and honorable voices that, as in Britain, can thoughtfully broach fundamental issues of community plan, penal code, morality, cultural tone, with some certainty of reaching a public forum and some possibility of being effective. For there is no other way of getting the best to lead, to have some conviction and even passionate intensity, to save America from going to managers, developers, and politicians by default.

Certainly right proportion, in a society tightly organized and conformist, requires a vast increase in the jealous safeguard of civil liberties, to put the fear of God back into local police, district attorneys, and the Federal Bureau of Investigation.

Here is a program of more than a dozen essential changes, all practicable, all difficult. A wiser and more experienced author could suggest a dozen more.

12.

Let me expand one of these: Making sense of adult leisure.

What are the present goals of the philosophers of leisure, for instance, the National Recreation Association? and now imagine those goals achieved. There would be a hundred million adults who have cultured hobbies to occupy their spare time: some expert on the flute, some with do-it-yourself kits, some good at chess and go, some square dancing, some camping out and enjoying nature, and all playing various athletic games. Leaf through the entire catalogue of the National Recreation Association, take all the items together, apply them to one hundred million adults—and there is the picture. (This costs *at present* forty billion dollars a year, according to the guess of Robert Coughlan in *Life*.) The philosophy of leadership, correspondingly, is to get people to participate—everybody must "belong."

Now even if all these people were indeed getting deep personal satisfaction from these activities, this is a dismaying picture. It doesn't add up to anything. It isn't important. There is no ethical necessity in it, no standard. *One cannot waste a hundred million people that way.*

The error is in the NRA's basic concept of recreation. Let me quote from a recent editorial in *Recreation*: Recreation is "any activity participated in . . . merely for the enjoyment it affords. . . . The rewards of recreational activities depend upon the degree to which they provide outlets for personal interests." (Outlets again, as in the Governor's prescription for the juvenile delinquents.) But enjoyment is *not* a goal, it is a feeling that accompanies important ongoing activity; pleasure, as Freud said, is always dependent on function.

From the present philosophy of leisure, no new culture can emerge. What is lacking is worth-while community necessity, as the serious leisure, the σχολή of the Athenians had communal necessity, whether in the theater, the games, the architecture and festivals, or even the talk.

That we find it hard to think in these terms is a profound sign of our social imbalance. Yet we do *not* need, as Dr. Douglass claimed in the passage we quoted above, "a new ethics, a new esthetic." For the activities of serious leisure are right there, glaring, in our communities, to avoid shame and achieve grandeur.

But the question is: If there is little interest, honor, or manliness in the working part of our way of life, can we hope for much in the leisure part?

13.

The best exposition of what I have been trying to say in this chapter is the classic of conservative thinking, Coleridge's *On the Constitution of the Church and State.* His point in that essay is simply this: *In order to have citizens, you must first be sure that you have produced men.* There must therefore be a large part of the common wealth specifically devoted to cultivating "freedom and civilization," and especially to the education of the young growing up.

CONCLUSION

I.

IT IS NORMAL for sober adult citizens to take the wildness and absurdities of the younger generation tolerantly and with a touch of envious admiration, just as those adults who are more inhibited and insecure always must deplore them and feel that things are going to the dogs. In solidly established Augustan ages, such as the period in England between 1688 and the Industrial Revolution, the excesses of well-brought-up young men are even socially obligatory, under the style of sowing wild oats. In outrageously bad ages, such as the period in Russia during the last half of the nineteenth century, rebellious youth is esteemed as the hoped-for agent of change.

These attitudes all make sense and apply in our times too. In this book I have no doubt been variously tolerant, envying, deploring, approving, and esteeming. It is not an interesting question whether or not our present Youth Problems are fundamentally different from those of other times, whether or not they will blow over; whether the Beats are a fad and the Delinquents no worse than in 1850. What I have tried to show, rather, is this: that such problems, by their form and content, test and criticize the society in which they occur. The burden of proof, as to who is "wrong," does not rest with the young but always with the system of society. Some societies bear it easily; our society is not outrageously bad, but it is far from adequate, and it stands the test poorly.

A poor showing is proved by the fact that young people are paid attention to as a group, as they must be if they are importantly "in the right"; and there are Fathers and Sons, or Flaming Youth, or Youth Problems. In America, our Flaming Youth and Youth Problems have occurred after great wars, for then the adults really disgraced themselves. (Appendix F contrasts these two periods.)

2.

We must distinguish between two kinds of special attention paid these days by the Americans to their young. The first is the effect of the disappointment and resignation of the older generation—it is a kind of Lear complex: they themselves have failed to be men and women; they are therefore both timid and guilty before the young. With respect to children, this adult resignation results in the child-centered suburb and the emphasis on "psychology." With regard to the adolescents, it appears as a craving for youth for oneself, to act like youth, to give in to youth, meaning by youth the teen-age foolishness that still has some vitality. This comes to the eleven-billion-dollar sales to teen-agers, for what can these kids think up except to imitate the customs of their elders? Naturally, once there is such a vast market, sales-minded publicists give most earnest attention to youth. This kind of youth is far from "problematic." It seems that it will be even more worthless than its parents, and God pity us.

But the second kind of attention is that claimed by the problematic who are importantly in the right. They are problematic because they try to vomit up the poisonous mores. They won't eat them— they are sick because they have eaten too many of them. And they are "in the right" because they are obviously in the right, everybody knows it.

3.

Flaming Youth of the twenties had salutary effects. It speeded the sexual revolution and the new permissive psychology of child care. It put the seal on the new simple prose. Our present round of Youth Problems has been dampened and delayed by war anxiety and disillusionment, yet even so it will have, it has already had, positive successes.

The young people have latched on to the movement in art that is the strongest in our generation, the so-called Action Painting or New York School. In music, the matching numbers are the percussive atonalists like Varèse, or the *musique concrète* made of the tapes. There is an Action Architecture. Artaud preached an Action Theater. I have tried to show that this disposition to go back to the material elements and the real situation, is intrinsic and spontaneous in the art action and poetry action of some of the young groups. This means that they are not off the main track. It can be said that this Action art lacks content, it does not carry enough humanity. I think this is true. But it is just its eschewing of a stereotyped or corrupt content while *nevertheless* affirming the incorruptible content of the artist's own action, that *is* its starved and brave humanity—a step beyond the nihilism of Dada—a beginning.

Young people have hit, too, on rituals of expression in face-to-face groups, and in provoking the public audience as a face-to-face group, that are clearly better than the canned popular culture or the academic culture. But these things are in line with what the best sociologists and community planners are also after. It is a move against anomie and the lonely crowd. Naturally it is drunken and threadbare.

The English Angry Young Men, again, have specialized in piercing the fraudulent speech of public spokesmen and in trying to force them to put up or shut up. They have learned to cry out "Shame!" When a million Americans—and not only young men—can learn to do this, we shall have a most salutary change.

Disaffected young groups in America, England, and France have also flatly taken direct action in race relations. They present racial brotherhood and miscegenation as a *fait accompli.*

More generally, all the recent doings of problematic youth, whether in the middle class or among the underprivileged juvenile delinquents, have had a stamp of at least partly springing from some existent situation, whatever it is, and of responding with direct action, rather than keeping up appearances and engaging in role playing. There is also among them a lot of phony role playing, but no more than in present acceptable society, and rather less than in the average young man or adolescent who has a "line." I think that the existential reality of Beat, Angry, and Delinquent behavior is indicated by the fact that other, earnest, young fellows who are not themselves disaffected and who are not phony, are eager to hear about them, and respect them. One cannot visit a university without being asked a hundred questions about them.

Finally, some of these groups are achieving a simpler fraternity, animality, and sexuality than we have had, at least in America, in a long, long time.

4.

This valuable program is in direct contrast to the mores of what we have in this book been calling "the organized system," its role playing, its competitiveness, its canned culture, its public relations, and its avoidance of risk and self-exposure. That system and its mores are death to the spirit, and any rebellious group will naturally raise a contrasting banner.

Now the organized system is very powerful and in its full tide of success, apparently sweeping everything before it in science, education, community planning, labor, the arts, not to speak of business and politics where it is indigenous. Let me say that we of the previous generation who have been sickened and enraged to see earnest and honest effort and humane culture swamped by this muck, are heartened by the crazy young allies, and we think that perhaps the future may make more sense than we dared hope.

APPENDICES

APPENDIX A

December 12, 1959

Commissioner of Education
Albany

Dear Dr. Allen,

I understand that the case of James Worley of Croton Falls has come
to you for review. Allow me to say something in his behalf.

In content, his original protesting action (refusing to prepare a
two-week lesson plan) seems to me beyond doubt correct. I myself
have taught every age from ten-year-olds through Ph.D. candidates
and older adults; it has been my universal experience that formal
preparation of a lesson plan beyond the next hour or two is not only
unrealistic but can be positively harmful and rigidifying, for it interferes with the main thing, the contact between the teacher and his
class. Worley's disagreement with the administrative order is, to me,
simply evidence that he is a good teacher and knows what the right
teaching relation is. A teacher who would *seriously* comply with the
order would likely be a poor teacher. (Our model must always be the
Socratic dialogue, for the aim is *not* to convey some information but
to get the information across as part of the student's nature and second nature, so he can make an individual and creative use of it.) On
the other hand, if the compliance is not serious it is a waste of time;
and, as you know well, teachers are burdened with paper work, much
of which is absolutely necessary.

In form, his protest was certainly insubordinate. But obviously each of us has the moral and social duty to draw the line somewhere against obedience to error. Worley has drawn it at a very crucial point, namely, where the order interferes with the right performance of the job. In the end this is the sacred and final obligation of every professional, to do the *work* and to defend the conditions under which the work can be done well.

The issue is of immense importance. Our country is being systematically emasculated by a sickening waste of human resources. The efforts of a Dr. Conant to salvage some scientific talent are ludicrously inadequate to the main problem, which is precisely the difficulties created by our social relations that keep the inventor from his materials, the workman from honest labor, the teacher from his students and subject matter, and the artist from his public. We cannot afford to throw away good teachers to save face for mistaken administrators. It is the glory of good administration precisely to *smooth the path* for objective work to proceed. Therefore I urge you to intervene in this case and reinstate Mr. Worley.

Copy to Gov. Rockefeller

Sincerely,
Paul Goodman
New York City

(The appeal of Mr. Worley was rejected by the Commissioner who said that, though he was much in the right, he ought to have acted through the proper channels.)

APPENDIX B

New Theater and the Unions*

I WANT to discuss a mistaken policy of certain theater craft-unions, and suggest a remedy. The matter has an importance in itself, because in recent years there has been a growth in new theater "off Broadway" that may, if it is encouraged, come to some real living theater. The union policy has been a discouragement—almost as bad as the unavailability of real estate—and it has been attacked with the usual jeering debater's points by the tribe unsympathetic to unionism as such. But especially I want to discuss this question because it is, *in parvo*, a remarkably apt case of what is becoming the chief problem of our contemporary culture: how to live and breathe creatively in a society whose technology and organizations unavoidably make for conformity.

Without mentioning names, let me tell the story concretely in a case where I happen to know the facts. Here is a company devoted to new theater that has now for nearly ten years kept at work under arduous conditions, in larger or smaller quarters as it could get or build them by their own and their friends' voluntary labor. The nucleus of the company is a group of theater-people, actors, musicians, dancers, and writers—some of them of great reputation—who have all of them, for from ten to fifty years, given themselves, often financially unrewarded, to the development of our modern art. They are a constellation comparable, for example, to the fine group that cooperated as the Provincetown Players. Nobody would question that

*From *Dissent*, Autumn, 1959.

they are devoted to the growth of theater and not to making money; they try to make enough to sustain themselves.

Now in casting their productions, they want to employ Equity actors. Many of those who voluntarily built the place they now occupy are Equity actors, and naturally, having laid the bricks, they want to act. By and large, professional actors belong to Equity and most of the best actors are professional, so you want to cast them. Now the situation among actors is as follows: (1) About 95 per cent are chronically unemployed. (2) Actors have a kind of hunger, a need, to act. (3) Understanding this, Equity permits its members to work, in certain circumstances, for as little as $40 a week, regarding this figure, I guess, as pretty near the decent subsistence minimum that a person must have, no matter what his enthusiasm or other satisfaction in the work. When, then, this company sends out a casting call in the professional journals, there are hundreds of responses from actors eager for any part, hoping to advance their careers by appearing and getting notices, and many of them glad to work in a cultured noncommercial atmosphere on intrinsically more interesting material, where they can learn something. That is, small noncommercial theaters of high standards, and trained professional actors, are mutually useful to one another; and Equity recognizes this obvious fact.

The professional theater, however, is organized also on the principle that Equity players may not act in a non-union play, a play whose staff is not union. In my opinion this principle is a correct one (for reasons I shall briefly mention in a moment). But unfortunately it works out as follows: When the director of the company goes to the various craft and staff unions to get a countersignature to allow Equity players to play, he is told that he must employ 1 union stagehand at $137 a week, 1 union press agent at $145, 1 union scene-designer at $40 per day (for at least 3 days); and whenever there is to be a little live music, there must be union musicians at similar figures. All this amounts to a financial burden out of all proportion to the company's other expenses, and to the profits they expect or even hope for; it is quite unfeasible. (The theater has less than 175 seats;

some are kept at $1, so students can come; figure it out.) In the case here, the burden happens to be particularly galling because the director himself is a gifted and well-known scenic designer; like all other artistic groups, they prefer to couch their press releases and other public relations in their own style; the work done by stagehands is what almost everybody connected with a little theater is skilled at and does with pleasure; and everywhere in integral theater there is a need for live music—it can never be omitted, and canned music is deathly.

The unions are inflexible in their demands; the company cannot fulfill them. In this impasse there is at once generated enormous heat and idiotic remarks. "If you don't have the money, stay out of the theater!" says a distinguished functionary of one of the unions. "You're a painter," he says to the director, "why don't you stick to pictures?" On the other side, the Equity actors connected with the company are in a rage and about to tear up their cards. Those who are politically hep point out that organized labor has fallen into the hands of racketeers. And the paranoid demonstrate that there is a conspiracy among the unions, the critics, and the owners of theater real estate, to prevent anything new and better from happening.

NECESSITY OF THE UNIONS

Let me insist that the principle of total theater unionism, including Equity, seems to me to be correct. This is simply because of the nature of the theater arts and crafts. Our city abounds in people of artistic talent, eager to exercise their separate talents. By disposition such people are free lances; and the state of serious art in our society is such that, until they make a lot of money, free artists have little status or security and cannot easily maintain their rights and dignity. As a group, then, they are peculiarly subject to being taken advantage of and exploited by producers who can give them any work at all; and when taken advantage of, they act effectually as scabs and lower the standards of honest employment. That is, it is precisely the intrinsic virtues of the talented, their hunger to work and their solitariness, that make them socially weak and liable to lower social standards. Poor gifted musicians, painters, poets, dancers, and actors are severally weak indeed; by insisting, even inflexibly and intransigently, on their union, one can give them collectively some strength.

What then? The principle of unionism lays an unbearable burden on any new noncommercial company; it works to the disadvantage of Equity actors; and yet the principle itself is a necessary one. Nevertheless, dispassionately considered, the solution to this dilemma is easy. Briefly, if we carefully consider the nature of theater, we shall see that new theater in general *cannot* make money and must overcome great obstacles in order to exist; and yet eventually it must in turn become immensely popular and make a lot of money, becoming the exciting novelty in commercial theater. The process has two steps, and mindful of their own interests the unions must have a dual attitude: positively to foster the new and noncommercial, and to protect their standards in the commercial; and there ought to be a definite rule to mark the passage from the first stage of the process to the second. There is no doubt that it is a vague or clear understanding of this that, in part, has led Equity to its own more flexible policy.

THE NATURE OF NEW THEATER

Reflect a moment on the following commonplace observations:

(1) The theater is a fine art for an immediate present public; and it is also a collaboration of many skills. Therefore, theater requires a large social effort, setting many people in motion, and a certain amount of social capital. (Not necessarily a large capital, compared, say, with architecture, where the very medium is expensive; but an even larger social effort than architecture.)

(2) Radically new theater, like any new art, cannot expect a mass popular response, for it presents what is unfamiliar and is even actively resisted as meaningless, perverse, or dangerous. The sign of

successful new theater is that the audience is torn between fascination and the impulse to walk out in disgust. The anxiety of new theater is greater than with other new art because theater demands a response in public, and its medium is exceptionally close to the animal and social behavior of life. The same anxiety, by the way, is felt even more by the players than by public, as any one who has rehearsed new theater with conventional actors can testify. Therefore, it is *only* from small, intensely personally involved groups, and a small public of the like-minded, that we can expect new theater to emerge.

(3) But conversely, once a new theatrical advance has been made, it is likely to become immensely popular, for it is shared excitement. A new advance in some other art need not become popular in this way, for, although humanly important, it may be specialist and learned; but theater art is common and simple.

(4) So-called "little theater" groups, making a great social effort and overcoming great obstacles, from real estate to interpersonal relations, and with little income to ease the path, are driven by an artistic fatality into the daring and the radically new. They are not dilettantes or amateurs; their aim is to achieve at least the excitement of the big professional entertainment—otherwise, why bother? Yet their means are limited. Therefore they explore new ways of handling limited means, to get as much meaning as if they had extensive means; this creates startling effects. Or alternately they make daring simplifications, and this creates startling effects.

Let me sum up these familiar propositions in a formula: The task of new theater is to find out and invent what must be unpopular and yet will soon be immensely popular; it is in this thorny task that it makes a great social effort against many obstacles. Naturally people are not too attracted by this prospect. Like most of the "off-Broadway" theater at present, people prefer the easier task of performing modern classics (the new theater of one or two generations ago); of importing European successes that are exotically safe; or of giving museum-like revivals, more properly the function of university players and dedicated amateurs. All that is off Broadway and fairly noncommercial, but it is not new theater. (I do not mean, by the way, that the company I am discussing is a pure model of new theater, but it is one of the best of a bad lot, and nothing is perfect here below.)

A PROPOSAL TO THE UNIONS

Bearing all this in mind, would not the wise, the statesman-like, attitude of the unions be for them to say something like this: "New theater! go to it and we hope you succeed. For if you do, there will be a new kind of immensely popular and paying theater; and if you don't, there will be only a dying theater. The policy of Equity, distinguishing a commercial and a noncommercial theater, is a sound one; but we, of course, are in a different situation from the actors: for our carpenters, electricians, press agents, musicians, and so forth, there is no psychological necessity to perform in theaters; unemployed in the theater, they could get other jobs; and we see no reason, therefore, to lower their standards in any way. But as for the actors, directors, and creative artists of scene, word, movement and music, who need the theater public to exercise their talents, we shall not stand in their way. On the other hand, as soon as you free artists begin to get into the money, then the situation is entirely different, and we have a right to take our place in the enterprise and exact our fair shares. We have the right because all wealth is social wealth, produced by society as a whole, and it must be apportioned according to the rules that society has come to at the present time, to achieve which we in labor have fought and suffered much. Therefore we shall, by some reasonable rule of thumb, set a figure, perhaps an income figure, perhaps a profit ratio, at which we think your free art has entered the cash nexus, a dividing line, at which the excitingly unpopular is beginning to be the immensely popular; and when any of your enterprises crosses that line, it must be total union. We reserve the right to examine your qualifications and check your books, and so you affiliate with us as your friends and pay a nominal dues."

This, I submit, is the wise, the statesmanlike, attitude that loses nothing for the unions, and that encourages the growth of theater. It can set a definite rule that fits the real nature of the case, unlike the present abstract "policy" or alternative nonpolicy of making "exceptions"; of sometimes being intransigent and sometimes shutting the eyes; of acting de facto as powerful critics and censors far beyond their competence. Instead, it gives the theater crafts a noble and protective role in the growth of the culture of the people.

A NEW RESPONSIBILITY

I said at the outset that this small question contains a great question; without further ado, let me generalize. The case is with us in America that, by and large, vast organizations, of state, capital, production, labor, communications, education, urbanism, etc., etc., have pre-empted the means of life. This is currently inevitable and doubtless in many ways desirable, though not so unquestionably desirable as most people think. (When *everything* is done according to a certain pattern, it is hard to imagine how some other pattern could work at all.) At the same time, it is resulting in a conformity that is by now inane and boring and will soon be dangerous, for nothing revitalizing can occur in an organizational plan, and when something occurs outside the plan it may not have space to grow. All this has become a familiar complaint.

I want to suggest simply that with their power, these organizations have acquired a new, strange, and troublesome responsibility: to limit the exercise of their power more intelligently than they are accustomed to, to stand out of the way in order that there can be a future also for themselves.

APPENDIX C
The Freedom to Go[*]

I HAVEN'T read John Keats' *The Insolent Chariots*, but I can see that it and Manfred Macarthur's critique of it provide an excellent example of a dual approach in recent sociology that is inevitable because we have a dual economy that is being analyzed. We have one society but two kinds of money: hard money and soft money, as somebody has called them (I don't know who first). Hard money is the old-fashioned money that you "really" work for, that is measured by labor time and surplus value, and that applies on the market, including the market for labor according to an iron law of wages. Soft money is mad money or sailor money that has at present, however, skyrocketed in amount; it is not only given away on TV for "personal appearances" or for nothing, and as wild salaries on Madison Avenue and in Hollywood; but also, very generally, it pours into fringe benefits, into long vacations with pay, giveaway foundations to avoid upper-bracket taxes, and even, in an important aspect, social insurance. Naturally these two moneys have different moralities, and contrasting moralists like Macarthur and Keats.

It is inevitable that we have these two kinds of money, because we have a surplus technology. The American machine is working at a small fraction of its productivity, and nevertheless there is a vast surplus of not very desirable wealth produced that simply must be bought up with the soft money. At the same time there is always a

_____
*From *Liberation*, January, 1959.

core of subsistence production, for men need bread and shelter, and to get this you have to pay, and work for, hard money. It does not seem to me sufficient to discuss this unique historical monster in terms of class exploitation, reinvestment, and the falling rate of interest—for the soft money pours to all classes. Yet, in power and control, our institutions still *do* work according to the old economic principles. If you omit the old economic analysis, in either your theory or your behavior, you lose out; but if you think and behave *in* those terms, you are quite out of touch with the facts of life, where bureaucratic and leisure values *are* paramount.

So we have two grand streams of social writing that are fantastically uncommunicating. There are the more academic and post-Marxist analysts of institutions, say, Mills or Ben Seligman or Lerner or Lundberg or Farrell; and there are the more journalistic and Freudian analysts of mass culture, like Riesman or Leites or Larrabee and Lynes or Spectorsky. Curiously, each group would probably think the other group is rather conservative and neglects the most important levers of social change. I myself don't know, I have not heard, a unified theory that avoids the overdetermination of these dual interpretations; and frankly, I don't see the need for one, so long as each author honestly works at what seems to him to be the main problem. There is plenty of injustice and folly for all.

My bias is that Keats and Macarthur both are perfectly right about the automobiles with their huge girth and long tails. I do think, however, that by overlooking the crucial factor of our surplus productivity—the President's anguished outcry that it is un-American not to buy, still rings in my soul—both authors are unfair and uncharitable toward our American problem. Keats seems (I have not read him) to neglect, or not sufficiently to stress, the basic need of the market for fashion and novelty that *underlies* the pandering to sex, speed, and prestige. There has to be *some* difference to make the year's model saleable. Put out the most efficient machine you want, and you will still have the problem of how to sell more of it than anybody needs. The experts at this problem are not engineers but "industrial designers." And if you say, stop making the needless cars, then what are you going to do with the productivity of America? I don't mean that there is no answer, but that *this* is the question.

Macarthur, on the other hand, seems to me to be very far from the reality with his puritanical remark about saving money and labor and taking trains and buses. Such Veblen-morals apply to an economy of scarcity. *Why* save the money and labor? To increase the time of leisure? But surveys (e.g., in Larrabee and Meyersohn's anthology *Mass-Leisure*) show that it is precisely for leisure that precisely a workingman's car is his chief salvation from absolute inanition. What if the car stands idle outside the plant because the lonely half-hour drive to and from work is the man's most precious hour of the day at either work or leisure? The car is his share in the superabounding wealth; what share would this author give him? On sunny holidays, the workingman will spend long hours "fixing the car"—it is his freedom to Go, though indeed he has nowhere to go, but parks outside the movie.

"The waste," concludes Macarthur, "is caused by lack of responsible over-all planning." If by planning he means socialist planning of production and distribution, I think that this is nonsense (for the American scene). We are already too efficient for our cultural resources. If, however, he means by planning an organic consideration of means and ends, and the education of the souls of men to be able to use practically the wealth of God and man, then, to his surprise, he will have to begin to think of sex and speed and power and all that.

APPENDIX D

The Freedom to be Academic[*]

A SPECIAL committee at Columbia University has worked for three years on the study of academic freedom, and here now are two books, by Richard Hofstadter and Walter Metzger, and by Robert MacIver, a history of the academic "freedom of inquiry" and a polemical defense of it against current attacks, especially in the social sciences. "Inquiry" is a term from the pragmatic vocabulary and denotes, roughly, a search to solve problems in the ongoing process of life; real, not "academic" problems, though not, of course, narrowly utilitarian problems. The question I want to raise is, to what extent do these authors seriously mean this and mean to defend it?

I.

Let me start by taking an annoying and apparently unfair tack. In discussing the case of Bertrand Russell, Professor MacIver says, "Actually...Russell was dealing, forthrightly and sincerely, with the most problematic of all areas of social relationship [sex]." (AF 156)[†]

---

[*]From *i.e., The Cambridge Review*, Number 5.

[†]Throughout, AF refers to *Academic Freedom in Our Time*, by Robert M. MacIver. N. Y., 1955. Columbia University Press. 304 pp.

Dev. refers to *The Development of Academic Freedom in the United States*, by Richard Hofstadter and Walter P. Metzger. N. Y., 1955. Columbia University Press. 506 pp.

This is an innocent passing remark in a relatively minor context in the book, but let us suddenly stop at it short and take the sentence at face value. If sexual relations is the most problematic of all areas of inquiry, we should expect that most or very many social scientists are inquiring and teaching here, or at least that the chairmen of departments are falling all over themselves to enlist experts for their staffs in this novel field; in the nature of the case much that these people are hypothesizing and affirming must be unconventional and socially unacceptable, for "in no other area of human behavior is there so unbridgeable a gulf between the officially sanctioned ethics and the socially accepted ways" (AF 157); and so there must here be lots of cases of infringement of academic freedom. But no such thing. In the three hundred pages of MacIver's book, six are some- what (mostly indirectly) concerned with such cases; in the five hun- dred pages of the history, none. Now this is not, I am convinced, because our authors are prejudiced on the subject or afraid of it; Pro- fessor MacIver, by his tone and remarks and the few times I have seen him, seems to me sensible and unusually frank. It is because indeed the most problematic area is not much an area of inquiry in the universities. Consider the following statement:

> We know of no cases where an educator, clearly convicted of flagrantly immoral behavior, defended his position by appeal- ing to the principle of academic freedom. Apart from the fact that such defense would be irrelevant, it is certain that his case would receive no support from his institution or from his col- leagues. (AF 150)

If his case would certainly receive no support, the educator would certainly be a fool to press it. But I should like to question the "fact" that such a defense would be irrelevant. The Professor Emeritus knows as well as I that it is not sexual immorality that gets teachers sacked, for this is condoned by his peers, it is among the "socially accepted ways"; but it is the publicity that sometimes accrues; and is this not tantamount to saying that it is not the thing but the proposition that is being penalized? (I know, for instance, of an even closer case, where a teacher in a small progressive college was refused reappointment not because of his delinquent behavior, which was at that place not uncommon and fairly public, but because of his "overt" claim to the right of it.)* Could not many such cases quite simply and relevantly be transformed into cases of infringement of academic freedom? But in this problematic area, the theory—in courses in anthropology—is kept far distant from the practice in the ongoing process of life.

In my opinion there is, in our times, a still more problematic area of social relationships: how to cope with war and the complex of issues around it, conscription, nuclear research, international diplomacy. Now in Professor MacIver's book, pacificism is accorded three pages; in the history, more interestingly, the cases of the First World War are given a large number of pages, but "academic freedom was relatively little affected during the Second World War." (Dev. 505) Why was it not? It seems to me that this area and the sexual area have an essential element in common: that in them a strong conviction tends to overt physical, not merely verbal, behavior; that is, the consequences of conviction tend to be dramatic and drastic, e.g., a young man may refuse the draft, a physicist may decline the job. Therefore these areas are sensitive, and therefore they are not much the objects of inquiry. But the suppression is not proximately extramural but intramural, and it is not forced by the president but by the faculty.

I am reasoning somewhat as follows: What is problematic for inquiry is always just beyond the known; in socio-psychological

---

*One major, and surprising, defect in these books is their omission of any discussion of the small radical colleges like Antioch, Black Mountain, Goddard, etc., founded on more liberal principles than the authors', and therefore with both a more intransigent standard of freedom and more embarrassment in being consistent. I should have thought their careers would be valuably relevant for comparison and contrast.

matters this is an area of confusion and anxiety, and of suppression and repression; then its exploration *must* involve interpersonal daring and personal risk, whether or not there is "acting out," and in these matters there is a generic tendency toward acting out. The vital social questions for inquiry are those you are likely to get jailed for messing with. When you are threatened with academic sanctions, it is a good sign that you are on the right track; when you are fired, it is better; but when you are beyond the pale of the academy and "will receive no support from your colleagues," then you are possibly touching the philosopher's stone. My point is not that universities are worthless, nor that they should not or cannot be free, but that one cannot seriously regard them as primarily places of inquiry nor found the case for academic freedom on freedom of inquiry.

Of course it is unrealistic, and it would be uncharitable, to object to the dropping of a man who by his theory and practice makes his colleagues anxious; after all, they have to live and breathe too and feel themselves part of a team.

> The situations with which we are mainly concerned are those in which an influential or power-holding group endeavors to make or succeeds in making its own predilections the official standards of fitness to teach, even though these predilections are particular to their own coterie or social class....Where such groups exercise control, the freedom of education is seriously infringed, and the more independent and freedom-loving members of the institution are likely to suffer most. It is the teacher who sets the highest value on intellectual freedom who is the most obnoxious to the authoritarians. The higher his standard of responsibility, the lower the respect in which they hold him. (AF 147)

Professor MacIver is here precisely not talking about the faculties of universities, but about their extramural oppressors; would he not, on reflection, extend the censure to the academic coterie as well?

2.

In the main these books seem to me to be written with a generous integrity and bona fides. They were occasioned, of course, by the recent investigations of communists and "communists"; and in such discussions, where every nuance of rhetoric and the penumbra of connotations are scrutinized by seasoned experts like Dr. Hook, it is impossible to satisfy anybody. But to my ear Professor MacIver's sermons—his book has very many pages of long sermons—all ring solid nickel. There is, however, one major topic in treating which there is evident embarrassment, avoidance, difficulties hinted at but not explored, and letting sleeping dogs lie with one eye open: this topic is the relation of knowledge and action. I do not find it credible that the meetings of so experienced a committee did not evoke more philosophic acumen on this subject than is here revealed.

On the one hand, Professor MacIver (the historians less so) lays great stress on "the intrinsic worthwhileness of the knowledge of things, the moral and spiritual values of the integrity of mind that steadfastly seeks the truth" (AF 14), the excitement of the infinite unknown, the grandeur of standing on the brink. He speaks of this with a religious fervor that makes us believe him but that also, I fear, takes it out of the context of a discussion of academic freedom at the University of Illinois or even the colleges of the Ivy League. For a seeker blessed and cursed with this much of the holy spirit will act accordingly with little help or hindrance from the opinions of presidents or from considerations of his own status and tenure; disciples will seek him out, and if we do not so much the worse for us. I think, too, the professor is too sanguine about the possibility of inculcating such an ideal by the ordinary processes of education in colleges; those who pick it up there have it in them to pick up.

On the other hand, all our authors are sold on the pragmatic theory of truth (I do not mean a utilitarian theory), namely, that truth is successful inquiry, and inquiry is an aggressive handling and coping with problems that claim attention; inquiry is experimental, it intervenes. This implies a close connection of knowledge and action. I am not here speaking of the consequences of inquiry but of the process itself. In the social sciences this must mean very often, must it not, sallying beyond the walls into areas that are troublesome, or even to making trouble where all seemed quiet. Certainly if we consider the masters of the century prior to our generations— whether Comte, Marx, Proudhon, Durkheim, Kropotkin, Sorel, Veblen, Lenin, Freud, Dewey, etc., etc.—we are struck by their activism, their actual or projected experimentation on a civic scale. Some of these men are unthinkable as academics and some had uneasy academic lives. The present-day preoccupation with careful methodology is academically praiseworthy, but it does not lead to intensely interesting propositions. One cannot help feeling that a good part of the current concern with statistics and polling is a way of being active in the "area" without being actively engaged in the subject matter. There is a good deal of sharpening of tools but not much agriculture.*

Professor Metzger eloquently expresses the very point I am trying to make. He is distinguishing the cases of Richard Ely and Edward Bemis who got into trouble on the theory and practice of labor organization during the '90s:

> A ... difference lay in the extent to which Ely and Bemis put their theories into action. For all his talk of the need for concrete reform, Ely's criticisms of the social order tended to be general, not specific; hortatory, not programmatic. For all his warm humanitarianism, he made no intimate contact with the multitude. "Only twice in my life," he wrote, "have I ever spoken to audiences of working men, and I had always held myself aloof from agitations as something not in my province—something for which I am not adapted." Replying to

---

*But consider the dilemma: Such massive research and experiment must be financed, if not administered, by Foundations; and those chosen by or for Foundations tend to be at least "sound" if not "safe."

the charge by Regent Wells that he *had* acted on his sympathies for labor, he issued a categorical denial. This author of a friendly history of the labor movement denied, at his trial, that he had ever entertained a walking delegate in his home, that he had ever counseled workers to strike, that he had ever threatened an anti-union firm with a boycott, or that he had ever favored the principle of a closed shop. Were these charges true, Ely wrote, they would "unquestionably unfit me to occupy a responsible position as an instructor of youth in a great University." These were the words of a very academic reformer. (Dev. 433)

When Ely was academically vindicated, Bemis wrote to him:

"That was a glorious victory for you.... I was only sorry that you seemed to show a vigor of denial as to entertaining a walking delegate or counselling strikers as if either were wrong, instead of under certain circumstances a *duty.*" This was the difference between them: Bemis was not only a partisan ... but an active party.... The subsequent careers of Ely and Bemis bear out the importance of this point. Ely survived (and in good part renounced) his spoken and written heresies. He remained in a state of academic grace for the rest of his life, taking a post at Northwestern in 1925 and one at Columbia in 1937. Bemis became an academic Ishmael with a reputation as a partisan and a malcontent that he was never able to live down. Except for his brief and ill-starred tenure at Kansas State, he received no further academic appointments. The trustees of the republic of learning could inflict on this kind of miscreant the terrible retribution of neglect. (Dev. 435)

All this is excellently and feelingly said. But it was an issue of sixty years ago, and today in this area a teacher has "the right to exercise the same political and civil liberties that are enjoyed by other citizens." (AF 238) My bother is that our authors do not extrapolate to present-day areas that must have the same borderline characteristics, and then look a little harder for academic-freedom cases which might look precisely not like academic-freedom cases as reported to the American Association of University Professors.

On this same topic of knowledge and action, let me raise another difficulty concerning the action of teaching itself and the teacher's responsibility for consequences. Our authors, especially the historians, are frequently scornful of the "assumption ... that a young man yields to the imprint of ideas as easily and uncritically as wax." (Dev. 411) They stress, rather, the development of freedom to learn, the opportunity to hear all and pick and choose. I do not think these are, in interesting cases, the real alternatives. The young mind is indeed not passive but intensely active, and its activity is to crystallize around an ideal, a system of ideas, or a nonfamilial personality, that serves as a parent substitute. Quite apart from sex, the relation of teacher and student is an erotic one, where for the student the attraction is in the excitement, particularly the rebellious excitement, of the system of propositions. The more excellent the teacher, the stronger the charismatic effect of his voice. In itself this is all to the good and is anyway inevitable; it cannot be prevented by doctrinal neutrality for then the very syntax of neutrality itself becomes adorable. But the attempt to prevent the effect or to disown responsibility for it, discourages the student and thwarts and embitters the teacher. Is not the situation familiar, that a powerful teacher is regarded by his colleagues, partly in envy and partly in anxiety, as a seducer of his students and indeed in a conspiracy with them to cast ridicule on themselves? On the other hand, if the strong teacher maintains his reserve, the student, whose needs are more frank, has indeed been rejected and will be either humiliated, disappointed, or angry, depending on his character. My guess is that every college term there is more infringement of the freedom to teach by academic timidity along these lines than in the whole history of cases here treated. Worse, is there not a great waste of natural human resources?

Our historians write of the liberation from "doctrinal moralism"

(Dev. 353ff), the idea that if, e.g., a man is an atheist he is no doubt a drunkard and unfit to teach: "in scientific criticism the dissociation of the man from his work has become a cardinal principle." This was indeed a great advance, for it heightened the respect for evidence and its accurate presentation and criticism. But I submit that the older theological view had the following merit: that a proposition was fraught with life consequences and had therefore the utmost seriousness; you knew a man by what he professed. I dislike appealing to the romantic and grisly past, but we must bear in mind that the adventure of inquiry has one quality when you are risking disgrace, imprisonment, and even death; and another when you are risking tenure; and quite another when you are risking nothing. Our secular society has great advantages, and even especially for inquiry, but its strong point is not the achievement of vocation or manliness. In his rhetoric of dedication to the Truth with a big T, Professor MacIver is harking back to Spinoza; I wonder if, by and large, he could comfortably use this rhetoric at the Faculty Club. Maybe I am wrong.

To sum up so far: I have tried in a quick and rude way to indicate that the professors fall short in two ways from a standard of inquiry as a phase of an experimental instrumental empiricism: they avoid problematic areas and they do not experiment their hypotheses. (Nothing of what I have said, let me remark, applies to more old-fashioned notions of academic freedom of inquiry. For instance, the notion of freedom of dialectic, as exemplified in, say, the *Parmenides,* where precisely the attachment and nonattachment to any proposition is used as a therapy of the soul. Or the Aristotelian freedom of curiosity, aimed at *theoria* as the highest happiness. Or the medieval *libertas philosophandi*, with its emphasis on disputation to let new air into an accepted world. Or finally to the Enlightenment's concept of freedom of criticism in the Kantian sense (*quo warranto?*), where the faculty of philosophy serves, as Kant says, as a kind of loyal opposition from the left. All of these base their claim on the proposition that the university is different from, perhaps better than, perhaps a servant of, the rest of the world.)

3.

I said I had started on an "apparently unfair" tack. Unfair because I chose an innocent sentence in a minor context, and I have been devoting myself to a matter of logic that Professor MacIver's book is mostly not about. Now what it is about is the defense of such inquiry as does exist from the current attacks upon it, and specifically and explicitly the communist hunting of the Cold War by many parties, from government agencies to self-constituted vigilantes. Let us then turn briefly to the overt book itself and see if I can show the relevance of the tack I have been taking.

Professor MacIver's findings on the Party and the investigations are the familiar ones of many liberals, and they warrant little fresh discussion here. Summarily: (1) The Party-communist teacher is unqualified, as authoritarian, suppressive, conspiratorial; but this disqualification is based on his activities, not on his theories. (Frankly, this distinction is idiotic, since what is a party that does not constrain to action?) (2) Past affiliation does not disqualify. (3) A communist, "whether he carries a Party card or not," may be dismissed "if he injects propaganda into his teaching or relationships with students"; but conversely, if he teaches a noncontroversial subject and is otherwise circumspect, it is better to let him be. (4) Investigation should be done by the faculty, not by the administration or outsiders. (5) "Any general investigation to uncover possible communists is wholly undesirable." (6) Loyalty oaths are "derogatory, injudicious, and futile." (7) Student organizations should be permitted to invite C.P. speakers. (8) Communist ideas do not disqualify the student.

It is useful to distinguish two strata in such a list: judgments that could be called anti-McCarthy and those that are anti-anti-anti-McCarthy. Objections to high-handed and unfair pressures, to informing, to lack of due process, to almost all restraints on freedom of speech: this is simple anti-McCarthyism; and at it are leveled charges of political naïveté, of being duped, of not seeing that this is a unique conspiracy, of locking the stable after the horse is gone, and so forth. The response to *these* charges, in turn, is anti-anti-anti-McCarthyism: granting that there are grounds for the investigations, yet their effect is so productive of fear and withdrawal and inhibition of useful functioning that they weaken the body politic rather than purge it; thus they play into the hands of the enemy, etc.

I think that it is this latter attitude, the prevalence of academic anxiety rather than any righteous indignation, that has prompted the books we are reviewing. For the fact seems to be—at least so it is agreed by all sides in this controversy except the investigators themselves—that the communist infiltration has been trivial, was never large, and has steadily waned for years; that the furor of investigation has been out of all proportion. The question, then, is why anything so groundless and inappropriate has been met by anything but simple manly rejection, either quiet, derisive, or indignant, depending on one's temperament. Why such big looks? Let me open MacIver at random and quote a few near-by passages:

There were evidences that in departments or faculties, here or there, disguised or subtle pressures had been applied to prevent the advancement of such noncomforming members or against the renewal of their appointments if they lacked tenure. It was not that the scholars who protested against the oath requirements were themselves nonconformists—there were very many good conservatives among them—but, whatever their economic viewpoints, alike they apprehended a growing peril to academic freedom. (AF 178)

No attack seems to be more disruptive than that which emanates from governing boards.... They rock the institution.... Governing boards are seldom prescient of the effect such edicts produce.... Often the disturbance that ensues comes to the governing boards as a complete surprise.... Censorial and inquisitorial action on the part of those who themselves are not devoted to the scholar's search for truth is for the true scholar a vital threat. (Ibid)

What concerns us here is that the Tenney warnings and threats and proposals created the most serious apprehensions among leading educators. (AF 179)

This new exercise of authority by a board over a faculty contained implicit threats against the status of the educator, against the two most vital interests of the profession. The pro-testing faculty members saw in the new requirement on the one hand a threat to academic freedom, on the other a threat to security of tenure. The pro-oath regents denied that any such threats were involved … but this lack of understanding is one of the two frequent consequences of the lack of rapport that exists in this country between faculties and governing boards. (AF 177)

I quote at random from adjacent pages; the book is thickly stud-ded with the like. One is ashamed to copy out the passages. What is one to make of this astonishing anxiety on the part of grownups, of professors, of supposedly dedicated scholars. "Disguised," "implicit threats," "rock the institution," "vital threat," "most serious appre-hensions," "lack of understanding," "they are not prescient"; and all this syndrome where in many cases admittedly no danger existed, and where altogether at the worst no great danger existed. Is it so hard to clear up misunderstanding by bearding the lion? or to force implicit threats to become explicit and have a bang-up fight? Could these persons really be so concerned about losing their jobs? And if they are really concerned for freedom as a principle and a vital need, is this the tone of such a concern?

I fear it is rather the tone of subordinate bureaucrats ridden by self-doubt and with plenty of projected hostility, unable to withstand the least pressure without anxiety. Then I cannot believe in the devo-tion to inquiry that gives them so little strength of self as this. And I cannot believe in the aggressive intensity of inquiry that gets them into so weak a feeling for the state of things. The job-clinging itself is not so much base as a pathetic symptom. How easily they are deflated of their status! What shall we say of an elite of competence that has so little pride and self-confidence? Is this our proud academic freedom? If I felt it was only this I would tear up my doctorate.

The fear of actual investigation, the paranoiac suspicion of fancied investigation, the economic panic, need for status, clinging to security: these have been familiar in the American middle classes during the past couple of generations; there is no need to discuss in the context of the academic community the causes that have been operating in the whole community. What is specific, however, is that these *are* doctors, with a proud tradition, sacred symbols, a culture far broader than average, the inspiration of beautiful subject matters and grand authors: in short, a self-transcending responsibility to history past and future that they (we) cannot finally betray without shame and self-betrayal. They *must* rally, even though the form of the rallying reveals the inner conflict of these books.

4.

It is remarkable how, in reading the vigorous and informative history of Professors Hofstadter and Metzger, one can see forming through the decades the lineaments of modern academic man, and an academic notion of inquiry defining itself. The authors call their book a "Development" and they rightly regard as an achievement the present concept of academic freedom with its bill of rights and its highly ramified national system of professional defenses. At the same time, being scrupulous and fairly philosophical and not at all homiletic, they note down the inevitable losses and sloughings-off that have occurred along the way. Now if instead of merely noting these losses, we accumulate them and form them into a picture: what a picture it is! so to speak, an ideal shadow of Western Academic Man that, we hope, haunts the modern American academic man, and sheds on him glory, and gives him a bad conscience. Let me collect half a dozen of these contrasts of development and loss.

(1) "At the time of their greatest independence," says Professor Hofstadter,

the universities lived in the interstices of medieval society, taking advantage of its decentralization and the balance of its conflicting powers to further their own corporate interests. [They were guilds of masters or students.] They appealed to king or council against pope, to pope against king or bishop, and to king and popes alike against truculent town governments. Moreover, they had weapons of their own that put them above the level of mere appellants and gave them independent bargaining power. Among these weapons were the cessation or suspension of lectures, the academic equivalents of the modern strike. A still more powerful device arose, oddly enough, from their very poverty. Unhampered...by physical apparatus, great libraries, worldly goods, and substantial college foundations, they could and on occasion did migrate, taking with them their large numbers of students and profitable trade.* (Dev. 7–8)

I suppose this could be taken as the zenith of academic liberty; just as the nadir would be a faculty of science, saddled with its cyclotron, supported 80 per cent by the War Department of a centralized state that dictates the avenues of research, and with a "personnel" subjected to a clearance arrived at by secret investigation.

(2) More than half of this history of universities is occupied with the decline of sectarian control of academic selection, thought, and action; the secularizing of learning. The other side, the loss, is of course that thought and action tend to come to us more lightly; few of us, though some, spend sleepless nights of doubt about a detail of phrasing in theory leading to an inconsistency in behavior perhaps publicly unnoticed anyway. Professor Hofstadter charmingly recounts a touching story of the resignation of the first president of Harvard, Henry Dunster, who had found in his heart that no infant

---

*So Black Mountain College was founded by a migration in the early 1930's, and the migrant faculty was thenceforth the owner of the college, without a governing board of trustees.

could properly be baptized and had to proclaim the same. (It seems to me, by the way, that this is an inevitable opinion for a college man who should set great store on learning and inquiry.) But Dunster was

> not dismissed, and he could have kept his job if he had promised to be silent about his unacceptable convictions, for everything in the case indicates that the magistrates and ministers never lost personal confidence in him. Dunster, however, submitted a curious letter of resignation which made no clear reference to religious issues but dwelled at some length on the recent investigation of the college and the expansion of the powers of the Overseers at the expense of the Corporation. The General Court gave Dunster the opportunity to take a month to reconsider. Evidently they still hoped that he could be persuaded to swallow his heresy. . . . But a month later Dunster closed his presidency with the utmost finality when he interrupted a baptismal service at Cambridge with a startling speech against infant baptism and the "corupcions stealing into the Church." (Dev. 89)

What is touching is not so much the president's earnest and dramatic witnessing, exactly in the style of Hawthorne, but the way in which the others respect their brother's right to wrestle with his god and their subsequent solicitude for him. It is unnecessary to mention contemporary contrasts.

(3) Again, in discussing the influence on America of the great German universities of the nineteenth century, the historian, Professor Metzger, beautifully analyzes on the one hand what was carried over, the methodic thoroughness, specific competence (but not the universality of interest), the freedom from utilitarian narrowness, dedication to absolute freedom of truth; and on the other hand what was sloughed off or suffered a sea change.

> We come to the heart of the difference when we compare the American and German conceptions of inner and outer

freedom.... The German idea of "convincing" one's students, of winning them over to the personal system and philosophical views of the professor, was not condoned by American academic opinion. Rather, as far as classroom actions were concerned, the proper stance for American professors was thought to be one of neutrality on controversial issues, and silence on substantive issues that lay outside of their competence. Innumerable utterances affirmed these limitations. Eliot, in the very address that so eloquently declared that the university must be free, made neutrality an aspect of that freedom: "... It is not the function of the teacher to settle philosophical and political controversies for the pupil, or even to recommend to him any one set of opinions as better than another.... The student should be made acquainted ... with the salient points of each system." (Dev. 400)

Professor Metzger goes on to argue that this norm of neutrality itself springs from an American bias of thought, its empiricism, resistant to intuition, speculation, fantasy—in the end, a suspicion of deliveries not fairly quickly verifiable.* I do not think he sufficiently estimates the disadvantages of the limitation to "neutrality" as against the German freedom to "convince." In the first place, with the American limitation, competence almost automatically becomes specialization, for what quickly verifiable fact is to connect the various parts of study? There is no system of facts, only systems of thought. Again, is Eliot's ideal of neutral presentation something that can possibly exist in a classroom? Have you ever listened to a convinced Whiteheadian trying to present the philosophy of Kant? Then is the teacher to have no conviction of his own? It is plausible

---

*This "neutrality" certainly has also a simpler and more traditional spring: the detachment of the wise and experienced, and the tradition of the academy as the home of the wise and experienced, with the motto *nil admirari*. Such an attitude is, of course, not neutral at all, but the provision of a background of security pre-different to controversial opinions, and relying on which, youth can risk having definite opinions.

for the school to be neutral and present all sides, but how can the teacher be neutral? But most important, Eliot and Professor Metzger do not see realistically the situation of the student in the face of neutrality and competence: his moral nature must have some culture or other, and if no ideal or moral connections are made in the university, this culture—unless he has had an unusually lucky upbringing—will fall to the first extramural propagandist, or intramural but extracurricular propagandist, or even worse, it will continue in an infantile set of prejudices and unconscious conventionalities while his intellectual life will be correspondingly arid and without vital strength and prone to panic before Senatorial committees or rabble rousers. As I have said above, the teacher is responsible either way, whether he freely exerts his influence or withholds it; and I think he does better not to worry about a standard of scientific certainty and impartiality, but, relying on the sense of his own integrity, to act forthrightly according to probabilities, keeping an open mind and heart. Best of all, no doubt, that he have a wisdom and learning that cuts under controversy and relieves its sharpness, but this is not a "stance" but a fact. It is a fact if the professor's urbane detachment, encyclopedic scope, urgent following-up, insistence on accuracy, or ability to make the controversy fascinating in itself (there are several admirable styles of teaching—none of them "neutral"), if these continually provide a new unsettling challenge to the student's wish to have an answer; but it is only a stance if the student feels he has come up against a limit of "no opinion." I don't think the majority of teachers are in fact this good. Finally, it seems likely that an important reason for the American standard of professorial neutrality has been the youth and sexual immaturity of our college students as contrasted with the German university students of that time; our students are more impressionable; but it is hard to see the logic of, on the one hand, dropping the older paternalism (or giving it over to administrative deans) and, on the other hand, discouraging discipleship; the students are told they are no longer children but young men, but they are forbidden the love affairs, both physical and intellectual, of young men. Yet where could such affairs be safer than at a university? Indeed, the contradiction is sometimes worse. There was a case at a famous Eastern college where in the aftermath of a sexual escapade the dean gave a student's name to the police; a great foreign teacher, who had once served as Rector of a European school, exclaimed indignantly, "We were not *in loco parentis* and we protected them; you act *in loco parentis* and you do not protect them!" There spoke eight hundred years.

(4) Another grievous loss for academic man occurred with the abandonment of the liberal arts course of classics for an elective system geared more to adjustment to the changing social scene. Professor Metzger handles this as follows:

> As the result of deeper social forces at work, the "conserving" function of the college no longer loomed so large. The unhinging of moral certainties by urban living, the fading out of the evangelical impulse, the depersonalization of human relations in the process of industrial expansion, were destroying that integral vision, that firm and assertive credulity, required of institutions devoted to conservation.... A good part of the pre-Civil War academic's opposition to a more secular university and a more vocationalized curriculum stemmed from the desire to protect very fragile values from the crush of a rough society. He sought the freedom not to acquiesce in the philistinism of his age. (Dev. 317)

I think this is wrongly put; it sounds like Allen Tate, who could say, justifiably enough, "Undo it!" At the beginning of *Academic Freedom in our Time* Professor MacIver analyzes the climate of opinion unfavorable to academic freedom and finds a major factor in the want of a common culture and a deep-going communication. Given Professor Metzger's analysis here, this is more and more inevitable, the University cannot cure it but rather tends to worsen it. What is common, integral, and humane is *ipso facto* out of date and fragile and needing conservation; meanwhile the University hastens on to new inquiry. Against this, the Great Books movement, associated with the names of Hutchins, Adler, McKeon, and Buchanan, has denied that the common culture is out of date; but they have made the contrary mistake, it seems to me, of claiming it is "eternal" and resides in the Great Books as "classics." All this is topsy-turvy and looking in the wrong place. The true classics are the structures, whether propositions or methods or habits, that are in fact operative in the present juncture, urban, industrial, depersonalized, or whatever. There is always a classical curriculum to be found, because what is classical is simply what is central, concrete, causally operative, underlying; and indeed in any new situation, the classics never look like "classics," nor, in the present state of literature, are they likely to be books. The Socratic dialogue is classic, and in our times it is to be found in the psychoanalytic group-session, where very soon one reaches what is integral, humane, and communicative. The experimental method is classic and chastens and unites us, but it must not be taught as a laboratory exercise nor in a course in logic, but rigorously applied to some real practical behavior. Eurhythmics and sports are classic. Mathematizing experience is classic. It is not classic to teach grammar, but it is classic to define the grammar of your speech. The mistake has been to study monuments of classical ages—the Greeks, the Medievals, the seventeenth century—rather than to assume that we are presently creating classics. I propose that this is what Dewey meant by reconstruction, to find-and-make ourselves classical techniques and a common culture by a philosophical handling of just where we are on our way. This is not what the university has been doing, and now nobody can teach classics and we do not know what classics we have.

(5) Another loss occurred to Academic Man when he became, and agreed to consider himself as, merely an academic man, without some other function and status of his competence in the larger society. The historians relate with too much satisfaction, it seems to me, the development of a specialist "profession" from a group of clergymen who perhaps temporarily accepted calls as teachers. But teach-

ing on the university level,* though it is surely a vocation and requires a special temperament and knack, is not a profession because it does not have a proper subject matter; it is a universal art applied to a proper subject matter; one might as well speak of a "professional orator." To the extent that the teacher inquires into the subject matter proper, however, he is not a teacher, and then why does he hang around the campus so much? One's suspicion is, alas, that the ancient maxim is true: "If you can't do it, teach it." Teaching is certainly a vocation and a responsibility of every expert; very few things are more beautiful to see than good teaching; perhaps nothing is more re-creative and enlarging for the expert himself, for he can teach with an integrity generally impossible in practice, and he gets to look at his habit of art with new eyes; even so, the scene of the same aging grownups hanging around while generations of youth pass by, has something in it that stinks in the nostrils. As for colleagues, the company of the like-minded is both stimulating and comforting, but to be immured with the like-minded is like—living at Princeton. A disadvantage of the professional situation, of course, is that the academic is economically tied; necessarily he is fearful of losing his tenure; he cannot, under stress, go off to his proper job where he is indispensable because he produces the goods. (In our society, of course, most of those goods do not fetch a price.) But perhaps a greater loss is that whole areas and provinces of science and scholarship have become merely intramural, they no longer importantly exist as the property of adult academies and learned societies, which in turn have tended to become merely honorary memberships that give prizes and sponsor social gatherings. Extramural science is bound to industry, extramural scholarship does not exist at all; yet it is simply by the accident that there are university libraries and laboratories and stipends that such activities are immured, with correspondingly irrelevant restrictions and duties that must be alleviated

---

*Teaching at the primary level is different, for there the emphasis is on teaching the pupil, not the subject matter; and there is then a profession of pedagogy analogous to medicine, and of which the remedial branch is psychotherapy.

by claims to "academic freedom." It is hard to know what to advise the scholar, hampered or often hampered by the atmosphere of colleges, in a society that does not much patronize the study of history, linguistics, and literature; nevertheless, to our ideal picture of the more heroic and free Academic Man we would do well to add the lineaments of the Humanist and the scientist of the seventeenth and eighteenth centuries, who were not professional academics. (Dev. 49, 195)

(6) Lastly, we must refer to a loss that has come with the coming of the Big University. Professor Metzger reads off the indictment from Veblen's *The Higher Learning in America:*

> Acutely, he discerned the trend toward bureaucratization was transforming the university's personnel, structure, and behavior. This change was already evidenced in the army of academic functionaries—the deans, directors, registrars, and secretaries—who had come upon the scene to manage the affairs of the university. It was evidenced in the organization of the faculty as a graded hierarchy of ranks within which passage was controlled by a series of official promotions. It was evidenced in the writing of rules that defined the rights and obligations of professors and trustees. It marked, though it did not cause, the end of an academic era in which the college had been a community and the faculty a body of peers. (Dev. 453)

Dealing with this and the rest of Veblen's jeremiad, Metzger seeks to prove, successfully enough, that Big Business as such was not the guilty agent, that the changes were socially pervasive and inevitable. But otherwise, I am baffled by the equanimity of his acquiescence. I should have thought that the faculty *is* the university, and if this university ceases to exist, what is there to write about as a continuing historical entity? We have come full circle from our first historical quotation, about the guild of scholars choosing the interstices of a plural society and willing to preserve itself by migrating bag and baggage; now we have, apparently, merely one wheel in a machine, that needs, to be sure, its own special oil and rules for successful operation, but we can hardly expect to hear from it any unique delivery of the creator spirit. This is not very interesting. If the brothers do not confront one another face to face and communally decide, nothing follows from their being brothers. Academic Man becomes the same as any other American man; this is just what one surmised from the passages of anxiety in MacIver's book—professors behaving like all the other sheep; it is uncharitable to level at them any special charges or to subject them to any special scrutiny; but then what is all the talk about a peculiar dedication? But I am sanguine enough to believe that the case is not so desperate as this.

The case is, it seems to me—and it is expressed in the tone and matter of both these stimulating books—that there is a double Academic Man.

Looming ever in the background is this ghostly presence or absence that we have been figuring forth by the accumulation of lost causes that can never be lost. I have tried to cull traits that show him in his extramural and intramural relations, in his personal responsibility and community, in his curriculum and livelihood. He is part of a band "intensely self-conscious and self-important," as Powicke said, and that carries colors and a coat of arms, not bashfully. He feels himself the carrier of Western culture and the champion of new invention. He has a deserved reputation as a stickler for antique tradition with excessive scrupulosity, and for stirring up entirely gratuitous innovations, just to make trouble. He is prone to terrible knockdown conflicts with his colleagues on the basis of mutual respect, and to erotic devotions, both lenitive and dangerous, toward his students. He goes abroad on his career in the world and sits on the faculty as an independent man of the world. This ghost, I say, is continually trying to break into reality and take over, but he is restrained—in many ways, let me hasten to add, *fortunately* restrained—by the circumstances of social history (very fully explained by our authors). Restrained and nonexistent, but he exerts an eerie fascination on the living body, rouses in him dreams, makes him touchy and irritable and suddenly ashamed and rebellious; and sometimes he gets hold of the speech and utters things like Professor MacIver's somewhat mesmerized sermons.

In the foreground and with us, is the other academic man, frightened by a noisy politician. Caught in a bureaucracy, ridden by authority from above and bullying others from below, he is afraid of a black mark against him, because if he loses his job here he won't have good references elsewhere; there is only one academic world and it is for him the only world. Weighed down by vast mortmain properties, corporately held and that make the living faculty a trivial force; and dependent for current expenses on alien interests that pay the piper and call the tune. Unerotic and at least publicly antisexual, naturally he is subject to anxiety. He uses lofty ethical terms to shame others, but gets remarkably little strength and animation from the reality pretended. He engages in plenty of intramural bickering and jockeying for position, but never in a bang-up fight. He does a good deal of obsessional counting and methodical busy work that is not very different from telling beads. He is not distinguishable, and circumspectly avoids becoming so by overt action. He and his fellows huddle together not as a totemic band but because it is cold. This is the academic man that speaks in Professor MacIver's reportage.

APPENDIX E

Review of On the Road*

IN THREE hundred pages these fellows cross America eight times, usually camping on friends or relatives; and they have kicks. The narrator tends to become saddened by it all, but gives little evidence of understanding why. The fellows seem to be in their middle or late twenties ("not long after my wife and I split up")—surprisingly, for the kicks are the same as we used to have less solemnly in our teens, between terms. Mostly they are from the middle class. Many other young men in their twenties and thirties call this book crazy and the greatest, as if it were their history: they were there. So let's look into it.

To an uncritical reading, *On The Road* seems worse written than it is. There are hundreds of incidents but, throughout most of the book, nothing is told, nothing is presented, everything is just "written about." Worse, the narrator seems to try to pep it up by sentences like, "That night all hell broke loose," when the incident is some drinking sailors refusing to obey an order; "this was the greatest ride I ever had," but nothing occurs beyond a fellow getting his pants wet trying to urinate from a moving truck; "this was exciting, this was the greatest"—but it's not exciting. Soon, when the narrator or some other character says "The greatest," we expect that he means "pretty fair"; but alas, he does not mean even this, but simply that there was *some* little object of experience, of whatever value, instead of the blank of experience in which these poor kids generally live.

For when you ask yourself what *is* expressed by this prose, by this

---

*From *Midstream,* Winter, 1958.

buoyant writing about racing-across-the-continent, you find that it is the woeful emptiness of running away from even loneliness and vague discontent. The words "exciting," "crazy," "the greatest," do not refer to any object or feeling, but are a means by which the members of the Beat Generation convince one another that they have been there at all. "I dig it" doesn't mean "I understand it," but, "I perceive that something exists out there." On me as a reader, the effect is dismay. I know some of these boys (I say "boys"; Jack Kerouac is thirty-five).

Last summer I listened to Kerouac's friend Allen Ginsberg read a passage from his *Howl;* it was a list of imprecations that he began pianissimo and ended with a thunderous fortissimo. The fellows were excited, it was "the greatest." But I sadly asked Allen just where in either the ideas, the imagery, or the rhythm was the probability for the crescendo; what made it a sequence at all and a sequence to be read just like that. The poet was crestfallen and furious; this thought had never occurred to him. And yet, during those few minutes they *had* shared the simple-minded excitement of his speaking in a low voice and gradually increasing to a roar; it was not much of a poetic experience, but it was something, it was better than feeling nothing at all that night. What Kerouac does well, not just writes about, is his description of the jazz musician who has hit on "it" and everybody goes wild shouting, "Go! Man! Go!" But they cannot say what "it" is. These boys are touchingly inarticulate, because they don't know anything; but they talk so much and so loud, because they feel insulted by the existence of the grownups who know a little bit.

"You can't *howl* a gripe, Allen. You can howl in pain or in rage, but what you are doing is griping." Perhaps the pain is too sore to utter a sound at all; and certainly their justifiable rage is far too dangerous for them to feel at all. The entire action of *On The Road* is the avoidance of interpersonal conflict.

One is stunned at how conventional and law-fearing these lonely middle-class fellows are. They dutifully get legal marriages and divorces. The hint of a "gangbang" makes them impotent. They never masturbate or perform homosexual acts. They do not dodge the draft. They are hygienic about drugs and diet. They do not resent being underpaid, nor speak up at all. To disobey a cop is "all hell." Their idea of crime is the petty shoplifting of ten-year-olds stealing cigarettes or of teen-agers joy riding in other people's cars. But how could it be otherwise? It is necessary to have some contact with institutions and people in order to rebel against them. It is necessary to want something in order to be frustrated and angry. They have the theory that to be affectless, not to care, is the ultimate rebellion, but this is a fantasy; for right under the surface, obvious to a trained eye, is burning shame, hurt feelings, fear of impotence, speechless and powerless tantrum, cowering before papa, being rebuffed by mama; and it is these anxieties that dictate their behavior in every crisis. Their behavior is a conformity *plus royaliste que le roi*.

One kid (age twenty-one) visited my home the other night, carrying his copy of *On The Road*. The salient feature was his expressionless mask-face, with the squared jaw of unconscious, suspicious watchfulness, the eyes in a fixed stare of unfelt hostility, plus occasional grinding of his back teeth at a vague projected threat. Even the hostility was hard to make overt, but his lips cracked in a small childish smile when he was paid attention to. "But nothing *can* be interesting from coast to coast, boy, if you do not respond to it with some interest. Instead all you can possibly get is to activate your rigid body in various towns, what you call kicks." He explained that one had to avoid committing oneself to any activity, lest one make a wrong choice.

It is useful to place this inexpressive face and his unoffending kicks in our recent literary genealogy. Great-granddaddy, I guess, is the stoical hero of Hemingway: Hemingway's young fellow understands that the grown-up world is corrupt and shattering, but he is not "Beat," for he can prove that he is himself a man by being taciturn, growing hair on his chest, and shooting elephants. He has "values" and therefore can live through a few books. His heir is Céline's anti-hero, a much shrewder fellow: he sees that to have those "values" is already to be duped by the corrupt adults, so he adopts the much more powerful role of universal griper and cry baby, to make everybody feel guilty and disgusted. The bother with his long gripe is that it is monotonous, there is a lot of opportunity for writing, but not even a single book. The next hero, and I think the immediate predecessor of being on the road, gives up the pretense of being grown-up altogether (a good case is Salinger's *Catcher in the Rye*): he is the boy in the very act of being mortally wounded by the grown-ups' corruption. This terrible moment is one book. But you can't cry forever, so you set your face in a mask and go on the road. The adolescent decides that he himself is the guilty one—this is less painful than the memory of being hurt—so he'd better get going. The trouble is that there is no longer any drama in this; the drama occurred before " *my wife and I split up*," before I lost my father.

Sociologically, the following propositions seem to me to be relevant: (1) In our economy of abundance there are also surplus people, and the fellows on the road are among them. There is in fact no man's work for them to do. (2) We are inheriting our failure, as an advanced industrial country, to have made reasonable social arrangements in the last century; now when there is no longer a motive to work hard and accumulate capital, we have not developed an alternative style of life. (3) The style that we do have, "Madison Avenue," is too phony for a young person to grow up into. (4) Alternatively, there is an attraction to the vitality (by comparison) of the disfranchised Negroes and now the Puerto Ricans; these provide a language and music, but this culture is primitive and it corrupts itself to Madison Avenue as soon as it can. (5) In family life there has been a similar missed-revolution and confusion, so that many young people have grown up in cold, hypocritical, or broken homes. Lacking a primary environment for the expression and training of their feelings, they are both affectless and naïve in the secondary environment. (6) The spontaneous "wild" invention that we may expect from every young generation has been seriously blighted by the anxieties of the war and the cold war (7) The style of life resulting from all this is an obsessional conformity, busy-ness without any urge toward the goals of activity, whether ideal goals or wealth and power. There is not much difference between the fellows "on the road" and the "organization men"—they frequently exchange places.

> I ate another apple pie and ice cream; that's practically all I ate all the way across the country, I knew it was nutritious and it was delicious, of course.

On other occasions, they eat franks and beans. More rarely hamburgers, malted milks, of course. That is, the drink-down quick-sugar foods of spoiled children, and the pre-cut meat for lazy chewing beloved of ages six to ten. Nothing is bitten or bitten-off, very little is chewed; there is a lot of sugar for animal energy, but not much solid food to grow on. I suppose that this is the most significant observation one can make about *On The Road*.

For nearly two-thirds of this book one is struck, I have said, by the lack of writing; the book is nothing but a conversation between the buddies: "Do you remember when?" and, "Do you remember how we?" "That was the greatest!" Here is confirmation that they, like Kilroy, were there; but not much distilled experience for the reader. But then (page 173) there *is* a page of writing, not very good and not original—it is from the vein of rhapsody of Céline and Henry Miller—nevertheless, writing. The situation is that the narrator finally finds himself betrayed, abandoned, penniless, and hungry in a strange city. The theme of the rhapsody is metempsychosis. "I realized that I had died and been reborn numberless times but just didn't remember"—and this theme is a happy invention, for it momentarily raises the road to a plane of metaphysical fantasy. And this is how the passage climaxes:

> In the window I smelled all the food of San Francisco.... Let me smell the drawn butter and lobster claws. There were places where they specialized in thick red roast beef *au jus* or roast chicken basted in wine. There were places where hamburgs

sizzled on grills and the coffee was only a nickel. And oh, that pan-fried chow mein ...

Here, at least in wish, is a piece of reality that is not just kicks and "the greatest"; he wants to *eat* this food. Silone was right when he said that we must learn again the words for Bread and Wine.

APPENDIX F
"The Crime of Our Century"*

Compulsion, by Meyer Levin
Nothing but the night, by James Yaffe

HERE ARE two recent books about the Leopold-Loeb case which Meyer Levin calls "the crime of our century." It occurred when Levin was in college (1924). James Yaffe is younger and takes the whole matter less seriously. Now the case is always considered the typical crime of the twenties, and I should like to set against these books for comparison a book of the twenties, Dreiser's *An American Tragedy* (1925), which retells a typical murder of the time of Dreiser's own youth, the case of Chester Gillette (1906). By this comparison I hope to say something about the twenties and the fifties, two decades of expansion.

I am not here making a literary evaluation, yet I must begin from a literary distinction. Of the two recent books, Yaffe's is quite worthless; by bowdlerizing, up-to-dating, stereotyping, and juvenilizing the events and persons of the case, he contrives to lose both artistic probability and any other interest. But *Compulsion* is not a bad book; by its earnest selection of the journalistic, medical, and legal material, often given verbatim, it presents an interesting and believable report; and Levin makes something touching and significant of the narrator's involvement in the action. Dreiser's book, however, is

---

*From *Midstream*, Summer, 1957.

of a different genre, it is a work of art; not (to my taste) a wonderful work, but a work of art in that it makes itself a world and this world is more important than the "case," it is the real case. The questions that I would ask are these: what would a book about the Crime of Our Century be like if it were worked as Dreiser worked? Would such a work get itself written and received? What, contrariwise, are Levin and Yaffe doing? And what does this tell us about the fifties and the twenties?

What strikes one immediately and persistently, is how Dreiser is *in* his story, in a way that our writers are not. He works as though all the motives and behaviors were immediately plausible, *unquestionable by either the author or the audience*, and therefore needing no explanation, only presentation. He may or may not have a theory of causation—we know that he had several—but he does not need one and he does not offer one; simply he shows us how first undeniably Clyde Griffiths did and suffered so and so, and then he did and suffered so and so. Instead of causation and the imputation of responsibility or compulsion, we get a solid and stolid probability that adds up to a real world; that's just how it was, like life only more so. (Dreiser carries this through admirably; the only episode that seems to me sketchy and a little fumbled is the temptation to the murder plan; but the author recovers.) Again, as a doctrinaire naturalist, Dreiser eschews every literary attitude except this narrowly selective "lifelike" presentation; there is no perspective, no irony, no wonder, no humor, no wisdom, compassion, admiration or contempt; no symbol, no formal surprise; certainly no sympathy. (But love, the love of undeviating attentiveness.) In all these ways Dreiser is not involved in the crime, but we shall see that just in these ways Levin and Yaffe are, each in his own fashion, involved. They cannot present the case as a naturalistic probability. Levin wisely makes little effort to do so and relies on the documents to move his story (that's how it was because that's how it was reported in the press); when Yaffe tries it, his story moves not at all.

When Dreiser succeeds in his art work of this kind, there follow two cultural consequences of the highest importance. In the first place he triumphantly vindicates the art act itself, for it is art and art alone that does human justice to Clyde Griffiths (and perhaps to his original Chester Gillette; but that no longer makes any difference). Here Dreiser is perfectly aware of what he is doing; he devotes his entire denouement to the varying attempts to understand and be fair to the young murderer: the trial, the appeal, the compassionate minister, the wise governor, the loving and sacrificing mother, and finally the confused boy himself trying honestly to assay himself. No one truly understands what occurred; but the author can say, "Nay, read here; *this* is what occurred." (Indeed, my bother with this good book is that Dreiser does not bring this poignant problem to the forefront soon enough; he does not show us until too far along the *confused* youth, longing to be understood and told what he is. Dreiser shows us always his vacillation and cowardice, but not enough his confused integrity; he sticks so close to what is like that particular life that he misses one transcendent tragedy of every life.)

But even more relevant to our present theme, when Dreiser succeeds in making a probable crime by accepting every usual presupposition, the social effect is revolutionary. If people do not like the outcome, they cannot simply reject it; they must reject the whole sequence *en bloc*; and since they have been patiently led along step by step, accepting every step as sensible, plausible, and like their lives, they must—must they not?—be shaken in their whole way of experiencing as a viable way of life. See, says the author, here is how *you* make sense, and it is not viable. Something is wrong. At this level, simply to entertain an alternative morality to the one that doomed Clyde, is to disavow the morality you grew up in. Historically, Dreiser's works were part of the revolutionary change in the sexual mores. The events of *An American Tragedy* would no longer be probable if retold today; this particular plot would occur today in a soap opera.

The authors of our books on Leopold and Loeb are not in those events, which are alien to them. There is no shared assumption of author and audience that this is, step by step, inevitable behavior leading up to what is quite unacceptable but must be accepted nev-

ertheless or all our sense rejected *en bloc.* Yaffe's book is merely manufactured on a causal theory, that such and such parental attitudes
lead to such and such juvenile delinquency: the premises are stereotypes, and the esthetic effect is the frigid one of having established a
possibility, for the sake of argument or to get a book written, that
such and such might occur; but there is never any probability or internal motion. Levin, much more masterfully, makes the chief thing
his own need to find out the cause, a fine theme, not unlike Proust's;
but then there is too much about Leopold and Loeb and not enough
about Meyer Levin. The esthetic effect of the major bulk, the crime,
is the harsh one of unpleasant newspaper reports. Both authors
make the philosophical error of trying to present a living process by
explaining it rather than by reliving it with us; their causes are *ex
post facto;* at every moment the protagonists might do otherwise but
don't happen to; afterward we can trace the trajectory they did follow, as if to say, "there must have been a compulsion"; we are certainly none the wiser about ourselves, or any urgent present matter.

Then there arises the question: What on earth makes two writers
devote so much effort to a narrative they cannot get on with, and
one of them to call it by such a title as the Crime of Our Century?
Why do they treat with it at all? This is a crucial question. They are
obviously fascinated. With what? It is fortunate that we have two
books, for unlike as they are in most respects, they prove to have a
couple of surprising attitudes in common, and these give us the clue
to the relevance of these books at this time in the fifties.

As alien as they are to the case, our authors feel even more alien
to the social milieu in which the case occurs. In Yaffe, who up-to-
dates the story, the disaffection is blatant from the beginning. He is
dealing with what would be normally a gloomy subject, yet with almost every character except the protagonists, his manner is usually
satirical and often sarcastic. One father is a frigid ass, the other is a
weak fool; one mother is sickly and timid, the other is a domineering
club woman and a fool; the principal is a pompous fool; the lawyer
is a vain conniver; the psychiatrists don't care; the judge is a sentimental fool. And as his story reaches its climax, Yaffe hits on the

pattern he is after: that nobody is concerned with the one important thing, the case, but this one is interested in his golf score, that one in his new article, another in his business prestige, etc. To drive it home, the author runs through the routine a second time.

Levin's disaffection is more touching; it is a slow growth to awareness of how pointless his own career as a man has been. Let me quote from his ending:

> ... As it happened, I never again reached the intense involvement and achievement—if achievement it may be called—of my first assignment. When something big comes to us early in our careers we have an expectation of exceeding and exceeding ourselves; yet for some this never happens, just as, for some, no later love has the quality of first love. I married, divorced, and during the war I was a correspondent with the Third Army. It was in the last weeks that the case came finally home to me.

Back in America he meets his first love.

> ... Looking at her, I was thinking, *It could have been.* It could all have been. . . . And I tended my job and married again, and we live in Norwalk.

But the social disaffection of both authors is evident also in their surprising attitude toward the two protagonists. They sympathize with, and admire, the dark funny-looking Jewish intellectual misfit (of course in Yaffe nobody is Jewish)—the one who wears the glasses and loses the glasses—the brooding one who has the fantasies of being a serviceable slave. They yearn to extenuate for him according to their own standards of decency, and Yaffe even contrives his metaphysical salvation. But toward the other, the fair good-looking youth, skilled in sports, dancing, and dramatics, sought after by the girls and boys, both authors are cold and even hostile; he is, somehow, to blame. What does this mean? Our authors look at themselves and at the world and its desirable roles, and they find nothing to admire and love—at most something to envy and be vindictive about—but certainly nothing that adds up to what you could be "intensely involved" in, or to "achieve" anything there. Yaffe, the younger, takes this pretty much for granted; Levin has learned it as he pursued his career and found that he, or it (it makes no difference), didn't come across. But there were those two rich and bright boys back in the twenties who "had everything," and they were wise to it already. They acted it out—it is fascinating—because one of them seduced the other into doing something spectacularly pointless, for the excitement; they committed the Crime of Our Century.

As is often the case, the opening page of *Compulsion*, before the author has a chance to develop his habitual defenses, tells more about the case and the real situation than all the rest. A professor is giving a brilliant cram lecture for the morrow's entrance examination to Law School. Judd, who killed the boy the day before, takes no notes; yet he is paying attention, because he seizes the first occasion to interrupt and bother the teacher and the class with his theory of the Superman; but he feels they don't understand his argument.... Levin here wants to portray the preoccupied youth, doodling a hawk, and unable to keep away from the area of the crime, and this is very well. But the salient psychological features of the scene are not these "unconscious" ones but much simpler and revealing ones: (1) What would seem to be "objectively" important, the cram lecture and the examination, is unimportant not only to Judd but also to the other students and to the teacher, for they rush at once into the time-wasting argument. (2) The aim of the young man is chiefly to claim attention, as if starved for attention, and to have something vital to him drawn forth and treated seriously, though not necessarily approved, even perhaps more to be refuted. (3) But since what he offers has no immediate practical content, there is no way to get himself understood. He wants to share his fantasy, which is his only creative act, but it is only a fantasy. We can be sure that, uninterested in the objective business of society—the examination—and unable to make contact with the other persons, he will pour his energy into lush fantasies indeed. (Of course I am not here speaking of Leopold and Loeb but of how they exist as fantasies of Meyer Levin.)

Now let me revert to the first question above: if our author were going to artifice a real world of the case, as Dreiser did in *An American Tragedy*, it is in these scenes of social behavior and how the protagonists are in them, and how they are *not* in them, that half the substance of the work would be. This is especially true for the outgoing, the socially successful youth (Artie). The author tells us, for instance, that Artie is a fine tennis player. In Yaffe's book the counterpart is manager of the baseball team. How is he *in* these sports? We get not a word. But Levin in one brief passage lets us know that Artie is impotent. Then we can envisage him on the field, or dancing hot jazz, throwing himself wildly into it for the relieving excitement of the muscular activity; excelling with the need to prove potency, and with the flash of triumph (and contempt) in doing so; but never, never with the total release of orgasm—having always something unfinished and the need, more fiercely next time, to repeat—and with this, the inability to get any of the quiet rewards of activity and success. He can do it and he proves it, but then it doesn't mean anything and he turns on his heel; or—more deeply—he turns on his heel in full flight from the anxiety of losing control and bursting into tears. Levin is concerned with explaining, and he is compassionate; but if he envisaged the real scenes and simply constructed them, there would be no need for explanation—any more than Dreiser explains anything—and the work itself would repair something, make it whole again, and this is the act of compassion.

Now the other half of such a reconstruction of the real case would, I think, deal with the proliferating fantasies, especially of the inward-turning youth. It happens that in our generation, by no accident, writers have learned to reconstruct such masturbation fantasies as a literary form. Genet is the most masterly. Henry Miller is more pedestrian. The essence of such reconstruction is that the physical and social reality, the "other's reality," enters the presented world with apparent caprice or is there only on the fringes; its meaning and value is the use it plays in beginning, maintaining, and heightening the fantasy. Certainly this is not far from the Leopold-Loeb "case" as told in the books we are considering; but our authors do not stay with the fantasist's world and therefrom lead us to the crime step by step as it really was; rather they persist in keeping the social valuation as their structural framework—and then the overt acts of fantasy occur as alien and require a causal explanation. And yet these same authors, as I have said, do not take that social reality seriously at all! Then what on earth are they doing? They are fascinated and they are avoiding.

In order to get something more nearly resembling what Dreiser did, we could structure this material as follows: On the one hand the scenes of the unsatisfactoriness of our social reality, made obvious and probable for us, the final pointlessness of the esteemed roles and careers, of the games and dates, the coldness of the families and fraternities, and the gnawing need to exceed. On the other hand, the rich reality of the fantasy world into which something looms from outside so that there begins to occur overt behavior continuous with the fantasy. It is in this matrix that the events occur that are reported in the newspapers as crime by those who have not gone step by step this whole road.

The youths kill a random boy for no reason, that is, for a trivial reason that would fit a trivial deed; but of course to them the deed is neither enormous nor trivial but of the order of their other acts; and their reason is not trivial, but to run the risk of being caught, exposed, punished. (It is hard to know what Levin means by "compulsion"—he seems to be saying that the death wish is compelling; but I think the usual psychological wisdom is that the thrilling excitement, the compulsion, is in the confrontation with the others. This is what the affectless repeat.) Yaffe and Levin seem to be peculiarly moved by the acts. They do not seem to understand how any principle of disaffection or estrangement, continuously operating, will take a person far afield; and not only negative principles, but such positive faculties as healthy lust or common sense in a crazy world will eventually lead a man to enormities of eccentricity; and the honest artistic need to touch a smug and debauched audience eventuates in dada. But these books keep the enormity of the act in the foreground; the crime is isolated. We continually feel their tug toward the crime as unfinished business for themselves—several times Levin says as much.

They cannot make the agents real and the act inevitable; they are too involved; they must explain it away. To sum up our comparison: in these books it is the crime we are to disavow and not the world of our assumptions; yet that world is not looked at squarely either, but avoided. But in *An American Tragedy* it was not the murder but the whole way of social life in which that murder was an incident that was recreated, and since our own experience of life allowed us to regard the sequence of events as probable, we had radically to disavow it, that is, to entertain alternatives.

Yet the book we have proposed in theory, portraying as plausible and probable so radical a disaffection from the accepted institutions and behaviors, and developing with sympathy the fantasies of perversity—such a book could not get itself accepted. People do not dare to disavow so frankly our conventionally desirable world, and therefore they would not admit the real scenes to be plausible; nor can they accept the fantasies of desire as what someone indeed might desire. It would all seem far-fetched and repugnant, rather than only too real and inadmissible *en bloc*. Yet the books that put the crime in the foreground—these exert a fascination.

Let me now generalize and compare the twenties and fifties as two periods of expansion. Both are marked by a booming productivity, much money to spend, a rising standard of living, and also by cultural adjustments to great technical innovations that offer exciting prospects; radio then and television now; flying the ocean and the geophysical year; relativity physics and psychoanalysis then and nucleonics and psychotherapy now. In both decades a vast increase in international travel and cultural exchange. Such things both support and give content to the expansion. At the same time the twenties and the fifties are marked by a profound disillusionment and disgust at the way our civilization has recently disgraced itself. No doubt the First World War was a more severe shock to moral preconceptions—we were inured by their experience of barbarism; yet we managed to turn up with crematoria and atom bombs. But these experiences, too, foster expansion in those who survive and in whom the shell shock thaws out, for people are purged, especially if there has been frank vomiting; and then more daring and radical notions can express themselves with a good conscience, since nothing an individual can think of would be so wicked as what everybody thought of collectively.

But there is also a dark contrast between the decades. The twenties were a time in which people thought (really believed) that there would never be another war. Great nations scuttled their warships according to a formula, and signed the Kellogg-Briand agreement. This element, of security, is of course capital to an expanding mood, for it is the absence of an external counterpressure.

If we consider the artistic creations of the twenties, they were indeed such as one would expect and hope for in a time of expansion and disgust. There was a flowering of advance-guard work, experimental, offensive, outrageous, bringing to a large public the esoteric efforts of several decades. And the standard style, as by that time *An American Tragedy* was in standard style, moved with serene self-confidence, immune from the need to explain, as if all the necessary radical positions had been securely conquered. In art as in politics, we had all the three elements necessary for the emergence of novelty: expanding energy, a rejection of the past, and security enough to tolerate confusion and anxiety.

Artistic creation today gives, rather, an impression of being balked, potential but unable to get along. There is a counterpressure that both opposes expansion and discourages it inwardly. Not only is there no peace, but no forth-right effort for it; the international community and even science are not free exchanges; and the increased standard of living no longer pays off in pride and joy, for people are avoiding some risk. There is not enough security, therefore not enough ability to tolerate anxiety, and therefore not enough risk of something startlingly new. At the same time; of course, there is too much disgust with the old, and too much new energy to burn, to allow for great conventional products. Instead there is a balked and teasing flirtation with something different, without daring to affirm it. It is in this ambience, I think, that books like *Compulsion* and *Nothing but the Night* get themselves conceived in fascination, executed defensively, and widely accepted by an audience that will not thereby change. They are widely accepted because everybody is in the same boat. Everybody *knows* better, but few dare to believe it and witness it.

Finally, let me return to the Case itself. The twenties had Flaming Youth; the fifties have Juvenile Delinquents. Leopold and Loeb were not Flaming Youth, they were juvenile delinquents a generation ahead of their time, and therefore they seem now to have committed the Crime of Our Century. Flaming Youth is rebellious youth astoundingly careless of the wisdom it rejects, claiming to be grown-up and untrammeled even while admitting it might be making mistakes to which it claims a right; but its aims are positive enough: sex, speed, and liquor to relax inhibition, ideal political doctrines, and frank answers in words of one syllable for thorny moral dilemmas. These are kids (they recur) looking for an honest adult to refute them. Meyer Levin's protagonists show some of this zeal, but I suspect that it is Levin who is looking for the honest adult. Our juvenile delinquents are not rebellious but resigned; and they are trapped and desperate. Since these young people do not know where to try to exercise their energies, they do mischief. The speed and liquor, and the PAL and the fan-clubs, are not the prelude to a quieter good time but to more desperate expedients toward excitement. Their philosophy would be *Existenz* and *L'Acte Gratuite*, except that to philosophize affirms an essence, truth, and it is not an *acte gratuite* but the property of a rational animal.

Dreiser's Clyde Griffiths is a dumb precursor of the rebel; he feels he is deprived, only he does not know how; and he is lovingly portrayed in a decade when they thought they knew what was wrong, and importantly did know, and were engaged in changing it. But our present protagonists "have" everything and it's no good; there is no point in their rebelling against their fathers for *they* don't have it either; and nobody demonstrates anything new for them in the bestsellers. They are rebels without a cause.

I am reminded of the commencement exercises some years ago at one of the superior academic high schools in New York: Music and Art. Senator Javits, then State's attorney, addressed the class and urged them to help combat juvenile delinquency by interesting the tough kids of their neighborhoods in their own cultural pursuits. Abstractly this was not a foolish proposal—even meaty for a commencement address. But the teen-agers to whom I listened thought it was ridiculous; that the delinquents were much in the right and they were stronger and would influence the good boys rather than the other way around; also—with a certain purity—that music and art should not be degraded to do police work, for they impugned the State's attorney's motives.

On Paul Goodman

I AM WRITING this in Paris, in a room about 4' by 10', sitting on a wicker chair at a typing table in front of a window which looks onto a garden; at my back is a cot and a night table; on the floor and under the table are manuscripts, notebooks, and two or three paperback books. That I have been living and working for more than a year in such small bare quarters, though not at the beginning planned or thought out, undoubtedly answers to some need to strip down while finding a new space inside my head. Here where I have no books, where I spend too many hours writing to have time to talk to anyone, I am trying to make a new start with as little capital as possible to fall back on.

In this Paris in which I live now, which has as little to do with the Paris of today as the Paris of today has to do with the great Paris, capital of the nineteenth century and seedbed of art and ideas until the late 1960s, America is the closest of all the faraway places. Even during periods when I don't go out at all—and in the last months there have been many blessed days and nights when I have no desire to leave the typewriter except to sleep—each morning someone brings me the Paris *Herald-Tribune* with its monstrous collage of "news" of America, encapsulated, distorted, stranger than ever from this distance: the B-52s raining mega-ecodeath on Vietnam, the repulsive martyrdom of Thomas Eagleton, the paranoia of Bobby Fischer, the irresistible ascension of Woody Allen, excerpts from the diary of Arthur Bremer—and, last week, the death of Paul Goodman.

I find that I can't write just his first name. Of course, we called each other "Paul" and "Susan" whenever we met, but both in my head and in conversation with other people he was never "Paul" or ever "Goodman" but always "Paul Goodman"—the whole name, with all the ambiguity of feeling and familiarity which that usage implies.

The grief I feel at Paul Goodman's death is sharper because we were not friends, though we coinhabited several of the same worlds. We first met twenty years ago. I was nineteen, a graduate student at Harvard, dreaming of living in New York, and on a weekend trip to the city someone I knew at the time who was a friend of his brought me to the loft on Twenty-third Street where Paul Goodman and his wife were celebrating his fortieth birthday. He was drunk, he boasted raucously to everyone about his sexual exploits, he talked to me just long enough to be mildly rude. The second time we met was four years later at a party on Riverside Drive, where he seemed more subdued but just as cold and self-absorbed.

In 1959 I moved to New York, and from then on through the late 1960s we met often, though always in public—at parties given by mutual friends, at panel discussions and Vietnam teach-ins, on marches, in demonstrations. I usually made a shy effort to talk to him each time we met, hoping to be able to tell him, directly or indirectly, how much his books mattered to me and how much I had learned from him. Each time he rebuffed me and I retreated. I was told by mutual friends that he didn't really like women as people—though he made an exception for a few particular women, of course. I resisted that hypothesis as long as I could (it seemed to me cheap), then finally gave in. After all, I had sensed just that in his writings: for instance, the major defect of *Growing Up Absurd*, which purports to treat the problems of American youth, is that it talks about youth as if it consists only of adolescent boys and young men. My attitude when we met ceased being open.

Last year another mutual friend, Ivan Illich, invited me to Cuernavaca at the same time that Paul Goodman was there giving a seminar, and I told Ivan that I preferred to come after Paul Goodman had left. Ivan knew, through many conversations, how much I admired Paul Goodman's work. But the intense pleasure I felt each time at the thought that he was alive and well and writing in the United States of America made an ordeal out of every situation in which I actually found myself in the same room with him and sensed my inability to make the slightest contact with him.

In that quite technical sense, then, not only were Paul Goodman and I not friends, but I disliked him—the reason being, as I often explained plaintively during his lifetime, that I felt he didn't like me. How pathetic and merely formal that dislike was I always knew. It is not Paul Goodman's death that has suddenly brought this home to me.

He had been a hero of mine for so long that I was not in the least surprised when he became famous, and always a little surprised that people seemed to take him for granted. The first book of his I ever read—I was sixteen—was a collection of stories called *The Break-up of Our Camp*, published by New Directions. Within a year I had read everything he'd written, and from then on started keeping up. There is no living American writer for whom I have felt the same simple curiosity to read as quickly as possible *anything* he wrote, on any subject. That I mostly agreed with what he thought was not the main reason; there are other writers I agree with to whom I am not so loyal. It was that voice of his that seduced me—that direct, cranky, egotistical, generous American voice.

Many writers in English insist on saturating their writing with an idiosyncratic voice. If Norman Mailer is the most brilliant writer of his generation, it is surely by reason of the authority and eccentricity of his voice; and yet I for one have always found that voice too baroque, somehow fabricated. I admire Mailer as a writer, but I don't really believe in his voice. Paul Goodman's voice is the real thing. There has not been such a convincing, genuine, singular voice in our language since D.H. Lawrence. Paul Goodman's voice touched everything he wrote about with intensity, interest, and his own terribly appealing sureness and awkwardness. What he wrote was a nervy mixture of syntactical stiffness and verbal felicity; he was capable of writing sentences of a wonderful purity of style and vivacity of language, and also capable of writing so sloppily and clumsily that one imagined he must be doing it on purpose. But it never mattered. It was his voice, that is to say, his intelligence and the poetry of his intelligence incarnated, which kept me a loyal and passionate addict. Though he was not often graceful as a writer, his writing and his mind were touched with grace.

There is a terrible, mean American resentment toward someone who tries to do a lot of things. The fact that Paul Goodman wrote poetry and plays and novels as well as social criticism, that he wrote books on intellectual specialties guarded by academic and professional dragons, such as city planning, education, literary criticism, psychiatry, was held against him. His being an academic freeloader and an outlaw psychiatrist, while also being so smart about universities and human nature, outraged many people. That ingratitude is and always was astonishing to me. I know that Paul Goodman often complained of it. Perhaps the most poignant expression was in the journal he kept between 1955 and 1960, published as *Five Years*, in which he laments the fact that he is not famous, not recognized and rewarded for what he is.

That journal was written at the end of his long obscurity, for with the publication of *Growing Up Absurd* in 1960 he did become famous, and from then on his books had a wide circulation and, one imagines, were even widely read—if the extent to which Paul Goodman's ideas were repeated (without his being given any credit) is any proof of being widely read. From 1960 on, he started making money through being taken more seriously—and he was listened to by the young. All that seems to have pleased him, though he still complained that he was not famous enough, not read enough, not appreciated enough.

Far from being an egomaniac who could never get enough, Paul Goodman was quite right in thinking that he never had the attention he deserved. That comes out clearly enough in the obituaries I have read since his death in the half-dozen American newspapers and magazines that I get here in Paris. In these obituaries he is no more than that maverick interesting writer who spread himself too thin, who published *Growing Up Absurd*, who influenced the rebellious American youth of the 1960s, who was indiscreet about his sexual life. Ned Rorem's touching obituary, the only one I have read that gives any sense of Paul Goodman's importance, appeared in the *Village Voice*, a paper read by a large part of Paul Goodman's constituency, only on page 17. As the assessments come in now that he is dead, he is being treated as a marginal figure.

I would hardly have wished for Paul Goodman the kind of media stardom awarded to McLuhan or even Marcuse—which has little to do with actual influence or even tells one anything about how much a writer is being read. What I am complaining about is that Paul Goodman was often taken for granted even by his admirers. It has never been clear to most people, I think, what an extraordinary figure he was. He could do almost anything, and tried to do almost everything a writer can do. Though his fiction became increasingly didactic and unpoetic, he continued to grow as a poet of considerable and entirely unfashionable sensibility; one day people will discover what good poetry he wrote. Most of what he said in his essays about people, cities, and the feel of life is true. His so-called amateurism is identical with his genius: that amateurism enabled him to bring to the questions of schooling, psychiatry, and citizenship an extraordinary, curmudgeonly accuracy of insight and freedom to envisage practical change.

It is difficult to name all the ways in which I feel indebted to him. For twenty years he has been to me quite simply the most important American writer. He was our Sartre, our Cocteau. He did not have the first-class theoretical intelligence of Sartre; he never touched the mad, opaque source of genuine fantasy that Cocteau had at his disposal in practicing so many arts. But he had gifts that neither Sartre nor Cocteau ever had: a genuine feeling for what human life is about, a fastidiousness and breadth of moral passion. His voice on the printed page is real to me as the voices of few writers have ever been—familiar, endearing, exasperating. I suspect there was a nobler human being in his books than in his life, something that happens often in "literature." (Sometimes it is the other way around, and the person in real life is nobler than the person in the books. Sometimes, as in the case of Sade, there is hardly any relationship between the person in the books and the person in real life.)

I always got energy from reading Paul Goodman. He was one of that small company of writers, living and dead, who established for me the value of being a writer and from whose work I drew the standards by which I measured my own. There have been some living European writers in that diverse and very personal pantheon, but no living American writer apart from him.

Everything he did on paper pleased me. I liked it when he was pig-headed, awkward, wistful, even wrong. His egotism touched me rather than put me off (as Mailer's often does when I read him). I admired his diligence, his willingness to serve. I admired his courage, which showed itself in so many ways—one of the most admirable being his honesty about his homosexuality in *Five Years*, for which he was much criticized by his straight friends in the New York intellectual world; that was six years ago, before the advent of Gay Liberation made coming out of the closet chic. I liked it when he talked about himself and when he mingled his own sad sexual desires with his desire for the polity. Like André Breton, to whom he could be compared in many ways, Paul Goodman was a connoisseur of freedom, joy, pleasure. I learned a lot about those three things from reading him.

This morning, starting to write this, I reached under the table by the window to get some paper for the typewriter and saw that one of the two or three paperback books buried under the manuscripts is *New Reformation*. Although I am trying to live for a year without books, a few manage to creep in somehow. It seems fitting that even here, in this tiny room where books are forbidden, where I try better to hear my own voice and discover what I really think and really feel, there is still at least one book by Paul Goodman around, for there has not been an apartment in which I have lived for the last twenty-two years that has not contained most of his books.

With or without his books, I shall go on being marked by him. I shall go on grieving that he is no longer alive to talk in new books, and that now we all have to go on in our fumbling attempts to help each other and to say what is true and to release what poetry we have and to respect each other's madness and right to be wrong and to cultivate our sense of citizenliness without Paul's hectoring, without Paul's patient meandering explanations of everything, without the grace of Paul's example.

—SUSAN SONTAG
September 21, 1972

TITLES IN SERIES

For a complete list of titles, visit www.nyrb.com or write to:
Catalog Requests, NYRB, 435 Hudson Street, New York, NY 10014

J.R. ACKERLEY Hindoo Holiday*
J.R. ACKERLEY My Dog Tulip*
J.R. ACKERLEY My Father and Myself*
J.R. ACKERLEY We Think the World of You*
HENRY ADAMS The Jeffersonian Transformation
CÉLESTE ALBARET Monsieur Proust
DANTE ALIGHIERI The Inferno
DANTE ALIGHIERI The New Life
WILLIAM ATTAWAY Blood on the Forge
W.H. AUDEN (EDITOR) The Living Thoughts of Kierkegaard
W.H. AUDEN W.H. Auden's Book of Light Verse
ERICH AUERBACH Dante: Poet of the Secular World
DOROTHY BAKER Cassandra at the Wedding*
J.A. BAKER The Peregrine
HONORÉ DE BALZAC The Unknown Masterpiece *and* Gambara*
MAX BEERBOHM Seven Men
STEPHEN BENATAR Wish Her Safe at Home*
FRANS G. BENGTSSON The Long Ships*
ALEXANDER BERKMAN Prison Memoirs of an Anarchist
GEORGES BERNANOS Mouchette
ADOLFO BIOY CASARES Asleep in the Sun
ADOLFO BIOY CASARES The Invention of Morel
CAROLINE BLACKWOOD Corrigan*
CAROLINE BLACKWOOD Great Granny Webster*
NICOLAS BOUVIER The Way of the World
MALCOLM BRALY On the Yard*
MILLEN BRAND The Outward Room*
SIR THOMAS BROWNE Religio Medici *and* Urne-Buriall*
JOHN HORNE BURNS The Gallery
ROBERT BURTON The Anatomy of Melancholy
CAMARA LAYE The Radiance of the King
GIROLAMO CARDANO The Book of My Life
DON CARPENTER Hard Rain Falling*
J.L. CARR A Month in the Country
BLAISE CENDRARS Moravagine
EILEEN CHANG Love in a Fallen City
UPAMANYU CHATTERJEE English, August: An Indian Story
NIRAD C. CHAUDHURI The Autobiography of an Unknown Indian
ANTON CHEKHOV Peasants and Other Stories
RICHARD COBB Paris and Elsewhere
COLETTE The Pure and the Impure
JOHN COLLIER Fancies and Goodnights
CARLO COLLODI The Adventures of Pinocchio*
IVY COMPTON-BURNETT A House and Its Head
IVY COMPTON-BURNETT Manservant and Maidservant
BARBARA COMYNS The Vet's Daughter
EVAN S. CONNELL The Diary of a Rapist
ALBERT COSSERY The Jokers*

* Also available as an electronic book.

ALBERT COSSERY Proud Beggars*

HAROLD CRUSE The Crisis of the Negro Intellectual

ASTOLPHE DE CUSTINE Letters from Russia*

LORENZO DA PONTE Memoirs

ELIZABETH DAVID A Book of Mediterranean Food

ELIZABETH DAVID Summer Cooking

L.J. DAVIS A Meaningful Life*

VIVANT DENON No Tomorrow/Point de lendemain

MARIA DERMOÛT The Ten Thousand Things

DER NISTER The Family Mashber

TIBOR DÉRY Niki: The Story of a Dog

ARTHUR CONAN DOYLE The Exploits and Adventures of Brigadier Gerard

CHARLES DUFF A Handbook on Hanging

BRUCE DUFFY The World As I Found It*

DAPHNE DU MAURIER Don't Look Now: Stories

ELAINE DUNDY The Dud Avocado*

ELAINE DUNDY The Old Man and Me*

G.B. EDWARDS The Book of Ebenezer Le Page

MARCELLUS EMANTS A Posthumous Confession

EURIPIDES Grief Lessons: Four Plays; translated by Anne Carson

J.G. FARRELL Troubles*

J.G. FARRELL The Siege of Krishnapur*

J.G. FARRELL The Singapore Grip*

ELIZA FAY Original Letters from India

KENNETH FEARING The Big Clock

KENNETH FEARING Clark Gifford's Body

FÉLIX FÉNÉON Novels in Three Lines*

M.I. FINLEY The World of Odysseus

THEODOR FONTANE Irretrievable*

EDWIN FRANK (EDITOR) Unknown Masterpieces

MASANOBU FUKUOKA The One-Straw Revolution*

MARC FUMAROLI When the World Spoke French

CARLO EMILIO GADDA That Awful Mess on the Via Merulana

MAVIS GALLANT The Cost of Living: Early and Uncollected Stories*

MAVIS GALLANT Paris Stories*

MAVIS GALLANT Varieties of Exile*

GABRIEL GARCÍA MÁRQUEZ Clandestine in Chile: The Adventures of Miguel Littín

ALAN GARNER Red Shift*

THÉOPHILE GAUTIER My Fantoms

JEAN GENET Prisoner of Love

ÉLISABETH GILLE The Mirador: Dreamed Memories of Irène Némirovsky by Her Daughter*

JOHN GLASSCO Memoirs of Montparnasse*

P.V. GLOB The Bog People: Iron-Age Man Preserved

NIKOLAI GOGOL Dead Souls*

EDMOND AND JULES DE GONCOURT Pages from the Goncourt Journals

PAUL GOODMAN Growing Up Absurd: Problems of Youth in the Organized Society*

EDWARD GOREY (EDITOR) The Haunted Looking Glass

A.C. GRAHAM Poems of the Late T'ang

WILLIAM LINDSAY GRESHAM Nightmare Alley*

EMMETT GROGAN Ringolevio: A Life Played for Keeps

VASILY GROSSMAN Everything Flows*

VASILY GROSSMAN Life and Fate*

VASILY GROSSMAN The Road*

OAKLEY HALL Warlock

PATRICK HAMILTON The Slaves of Solitude

PATRICK HAMILTON Twenty Thousand Streets Under the Sky

PETER HANDKE Short Letter, Long Farewell

PETER HANDKE Slow Homecoming

ELIZABETH HARDWICK The New York Stories of Elizabeth Hardwick*

ELIZABETH HARDWICK Seduction and Betrayal*

ELIZABETH HARDWICK Sleepless Nights*

L.P. HARTLEY Eustace and Hilda: A Trilogy*

L.P. HARTLEY The Go-Between*

NATHANIEL HAWTHORNE Twenty Days with Julian & Little Bunny by Papa

GILBERT HIGHET Poets in a Landscape

JANET HOBHOUSE The Furies

HUGO VON HOFMANNSTHAL The Lord Chandos Letter*

JAMES HOGG The Private Memoirs and Confessions of a Justified Sinner

RICHARD HOLMES Shelley: The Pursuit*

ALISTAIR HORNE A Savage War of Peace: Algeria 1954–1962*

GEOFFREY HOUSEHOLD Rogue Male*

WILLIAM DEAN HOWELLS Indian Summer

BOHUMIL HRABAL Dancing Lessons for the Advanced in Age*

DOROTHY B. HUGHES The Expendable Man*

RICHARD HUGHES A High Wind in Jamaica*

RICHARD HUGHES In Hazard*

RICHARD HUGHES The Fox in the Attic (The Human Predicament, Vol. 1)*

RICHARD HUGHES The Wooden Shepherdess (The Human Predicament, Vol. 2)*

MAUDE HUTCHINS Victorine

YASUSHI INOUE Tun-huang*

HENRY JAMES The Ivory Tower

HENRY JAMES The New York Stories of Henry James*

HENRY JAMES The Other House

HENRY JAMES The Outcry

TOVE JANSSON Fair Play *

TOVE JANSSON The Summer Book*

TOVE JANSSON The True Deceiver*

RANDALL JARRELL (EDITOR) Randall Jarrell's Book of Stories

DAVID JONES In Parenthesis

KABIR Songs of Kabir; translated by Arvind Krishna Mehrotra*

FRIGYES KARINTHY A Journey Round My Skull

HELEN KELLER The World I Live In

YASHAR KEMAL Memed, My Hawk

YASHAR KEMAL They Burn the Thistles

MURRAY KEMPTON Part of Our Time: Some Ruins and Monuments of the Thirties

RAYMOND KENNEDY Ride a Cockhorse*

DAVID KIDD Peking Story*

ROBERT KIRK The Secret Commonwealth of Elves, Fauns, and Fairies

ARUN KOLATKAR Jejuri

DEZSŐ KOSZTOLÁNYI Skylark*

TÉTÉ-MICHEL KPOMASSIE An African in Greenland

GYULA KRÚDY The Adventures of Sindbad*

GYULA KRÚDY Sunflower*

SIGIZMUND KRZHIZHANOVSKY The Letter Killers Club*

SIGIZMUND KRZHIZHANOVSKY Memories of the Future

MARGARET LEECH Reveille in Washington: 1860–1865*

PATRICK LEIGH FERMOR Between the Woods and the Water*
PATRICK LEIGH FERMOR Mani: Travels in the Southern Peloponnese*
PATRICK LEIGH FERMOR Roumeli: Travels in Northern Greece*
PATRICK LEIGH FERMOR A Time of Gifts*
PATRICK LEIGH FERMOR A Time to Keep Silence*
PATRICK LEIGH FERMOR The Traveller's Tree*
D.B. WYNDHAM LEWIS AND CHARLES LEE (EDITORS) The Stuffed Owl
GEORG CHRISTOPH LICHTENBERG The Waste Books
JAKOV LIND Soul of Wood and Other Stories
H.P. LOVECRAFT AND OTHERS The Colour Out of Space
DWIGHT MACDONALD Masscult and Midcult: Essays Against the American Grain*
NORMAN MAILER Miami and the Siege of Chicago*
JANET MALCOLM In the Freud Archives
JEAN-PATRICK MANCHETTE Fatale*
OSIP MANDELSTAM The Selected Poems of Osip Mandelstam
OLIVIA MANNING Fortunes of War: The Balkan Trilogy
OLIVIA MANNING School for Love*
JAMES VANCE MARSHALL Walkabout*
GUY DE MAUPASSANT Afloat
GUY DE MAUPASSANT Alien Hearts*
JAMES MCCOURT Mawrdew Czgowchwz*
HENRI MICHAUX Miserable Miracle
JESSICA MITFORD Hons and Rebels
JESSICA MITFORD Poison Penmanship*
NANCY MITFORD Madame de Pompadour*
NANCY MITFORD The Sun King*
HENRY DE MONTHERLANT Chaos and Night
BRIAN MOORE The Lonely Passion of Judith Hearne*
BRIAN MOORE The Mangan Inheritance*
ALBERTO MORAVIA Boredom*
ALBERTO MORAVIA Contempt*
JAN MORRIS Conundrum
JAN MORRIS Hav*
PENELOPE MORTIMER The Pumpkin Eater*
ÁLVARO MUTIS The Adventures and Misadventures of Maqroll
L.H. MYERS The Root and the Flower*
NESCIO Amsterdam Stories*
DARCY O'BRIEN A Way of Life, Like Any Other
YURI OLESHA Envy*
IONA AND PETER OPIE The Lore and Language of Schoolchildren
IRIS OWENS After Claude*
RUSSELL PAGE The Education of a Gardener
ALEXANDROS PAPADIAMANTIS The Murderess
BORIS PASTERNAK, MARINA TSVETAYEVA, AND RAINER MARIA RILKE Letters, Summer 1926
CESARE PAVESE The Moon and the Bonfires
CESARE PAVESE The Selected Works of Cesare Pavese
LUIGI PIRANDELLO The Late Mattia Pascal
ANDREY PLATONOV The Foundation Pit
ANDREY PLATONOV Soul and Other Stories
J.F. POWERS Morte d'Urban
J.F. POWERS The Stories of J.F. Powers
J.F. POWERS Wheat That Springeth Green
CHRISTOPHER PRIEST Inverted World

CHRISTINA STEAD Letty Fox: Her Luck

GEORGE R. STEWART Names on the Land

STENDHAL The Life of Henry Brulard

ADALBERT STIFTER Rock Crystal

THEODOR STORM The Rider on the White Horse

JEAN STROUSE Alice James: A Biography*

HOWARD STURGIS Belchamber

ITALO SVEVO As a Man Grows Older

HARVEY SWADOS Nights in the Gardens of Brooklyn

A.J.A. SYMONS The Quest for Corvo

ELIZABETH TAYLOR Angel*

ELIZABETH TAYLOR A Game of Hide and Seek*

HENRY DAVID THOREAU The Journal: 1837–1861*

TATYANA TOLSTAYA The Slynx

TATYANA TOLSTAYA White Walls: Collected Stories

EDWARD JOHN TRELAWNY Records of Shelley, Byron, and the Author

LIONEL TRILLING The Liberal Imagination*

LIONEL TRILLING The Middle of the Journey*

IVAN TURGENEV Virgin Soil

JULES VALLÈS The Child

RAMÓN DEL VALLE-INCLÁN Tyrant Banderas*

MARK VAN DOREN Shakespeare

CARL VAN VECHTEN The Tiger in the House

ELIZABETH VON ARNIM The Enchanted April*

EDWARD LEWIS WALLANT The Tenants of Moonbloom

ROBERT WALSER Berlin Stories*

ROBERT WALSER Jakob von Gunten

REX WARNER Men and Gods

SYLVIA TOWNSEND WARNER Lolly Willowes*

SYLVIA TOWNSEND WARNER Mr. Fortune*

SYLVIA TOWNSEND WARNER Summer Will Show*

ALEKSANDER WAT My Century

C.V. WEDGWOOD The Thirty Years War

SIMONE WEIL AND RACHEL BESPALOFF War and the Iliad

GLENWAY WESCOTT Apartment in Athens*

GLENWAY WESCOTT The Pilgrim Hawk*

REBECCA WEST The Fountain Overflows

EDITH WHARTON The New York Stories of Edith Wharton*

PATRICK WHITE Riders in the Chariot

T.H. WHITE The Goshawk*

JOHN WILLIAMS Butcher's Crossing*

JOHN WILLIAMS Stoner*

ANGUS WILSON Anglo-Saxon Attitudes

EDMUND WILSON Memoirs of Hecate County

RUDOLF AND MARGARET WITTKOWER Born Under Saturn

GEOFFREY WOLFF Black Sun*

FRANCIS WYNDHAM The Complete Fiction

JOHN WYNDHAM The Chrysalids

STEFAN ZWEIG Beware of Pity*

STEFAN ZWEIG Chess Story*

STEFAN ZWEIG Confusion *

STEFAN ZWEIG Journey Into the Past*

STEFAN ZWEIG The Post-Office Girl

BOLESŁAW PRUS The Doll*

RAYMOND QUENEAU We Always Treat Women Too Well

RAYMOND QUENEAU Witch Grass

RAYMOND RADIGUET Count d'Orgel's Ball

JULES RENARD Nature Stories*

JEAN RENOIR Renoir, My Father

GREGOR VON REZZORI An Ermine in Czernopol*

GREGOR VON REZZORI Memoirs of an Anti-Semite*

GREGOR VON REZZORI The Snows of Yesteryear: Portraits for an Autobiography*

TIM ROBINSON Stones of Aran: Labyrinth

TIM ROBINSON Stones of Aran: Pilgrimage

MILTON ROKEACH The Three Christs of Ypsilanti*

FR. ROLFE Hadrian the Seventh

GILLIAN ROSE Love's Work

WILLIAM ROUGHEAD Classic Crimes

CONSTANCE ROURKE American Humor: A Study of the National Character

TAYEB SALIH Season of Migration to the North

TAYEB SALIH The Wedding of Zein*

GERSHOM SCHOLEM Walter Benjamin: The Story of a Friendship*

DANIEL PAUL SCHREBER Memoirs of My Nervous Illness

JAMES SCHUYLER Alfred and Guinevere

JAMES SCHUYLER What's for Dinner?*

LEONARDO SCIASCIA The Day of the Owl

LEONARDO SCIASCIA Equal Danger

LEONARDO SCIASCIA The Moro Affair

LEONARDO SCIASCIA To Each His Own

LEONARDO SCIASCIA The Wine-Dark Sea

VICTOR SEGALEN René Leys

PHILIPE-PAUL DE SÉGUR Defeat: Napoleon's Russian Campaign

VICTOR SERGE The Case of Comrade Tulayev*

VICTOR SERGE Conquered City*

VICTOR SERGE Memoirs of a Revolutionary

VICTOR SERGE Unforgiving Years

SHCHEDRIN The Golovlyov Family

ROBERT SHECKLEY The Store of the Worlds: The Stories of Robert Sheckley*

GEORGES SIMENON Act of Passion*

GEORGES SIMENON Dirty Snow*

GEORGES SIMENON The Engagement

GEORGES SIMENON The Man Who Watched Trains Go By

GEORGES SIMENON Monsieur Monde Vanishes*

GEORGES SIMENON Pedigree*

GEORGES SIMENON Red Lights

GEORGES SIMENON The Strangers in the House

GEORGES SIMENON Three Bedrooms in Manhattan*

GEORGES SIMENON Tropic Moon*

GEORGES SIMENON The Widow*

CHARLES SIMIC Dime-Store Alchemy: The Art of Joseph Cornell

MAY SINCLAIR Mary Olivier: A Life*

TESS SLESINGER The Unpossessed: A Novel of the Thirties*

VLADIMIR SOROKIN Ice Trilogy*

VLADIMIR SOROKIN The Queue

DAVID STACTON The Judges of the Secret Court*

JEAN STAFFORD The Mountain Lion